D1499282

Semantics, Tense, and Time

Semantics, Tense, and Time   Peter Ludlow

An Essay in the Metaphysics
of Natural Language

A Bradford Book
The MIT Press
Cambridge, Massachusetts
London, England

© 1999 Massachusetts Institute of Technology

Set in Times Roman by The MIT Press.
Printed and bound in the United States of America.

Library of Congress Cataloging-in-Publication Data

Ludlow, Peter, 1957–
Semantics, tense, and time : an essay in the metaphysics
of natural language / Peter Ludlow.
p.   cm.
"A Bradford book."
Includes bibliographical references and index.
ISBN 0-262-12219-7 (alk. paper)
1. Semantics. 2. Language and languages—Philosophy. 3.
Time. 4. Metaphysics. 5. Grammar, Comparative and
general—Tense. I. Title.
P325.L754   1999
401'.43—dc21   99-13958
                                                           CIP

for Robert B. Ludlow

...For, believe, the secret of existence is: to *live dangerously!*
Build your cities under Vesuvius! Send your ships into uncharted seas!

Live at war with your peers and yourselves!
Be robbers and conquerors, as long as you cannot be rulers and owners, you lovers of knowledge!

—F. Nietzsche

Contents

Contents

Preface

In one of the most infamous episodes of twentieth-century intellectual history, the linguist-anthropologist Benjamin Lee Whorf argued (i) that language shapes thought and reality, (ii) that the tense system of a language can tell us about the metaphysics of time entailed by that language, and (iii) that for the Hopi, among other cultures, the tense system (if it can be called that) is so radically different from ours that those cultures may not have a concept of time at all. "I find it gratuitous," writes Whorf (1956, p. 57),

to assume that a Hopi who knows only the Hopi language and only the cultural ideas of his own society has the same notions, often supposed to be intuitions, of time and space that we have, and that are generally assumed to be universal. In particular, he has no general notion or intuition of TIME as a smooth flowing continuum in which everything in the universe proceeds at an equal rate, out of future, through a present, into a past; or, in which, to reverse the picture, the observer is being carried in the stream of duration continuously away from a past and into a future .... The Hopi language is seen to contain no words, grammatical forms, constructions or expressions that refer directly to what we call "time," or to past, present, or future or lasting, or to motion as kinematic rather than dynamic (i.e. as a continuous translation in space and time rather than as an exhibition of dynamic effort in a certain process), or that even refer to space in such a way as to exclude that element of extension or existence that we call "time," and so by implication leave a residue that could be referred to as "time." Hence, the Hopi language contains no reference to "time," either explicit or implicit.

I think that Whorf was more right than wrong in the above passage. Oh, I don't mean that he was right in thinking that the Hopi are so different from us. The past few decades' work in generative grammar has shown us that the differences among human languages are superficial at best. Moreover, it is now pretty clear that even on the surface the Hopi have a temporal system not unlike our own. (See Malotki 1983 for a discussion.) Still, I think Whorf was on target on a number of points. I think he was correct in thinking that one can argue from the structure of human language to the nature of reality, and I think he was most likely correct in seeing a close connection between language and thought.

But there is another point on which I think Whorf was right in the above passage. I think that on a certain level of deep analysis his description of the Hopi tense system was basically correct—not just for the Hopi, but for all of us. That is, I think that a close study of English does not support the thesis that there is such a thing as tense—at least not the sort of tense system that is compatible with currently favored philosophical theories of time. More to the point, I doubt that *we* actually have a "general notion or intuition of TIME as a smooth flowing continuum in which everything in the universe proceeds at an equal rate, out of future, through a present, into a past." I am also quite sure that *we* have "no words, grammatical forms, constructions or expressions that refer directly to what we call "time," or to past, present, or future."

These are pretty provocative claims. At least Whorf had the good sense to restrict his claims to (in our eyes) exotic peoples, thus allowing us room to concede that exotic peoples may have exotic realities. But who would suppose that *we* don't have a tense system that allows us reference to past and future, etc.? Isn't it obvious that we do?

Even if it could be shown that our tense system lacks reference to future and past events, why should we draw conclusions about time itself—about the nature of reality? Can't we simply say that there is tense, and there is time, but they don't have much to do with each other?

What I will try to show is that Whorf's unargued intuition—that there is a close connection between language and reality—is basically correct. His error was in exaggerating the differences between natural languages. Once that error is corrected, there is no reason for us to be driven to the kind of cultural relativism that followed from Whorf's original thesis. The structure of language does have metaphysical consequences, but the structure of language does not differ in relevant ways between English and Hopi, between French and Farsi, or between Chinese and Urdu. It follows that humans all share the same metaphysics—the same reality.

Thus, one of the central goals of this book is to illustrate how one can study metaphysical questions from a linguistic/semantical perspective. The specific issue that I have chosen to investigate is the well-entrenched dispute between A-theorists and B-theorists about the nature of time.

According to B-theorists, there is no genuine change; rather, there is a permanent sequence of unchanging events, ordered (lined up, if you will) by an earlier-than/later-than relation. For example, World War I (and all the sub-events contained in it) is just as real as the event of your reading this preface, which in turn is just as real as the event of the death of the sun. When we say that World War I is past, we mean that it is earlier than the event of our utterance that

World War I is past. When we say that the death of the sun is future, we mean that the death of the sun is later than our utterance that the death of the sun is future. In this sense, B-theorists consider reality to be "untensed"—events are not intrinsically past, present, or future; rather, they simply exist (out there, somewhere), and 'past' and 'future' are merely ways of talking about where those events lie relative to the utterance events in which we speak about them. This view may seem counterintuitive, but it is most likely the received view in both physics and philosophy, having been advocated (or said to have been advocated) by figures ranging from Albert Einstein to Bertrand Russell.

According to A-theorists, on the other hand, time is not a frozen sequences of unchanging events. The picture given by A-theorists varies from theorist to theorist, but I will be defending an alternative due to A. N. Prior (and perhaps to Saint Augustine before him) in which, strictly speaking, there is no future and no past "out there" or anywhere. We can say that it will be true that a certain state of affairs (say, the death of the sun) will hold and that it was true that a certain state of affairs (say, World War I) held, but that this does not involve our referring to future and past events or to there being such events for us to refer to. According to this idea (often called *presentism*), what makes something future or past is how the world stands right now.

The alleged problems with each of these two positions are now fairly well mapped out. The chief problem with the B-theory is that it fails to account for the indexical nature of our temporal discourse. As an illustration, suppose that I know I have an important appointment at 2 o'clock, but that because my watch has stopped I do not know that it is now 2 o'clock. I blissfully think out loud: "I have an appointment at 2 o'clock." Suddenly, the radio announces that it is 2 o'clock. I now think out loud: "Oh no, I have an appointment *now!*" The alleged problem for the B-theorist is that there is no way to distinguish the content of these thoughts/utterances with B-theory semantical relations. As far as the B-theory is concerned, 'now' just means the same as 'the time of this utterance', which is just to say '2 o'clock'. Something has gone wrong.

The response strategies of the B-theorists are limited to two general routes. First, one can say that semantics doesn't have anything to do with metaphysics, so we can allow indexicality in the semantics without it infecting our metaphysics. Second, one can say that the two sentences in my example of the 2 o'clock meeting, despite appearances, actually have the same semantics, or at least the same semantic "content." The extra "meaning" supplied in the sentence with the indexical is not really semantical; however, it may be psychological, and psychology does not have the same metaphysical commitments that semantics does. In this book I will argue that both of these strategies fail—that semantics cannot be divorced from metaphysics, and indexicality cannot be divorced from semantics. My conclusion will be that a B-theory metaphysics is inherently defective.

On the other side, there are two central objections to the A-theory: first, that it allegedly falls victim to a logical paradox observed by J. M. E. McTaggart, and, second, that it can't be integrated within a semantics of tense because it cannot account for temporal anaphora (expressions, such as 'then', that apparently refer to times in the past and future) and therefore it also can't account for complex tenses (e.g., the past perfect). I will argue that the objections related to temporal anaphora and McTaggart's objections turn out to be related, and that a theory of temporal anaphora can be incorporated into a semantics of tense that does not have future and past events. The idea will be to develop a theory of "E-type temporal anaphora" in which temporal anaphors are not referring expressions but rather stand proxy for temporal conjunctions—e.g., when-clauses (which can then be treated in a nonreferential way). My conclusion will be that there are no compelling semantical objections to the A-theory.

My case for the A-theory will not end there. If there is a fact of the matter as to what semantical theory a language user is exploiting (and how the language user is representing that knowledge), and if language users actually have (tacit) knowledge of their semantical theory (and of how they are representing it), then there may be psycholinguistic probes that can help us determine whether the speaker is using an A-theory semantics or a B-theory semantics. As we will see, evidence from language acquisition and from acquired linguistic deficits supports the idea that the structure of our semantical knowledge is consistent only with the A-theory picture.

The main theses of this book are, then, the following:

• We can gain insight into the metaphysics of time by studying the semantics of natural language, where this constitutes (in part) our knowledge of language-world relations and how we represent that knowledge.
• The B-theorist cannot account for the semantics of temporal indexicals; hence, the possibility of a B-theory metaphysics is undermined.
• The A-theorist *can* answer semantical objections about temporal anaphora and metaphysical objections about the McTaggart paradox.
• Psycholinguistic evidence about the semantical theory that humans actually employ also favors the A-theory semantics and hence favors A-theory metaphysics.

Defending some of these theses will obviously require that we do some technical work, both on the philosophical end and on the linguistic end. This need to go into technical matters has presented me with a dilemma. Philosophers will puzzle over the need for formal fragments and will find the empirical discussion of grammatical tense and anaphora to be mind-numbingly detailed. Linguists will puzzle over all the attention given to the McTaggart argument and truth-value links, and will find the empirical discussion of tense phenomena and anaphora surprisingly condensed. There is no helping this, I'm afraid. I have tried to give the minimum level of detail necessary to secure my argument, and I have relied heavily on notes to point the way to further discussion of many crucial issues. Readers interested in digging deeper will have to pursue the references. My goals here are simply to lay out the form of the argument and to give enough detail to show how the pieces hang together.

As I have already hinted, my central concern in this project is not with the A-theory and the B-theory, or even with the philosophy of time. Rather, my goal in this exercise is to illustrate an approach to metaphysics in which semantical theory and the philosophy of language are central. Fifty years ago perhaps no one would have bothered making this final point, since analytic philosophers then took it for granted that language (and the philosophy of language) would stand at the center of any philosophical endeavor. In subsequent decades the philosophy of language was removed from this central position, sometimes to be replaced by the philosophy of mind and sometimes to be replaced by nothing at all (leaving the various sub-branches of analytic philosophy to spin off in numerous unrelated directions).

It is not all bad that the philosophy of language lost its place at the center of analytic philosophy. The view of language that guided most of the mid-century research was, in my view, fundamentally mistaken. Further, many of the supposed consequences which were to flow from the philosophy of language were tenuous at best. Today, if the philosophy of language has some claim to make in metaphysics or elsewhere, it must be carefully argued, and that is all to the good.

Yet, as the century draws to a close the philosophy of language has returned in a new form. It has been successfully naturalized, in my view, and integrated into the semantics of natural language and linguistic theory. (For a survey of relevant literature and a gloss on this naturalization project, see Ludlow 1997a.) Returning in this form, the philosophy of language *does* have powerful claims to make about our various philosophical endeavors, not just in the metaphysics of time, but also in the theory of causality, in the theory of action, and in value theory. I hope that this book will serve to illustrate just how central the philosophy of language is, and how, executed correctly, the philosophy of language deserves to reclaim its place at the very heart of analytic philosophy.

Acknowledgements

When I conceived of this project, in 1991, the idea was to put together a short manuscript that would develop two different theories of tense within an absolute semantics for natural language and would show the connection between those theories and two leading theories of time. In 1992 I circulated a short draft manuscript that contained the core of the idea (although not worked out in detail). That draft received a number of helpful comments from Barry Schein, Ed Zalta, and Richard Larson, which led to some significant revisions.

In the fall of 1993 the revised material was presented at a series of lectures at the University of Padua, and it benefited greatly from the criticisms and comments of some of the participants (including Paolo Leonardi, Mario Mignuce, and Ernesto Napoli). These lectures (and the discussion periods) led to the first 1994 draft, which I again circulated narrowly. Again I was fortunate to have important feedback from Richard Larson and Barry Schein, and in particular from Ernie Lepore. Incorporating those comments, I revised the manuscript again. Late in 1994 I submitted it to The MIT Press. Although I received helpful comments from two anonymous reviewers, and although the project was "green lighted," it was clear to me that a lot of technical problems remained to be worked out.

Subsequent revisions of this material, particularly the development of the technical details, were presented in a course on the semantics of tense which I taught at in the Diploma Program in Philosophy of Language and Linguistics at the University of Venice in the summer of 1995, and at a seminar on tense which I taught in the Department of Linguistics at Stony Brook in 1996. The less technical portions of this material were presented in mini-courses that I taught at the University of Novi Sad, Jugoslavia in 1997 and at the Fourth Central European Summer School in Generative Linguistics, in Olomouc, the Czech Republic, 1997.

Portions of chapters 5–10 were presented in talks at the Department of Philosophy at the University of Maryland (1995), at the Department of Linguistics, Humboldt University in Berlin (1995), at the Inter-University Center Conference on Truth in Bled, Slovenia (1996), at the Conference on the Question of Temporality at the University of Venice (1996), and at the Moral Sciences Club at Cambridge University (1997).

The penultimate draft, completed in late 1997, was again circulated for comments. Once again, invaluable assistance and encouragement came from Richard Larson and Ernie Lepore, as well as from Lori Repetti, Gabe Segal, and Jason Stanley. Crucially, Larson and Repetti both convinced me that, while I had perhaps ironed out the theory to my satisfaction, the exposition was utterly opaque. I accordingly spent the next six months trying to streamline the manuscript, remove technical details, and in general make the book more user friendly. To this end, in the spring of 1998 I used several venues to experiment with ways of presenting the material: the University of Milan, the Scuola Normale Superiore in Pisa, and a workshop on tense sponsored by UCLA's Department of Linguistics.

The last year and a half of work on this book was done in some idyllic settings. In the spring of 1997 I was a visiting scholar at Cambridge University, where apart from the MSC talk, I benefited greatly from discussing these issues with Hugh Mellor, Jeremy Butterfield, Isaac Levi (who was also visiting), and Michael Potter. (I might add that the office I was provided at Cambridge was furnished with portraits of J. M. E. McTaggart, C. D. Broad, and G. E. Moore— quite inspirational for someone working on the reality of time.) In the fall, work continued at the University of Venice, where I held the Fulbright Chair in Philosophy of Language/Linguistics. I am indebted to Anna Cardinaletti, Michal Starke, and Guglielmo Cinque for logistical and intellectual support while in Venice. I am also indebted to my department chair, Ed Casey, and to the administration at SUNY Stony Brook for supporting my leaves of absence during this period.

Certain individuals deserve thanks for contributions that are somewhat more existential in nature. Lori Repetti and our daughter Chiara deserve some sort of award for tolerating me while I worked on this. Fortunately for Chiara, she was not around during the first four years of this effort. I should add that Lori provided not only existential support but also some crucial additions and corrections—particularly in the sections on the nature of I-language and in the section on eliminating grammatical tense. A different sort of existential contribution came from Noam Chomsky and Richard Larson, who (apart from providing me with comments on portions of the manuscript) taught me to be courageous in my thinking, and more importantly, by their examples, taught me how to have the kind of mental strength necessary to grind out the arguments required of a minority intellectual position. I now realize, however, that the foundation of what I learned from them I had already learned from my father. It was he who taught me about having at least one new idea every day, and how to stay with each new idea, sometimes for years, reworking it until it came to fruition. He also taught me that, even after all this work, one has to expect a high rate of failure among radical ideas. As this project is way out on several philosophical limbs and could, even tomorrow, crash in a most spectacular way, the only person I can imagine dedicating this book to is my father. If the project in this book succeeds, no one else is more deserving of having it dedicated to them. If the project fails... well, as my father would say, "it's all in a day's work."

Semantics, Tense, and Time

Introduction

The A-Series vs. the B-Series

Metaphysics is, in part, the study of what is real. The layperson often supposes that when philosophers worry about what is real they must worry about whether tables, chairs, and dinner plates are real. Some philosophers do worry about these questions, but there are a number of other metaphysical issues that philosophers worry about too.

Among the areas of interest is a class of metaphysical questions surrounding the nature of time. For example, is time real? If so, is the future as real as the past? Can we change the future? If yes, why? If not, why not? If time is real, then what exactly is it? Is time, as some have suggested, really just physical change? If so, then how do we make sense of this change apart from its occurring in time? But if change takes place in time, then how can time be change? As with other metaphysical questions, questions about the nature of time are notoriously difficult. Certain problems posed by the pre-Socratic philosophers are still debated, and the number of metaphysical puzzles surrounding the nature of time continues to multiply.

This work will focus on just one of the many issues in the philosophy of time. The issue, which in some form was discussed as far back as the third century (by the Neoplatonist Iamblichus[1]), has been at the center of the twentieth-century discussion of the philosophy of time. Briefly, the problem is as follows: Two broad approaches to the philosophy of time can be distinguished. According to one approach, adopted by Russell, Einstein, Reichenbach, and others, time is simply a sequence of unchanging and tenseless events. Future events, past events, and present events are all equally real. McTaggart (1908) called this the *B-series* conception of time; others, including Mellor (1981), have called it the *untensed* conception. According to the *alternative* approach, it is fundamental to the notion of time that events, or perhaps propositions, have genuine temporal status. So, for example, there is a fundamental metaphysical distinction between events that are future and those that are present or past. This fundamental difference is supposedly deeper than a simple ordering of events by the earlier-than/later-than relation. McTaggart referred to this as the *A-series* conception of time; others have characterized it as the *tensed* conception.

Following Gale (1967), we might find it useful to distinguish the A-series and the B-series according to the following criteria.

A-series	B-Series
The B-series is reducible to the A series.	The A-series is reducible to the B series.
Temporal becoming is intrinsic to all events.	Temporal becoming is psychological.
There are important ontological differences between past and future.	The B-series is objective. All events are equally real.
Change is analyzable solely in terms of A-series relations (past, present, future).	Change is analyzable solely in terms of B-series relations (earlier-than, later-than).

As we will see, these criteria do not provide necessary and sufficient conditions for identifying the A-series and the B-series; indeed, some of the criteria will have to be relaxed if logical conundrums are to be averted. For now, however, they can provide us with a useful way of thinking about the distinction. But what exactly is at stake in this distinction?

Questions like these have been pursued throughout the history of philosophy, not just because of their intrinsic interest but also because metaphysics has often been seen as a point of departure for other philosophical investigations. Questions about the metaphysics of time have been thought to have consequences for the philosophy of language, the philosophy of mind, the philosophy of religion, the philosophy of science, epistemology, and other branches of philosophy.

As we will see in chapter 10, the decision between the A-theory and the B-theory is rich in consequences. But how does one decide between alternatives like these? One answer would be that questions about the nature of time are best addressed by physicists. For example, Einstein held a B-series conception of time.[2] He presumably had good physical reasons for doing so. Shouldn't we therefore defer to Einstein, or to whatever current physical theory dictates? Putnam (1967, p. 247) appears to adopt such a view:

I conclude that the problem of reality and the determinateness of future events is now solved. Moreover, it is solved by physics and not by philosophy. . . . Indeed, I do not believe that there are any longer any *philosophical* problems about Time; there is only the physical problem of determining the exact physical geometry of the four-dimensional continuum that we inhabit.

On the other hand, Sklar (1981, p. 249[3]), specifically addressing this passage from Putnam, notes that such a position reflects some ignorance of the nature of the scientific enterprise:

I think that such a naive view is as wrong as it can be. Just as a computer is only as good as its programmer ('Garbage in, garbage out') one can extract only so much metaphysics from a physical theory as one puts in. While our total world-view must, of course, be consistent with our best available scientific theories, it is a great mistake to read off a metaphysics superficially from the theory's overt appearance, and an even graver mistake to neglect the fact that metaphysical presuppositions have gone into the formulation of the theory, as it is usually framed, in the first place.

If Sklar is correct, there is still a philosophical investigation to be undertaken, even if it is to be a part of the scientific program of physics.[4] Others have argued that subject matter called "time" in physics really has nothing to do with the metaphysical conception of time but is just an appropriation of the term to discuss certain aspects of light relations within the theory.[5]

Perhaps the most telling problem is that it is not obvious that current physics (as opposed to physicists) actually favors one position over the other. As Sklar (1974, p. 275) has noted, the scientific theory can "change the philosophy and put the dispute [between the A-theory and the B-theory] in a new perspective, but it cannot resolve the dispute in any ultimate sense." Furthermore, Sklar (1981), Stein (1968), Dieks (1988), and Shimony (1993) have argued that non-B-theory interpretations of the special theory of relativity are possible.[6]

In sum, even if philosophers wish to pass the burden of metaphysical inquiry onto the physicist, the physicist simply cannot shoulder the burden. There are still metaphysical questions to be answered, and it is not up to physicists alone to answer them.[7]

But what exactly can philosophy bring to the table? Philosophers, after all, have been debating metaphysical puzzles for more than 2000 years without much apparent success. Dummett (1991, p. 12) puts the situation as follows:

The moves and counter-moves are already familiar, having been made repeatedly by the philosophers through the centuries. The arguments of one side evoke a response in certain of the spectators of the contest, those of the other side sway others of them; but we have no criterion to decide the victors. No knock-out blow has been delivered. We must award the decision on points; and we do not know how to award points.

Or, as Voltaire put it (less pugilistically) 200 years earlier, metaphysics is a dance of elegant steps in which we end up back where we started. Is there anything a philosopher can bring to this dance besides pure speculation and elegant steps?

One strategy in philosophy has been to reject the idea of metaphysics as a starting place and to argue for moving from the bottom up—from the theory of thought to metaphysics.

The general idea is broadly Kantian in character. We can never know things as they are "in themselves," since the mind is actively involved in organizing our experience. The best we can do is elucidate the categories or structure of reason. For example, according to Kant, time was not itself a property of things in themselves; rather, it was imposed upon our experience by the mind. Of course, from this perspective it would be futile to begin an investigation into the nature of time apart from a consideration of the nature of thought or reason. And indeed, after an investigation into the nature of time as a category of human reason had taken place, there would be little left to do in the way of metaphysics, save perhaps to dot the i's and cross the t's. Or, to use a metaphor due to Dummett, the philosopher's task is like that of the optometrist, who cannot tell us what we will see when we look about, but who, by providing us with adequate corrective lenses, can nonetheless help us to see more clearly.

In the twentieth century, a number of analytic philosophers have conceded to Kant the general view in which an investigation into metaphysics cannot be conducted apart from an investigation into the nature of thought, but have rejected Kant's conception of thought, with its attendant categories of reason. In its place, they have proposed that thought is inherently linguistic in nature. Thus, they have proposed that the proper starting place for investigation should be the language in which we think, and this has generally been taken to be natural language.[8]

Interestingly, the B-theory and A-theory approaches to the philosophy of time parallel two distinct approaches to the semantics of tense in natural language. On the one hand, there are approaches to the semantics of tense (see, e.g., Reichenbach 1947) that appeal to reference events in accounting for complex tenses and temporal anaphora. On the other hand, there are approaches to tense that are more in the spirit of Prior (1967, 1968)—approaches in which 'past', 'present', and 'future' are primitive operators, and in which there are no past and future events per se.[9]

If one supposes that there is an interesting connection between metaphysics and the semantics of natural language, and if one supposes that the semantics of natural language can help illuminate our metaphysics, then one might hope that the semantics of tense can help illuminate the metaphysics of time. For example, one might suppose that the choice between Reichenbach's theory of tense and Prior's theory of tense might have profound metaphysical consequences (favoring either the B-series or the A-series conception of time).

Here I am not advocating an approach, like that of Dummett (1991), in which we are supposed to reason bottom-up from the theory of meaning to metaphysics. It seems to me that the construction of a theory of meaning without some prior sense of ontology would have us climbing blind. That is, without some sense of the constituent structure of the world we would have no idea of how the theory of meaning is to link up our language with the world. Nor am I advocating the opposite position in which we are to sort out our ontology before we undertake the construction of a theory of meaning. It is only through the theory of meaning that we are able to differentiate the elements of our ontology. For example, even if a priori metaphysics is able to tell us that something in the world has an abstract property *foo,* what in our ontology tells us that *foo* is a *temporal* property—that it has something to do with the nature of *time?*

Accordingly, I assume that we have partial knowledge of the nature of reality and partial knowledge of the theory of meaning, and that our task is to solve a kind of complex equation involving information from semantics on the one side and metaphysics on the other. What we know about the nature of reality will help shape our semantic theories, but it is also the case that semantic theory will help to shed light on the nature of reality.

Of course many philosophers will hold that either metaphysics or the theory of meaning must be more fundamental than the other, but to me this has all the makings of a "chicken or egg" argument. There may be some deep truth about whether chickens or eggs are more fundamental, but no serious biologist would engage in such a debate, nor (I hope) would any serious philosopher be exercised by the question. Likewise, in my opinion, philosophers should worry less about whether metaphysics or the theory of meaning is more fundamental and should worry more about the relations that must hold between them in view of what we already know about each.

Roughly, when I say that there is an interesting relation holding between metaphysics and semantics I mean that concrete questions about the nature of reality can be illuminated by what we know about semantic theory, and that important questions in semantic theory may be adjudicated by certain of our metaphysical intuitions about the constitution of reality. Clearly more needs to be said, and chapter 4 will take up the issue in detail. Of course, this book is intended to serve as an illustration of this general point.

Indeed, the goal of this book is to provide a semantical argument in support of the A-theory conception of time. Or, better, the goal is to argue simultaneously for the A-theory conception of time and for a theory of tense that I will call the A-theory of tense. As will be seen, if the connection between language and the world holds up, then these two doctrines will be mutually reinforcing.

My main argument will be as follows: First, there are certain semantical weaknesses inherent in the B-theory semantical position. Specifically, the B-theorist cannot adequately account for the indexical nature of temporal discourse. Since the B-theory of time cannot be detached from the B-theory semantics, this effectively undermines the B-theory metaphysics.

On the other side, it has been held that the A-theory semantics has weaknesses of its own. Accordingly, I argue that those weaknesses, to the extent they exist, are easily repaired. The A-theory conception of time thus remains a plausible and undamaged alternative to the B-theory conception.

But I will argue further that independent psycholinguistic evidence supports the thesis that the A-theory semantics is in fact the semantical theory that users of natural language internalize and "know" (in a sense to be spelled out in chapter 2).

To get a better idea of how this argument will unfold, let us first briefly review the semantical challenges facing both the A-theory and the B-theory.

The Semantical Challenge for the B-Theorist: Temporal Indexicals

My wedding anniversary is March 12. Suppose that I have memorized this date. Maybe I had it inscribed in my wedding ring. So I know the following: My wedding anniversary is March 12.

Now suppose I am in my office late in the afternoon one day next March. I may say to myself: "My fifth anniversary is March 12. I should think about buying my wife an anniversary present." I might then wonder how much time I have. I take out a calendar to find today's date and discover to my horror that it is March 12! I shout "My fifth anniversary is today!"

In this little episode it is clear that I had two distinct utterances:

(1)
My fifth anniversary is March 12.

(2)
My fifth anniversary is today.

It is also clear that when I uttered (2) I had knowledge that I did not have when I uttered (1), and this extra knowledge appears to be reflected in the difference between (1) and (2). Thus, it is arguable that (1) and (2) have different semantical contents. As intuitive as this may seem, there are some powerful arguments designed to show otherwise—to show that the semantic contents of (1) and (2) are the same.

Indeed, the standard philosophical treatment of indexicals—for example, by Perry (1969, 1977) and Kaplan (1977, 1979, 1990)—has been to argue for a distinction between the content of a demonstrative expression and its *character* or *role*. The content would be the individual or object referred to by the demonstrative, and the character/role would be the additional cognitive significance (sometimes the expression "linguistic meaning" is used to characterize the extra element) supplied by the indexical in cases like (2). Although the literature is sometimes unclear on this point, it appears that these authors are advocating that character/role should not be part of the semantic content (or literal truth conditions) of the utterance.

What does that mean? If the semantics of natural language takes the form of a T-theory, and hence the semantics of a sentence is given by theorems like (3), then the right-hand side of the theorem—the portion following 'if and only if'—states the literal truth conditions of the sentence on the left-hand side.

(3)
'Snow is white' is true if and only if snow is white.

In this case, the truth conditions are that snow is white. If we assume a framework of this kind (I will explain and argue for it in chapter 2), then one way of taking the Kaplan-Perry thesis is as saying that character/role does not make it into the right-hand side of a T-theory theorem.[10] For example, the truth conditions of a sentence like 'I am hungry' would be not as in (4) but akin to (5).

(4)
'I am hungry now' is true if and only if I am hungry now.

(5)
An utterance u, at time t, by speaker s, of 'I am hungry now' is true if and only if s is hungry at t.

Here the only things that make it into the truth conditions are the individual s and the time t. The extra indexical element found in 'I' and 'now' must lie somewhere outside the semantics proper.

As we will see in chapter 3, there are many arguments for keeping the semantics free of character/role. For starters, having it in the semantics leads to headaches in modal constructions. But, as we will also see, these headaches can be ameliorated—there are ways to retain indexicality in the semantics and also cope with technical problems about modality.

Accordingly, I am going to argue that the received treatment of indexicality is mistaken—that indexicality should not be divorced from semantics. Obviously, this is not an argument that can be made carelessly, and a great deal of groundwork concerning the nature of language will have to be laid.

For example, leaving indexicality in the semantics leads to certain analyses that appear shockingly naive. A case in point would be (4) above. This is allegedly naive, since an utterance of 'I am hungry' by me to a hearer H can hardly be interpreted by H using (4)—that would force H to conclude that I am saying that H is hungry. The advice we are given by Perry and Kaplan, therefore, is to sweep away this naive view of indexicals and retain only the contents within the truth conditions (as in (5)).

The problem with this brief chain of reasoning is that it rests on assumptions about the nature of language that I consider to be fundamentally mistaken. If the function of language is communication, then the objection has some merit. But why should we suppose that language is *for* communication as opposed to, say, representing our thoughts? Indexicals will be discussed at length in chapter 3, but it is already evident that certain assumptions about the nature of language will have to be laid our first. This will be done in chapter 1, which will lay the foundations for the discussion of the nature of semantics in chapter 2 and for the treatment of indexicals in chapter 3. Later, in chapter 6, we will see precisely why this problem is insurmountable for the B-theorist.

The Challenges for the A-Theorist

There are two central challenges for the A-theorist. The first is a philosophical challenge involving an alleged paradox originally discussed by McTaggart. The second challenge—more semantical in nature—is that the A-theorist has no way of accounting for temporal anaphora. These two problems turn out to be related, but we can begin by treating them separately.

The McTaggart Paradox: Is the A-Theory Contradictory?
One of the earliest and most influential critiques of the A-theory is found in McTaggart's (1908, 1927) argument for the unreality of time. McTaggart's argument begins with the observation that certain pairs of properties are such that it would be inconsistent for one object to have both properties. For example, although a table can be both round and red, it cannot be both round and square, for roundness and squareness are inconsistent properties. Likewise, according to McTaggart, it would be inconsistent for certain events (e.g., the death of Queen

Anne) to be both past and future. Thus, in such cases, if we affirm (6), we have stated something that is inconsistent if not contradictory.

(6)
future(X) & past(X)

But according to McTaggart this is exactly what the A-theory entails, for a given event E will at some point be past, at some point be present, and at some point be future.[11] Thus, we have the following conjunction:

(7)
future(E) & past(E) & present(E)

The initial reaction to this part of the argument is often that it is absurd, for surely one is not saying that E is always future and always past and always present, but rather one is asserting (for example) that E is future at a certain time segment t, present at some time t*, and past at another time segment t'. But according to McTaggart this move is a cheat; it amounts to smuggling in B-theory resources; the A-theorist can't appeal to a sequence of events or times. The B-series time line cannot be introduced here to save the A-theorist.

Let us set this paradox on the back burner for the moment and turn to the problem of temporal anaphora. As we will see, the two problems are linked, and only by solving the problem of temporal anaphora for the A-theorist can we come to grips with the McTaggart argument.

The Problem of Temporal Anaphora
Consider the following example (Partee 1973, 1984):

(8)
I turned off the stove.

Clearly (8) does not merely mean that at some time in the past I turned off the stove. Without a doubt there have been many such episodes in my past. According to Partee (1973), (8) is informative because there is an implicit reference to some time or some reference event. I might equally well have uttered 'I turned off the stove then' (with 'then' serving as a temporal anaphor referring to some segment of time or event in the past).

This problem seems to lie at the heart of another objection to Priorean theories: that they are not able to account for complex tenses. The objection is that, for example, [PAST[PAST[S]]] simply collapses into the simple past. To see this, first consider the case where time is discrete. Let us call the minimum unit of time a "chronon." Then, at best, [PAST[S]] is true iff S was true at least one chronon ago. But then [PAST[PAST[S]]] is true iff S was true more than one chronon ago. But this doesn't seem to capture what we intended to say by a past perfect sentence like 'I had left'.

One might try to get around this difficulty by talking about degrees of pastness, but even this move is bound to fall short. 'I had left' might be about an event at any arbitrary distance in the past. Plus, there is the strong intuition that there really is a reference event here—that one could very well continue 'I had left...' with 'when Smith arrived'. How is *that* to be cashed out on a Priorean theory if there is no way to avail ourselves of temporal reference?

The Solution
The solution that I will propose to the problem of temporal anaphora is to develop a notion of E-type temporal anaphora—essentially a theory of temporal anaphora that does not involve reference to times or events.

In the case of ordinary E-type pronominal anaphora, as in (9), the idea is that the pronoun 'He' does not refer to some salient individual, but rather stands proxy for a definite description, so that the analysis of (9) is something along the lines of (9').

(9)
A man came in the room. He tripped over the chair.

(9')
A man came in the room. The man who came in the room tripped over the chair.

Crucially, 'The man who came into the room' is a Russellian description, not a referring expression; hence, the second sentence in (9') is not about some particular individual but makes a general claim about the world—i.e., that the world contains exactly one man who came into the room, and he tripped over the chair. We can say that the second sentence in (9') is therefore a *general* proposition and not a *singular* or *object-dependent* proposition. This difference may not seem like a big deal; however, as we will see, it is very important in certain contexts—for example, within the scope of modals and propositional-attitude verbs. For example, consider (10).

(10)
I believe that a unicorn is in the garden and that it is eating my roses.

If the pronoun 'it' is a referring expression and I have successfully uttered an object-dependent proposition, then it appears that we are committed to the existence of unicorns. However, if the pronoun stands proxy for a description, as in (10'), then if we treat descriptions à la Russell (1905) we are not forced to admit the existence of unicorns.

(10')
I believe that a unicorn is in the garden and that the unicorn in the garden is eating my roses.

A similar strategy can be executed for temporal anaphora. The operative idea is that temporal anaphors like 'then' do not refer to times but rather stand proxy for temporal conjunctions like when-clauses. So, for example in (11), the pronoun 'then' does not refer to a time, but is a place holder for a when-clause that might be extracted from the text. Thus, (11) might have the gloss given in (12).

(11)
Sam addressed Bill. Bill didn't respond then.

(12)
Sam addressed Bill. Bill didn't respond when Sam addressed him.

Crucially, on this proposal, the when-clause does not refer to a time, but will express a general proposition (at least general in the sense that the proposition is not dependent upon particular times or events described therein). Furthermore, the general nature of these propositions will be crucial when they are embedded in intensional environments like those created by modals and by propositional-attitude verbs, and also, I shall argue, in the scope of temporal operators like 'past' and 'future'. In brief, when general propositions are embedded in such environments the results are innocent claims to the effect that states of affairs matching certain descriptions did hold or will hold. Nothing follows about there being past or future events or times.

I realize that so far this is a big promissory note. It certainly sounds incredible that a when-clause need not refer to a time. But, as we will see, the idea can be cashed out handily using only off-the-shelf philosophical resources. These resources (including the distinction between general and singular propositions) will be introduced and incorporated into a full theory of E-type temporal anaphora in chapter 8.

Of course, in most cases the temporal anaphor is implicit (as in 'Bill didn't respond') and the number and range of temporally anaphoric constructions is vast. I will not be able to chart the entire territory, but I will survey enough of them in chapter 8 to suggest how the theory of E-type temporal anaphora might be developed. In addition, one of the central hypotheses of chapter 8 will be that *every* sentence has a when-clause, or a temporal adjunct of some form (e.g. 'before...', 'after...'), or a temporal anaphor that stands in for a when-clause. Accordingly, every sentence in natural language has either an explicit or an implicit temporal adjunct clause.

This insight turns out to lie at the root of the connection between temporal anaphora and McTaggart's paradox. The idea, very simply, is that one's initial intuition about the McTaggart argument was basically on track. One wants to say that it is possible to avoid the contradiction in (6) by adding that X is future at a certain time and past at another.

(6)
future(X) & past(X)

That move is certainly blocked for the A-theorist if times are construed in a B-series way, but that does not mean that there is no analogous A-theory maneuver. The idea, in short, is that the A-theorist will want to invoke E-type temporal anaphora.

Here is the gambit: (13) is shorthand for a representation of the form given in (13'why).

(13)
X is future.

(13')
X is FUT when [...].

But then the semantics delivers the following truth conditions for (13'):

(13*)
'X is FUT when [...]' is true iff X will be true when [...].

Similar considerations apply to (14).

(14)
X is PAST.

It will have the following truth conditions:

(14*)
'X is PAST when [...]' is true iff X was true when [...].

The trouble is that we can never get to the point where we have a conjunction of two conflicting A-theory tensed claims. Clearly (13*) and (14*) are not incompatible, since the when-clauses will have different contents. In short, once we introduce E-type temporal anaphora, the McTaggart argument will fail to get off the ground.

The Plan of the Book

Clearly, the lines of argument I will be taking on temporal indexicals and temporal anaphora lead us directly to the semantics of indexicals and anaphors generally, and ultimately to the very foundations of semantics. There is no question that the arguments given by B-theorists like Mellor have rested upon a very respectable semantical foundation: the work of David Kaplan and John Perry on indexicals. for example. However, for all its respectability, I believe that it is a foundation of sand, not rock, and that it is fundamentally unstable. Accordingly, I will begin with a detailed discussion of the nature of semantics.

Nothing I say about the foundations of semantics is going to be original; for the most part, it will involve elucidating a number of ideas about indexicals and anaphors that have been advanced by Gareth Evans, and it will also incorporate a general semantical picture that has been proposed by James Higginbotham and developed by a number of my peers in the philosophy of language. This work remains a minority position, however, and I will need to develop and defend the leading ideas in some detail here.

Underlying this alternative approach to the semantics of indexicals, for example, there is an even deeper philosophical issue about the nature of language. Is it a social object constructed for purposes of communication? Or, as Chomsky has proposed, is language a natural object which is part of our biological endowment and not necessarily *for* communication at all? My answer to this question will have consequences for the semantics of indexicals, so my first steps will have to be though this terrain.

Accordingly, the general plan will be to move gradually from a discussion of the nature of language to a general discussion of the semantics of natural language. After adding some needed technical resources to the semantics, I will take up the general issue of the connection between language and the world, then develop the A-theory and B-theory semantical theories, and then proceed to a discussion of the challenges faced by the A-theory and the B-theory.

All these preliminaries may seem like a very "long march" just to arrive at a discussion of the problem posed by indexicality for the B-theorist and the problem posed by temporal anaphora for the A-theorist, but in my view the march is unavoidable. The issues here are very subtle and very deep, and any attempt to skirt foundational questions is going to result in an exchange of uncompelling claims and counterclaims.

Impatient readers may want to begin with the challenge to the B-theory in chapter 6 and the defense of the A-theory in chapters 7 and 8 and then work backward. That's fine by me. The order of exposition here reflects my understanding of the logical precedence of the issues, not necessarily the friendliest or most enticing path for the reader.

Here, then, is the complete organization of the book.

In chapter 1, I first take up general considerations about the nature of language, opting for a conception of language (called "I-language" by Chomsky) as an innate computational/representational system that is part of our biological endowment but is not necessarily evolved for purposes of communication. I then discuss the possibility that I-language might the language of thought.

In chapter 2, I begin to develop the semantic theory at a very simple level, beginning with a discussion of why a referential semantics should take the form of an absolute truth-conditional semantics. Among the issues that will be pivotal in later chapters is the question of whether T-theories can display senses (and if so, how), the distinction between modest and robust T-theories, and the possibility of ontologically parsimonious theories of predication—theories that don't require reference to properties.

In chapter 3, I devote some time to showing how resources for propositional-attitude environments and for the theory of indexicals can be incorporated into an absolute semantics. (Both sets of resources will be necessary to develop my semantics of tense.) Crucially, I will argue for an analysis of indexicals in which they are treated disquotationally. Following Gareth Evans, I will also argue that we can rely on certain tracking abilities to underwrite our knowledge that 'I am hungry now' expresses the same proposition as 'I was hungry yesterday' said a day later. Of course the real challenge for any alternative theory of indexicals is whether it can handle modal environments as well as Kaplan's theory can. Hence, I also discuss possible lines of investigation that would allow an Evansian semantics of indexicals to accommodate the modal environments that have been brought to attention by Kaplan and others.

In chapter 4, I return to the question of the metaphysical commitment of semantic theory, showing exactly where the metaphysical commitments arise when one is utilizing an absolute semantical theory and exploring certain example cases.

In chapter 5, I extend the general semantical apparatus to include a semantics of tense in the spirit of Reichenbach (1947). As we will see, this semantical theory has robust metaphysical consequences—in particular, it is committed to a B-theory metaphysics of time in the sense of McTaggart (1908).

In chapter 6, I develop the criticism of the B-theory semantics by constructing the problem of indexicality. I argue that there are profound difficulties surrounding the analysis of temporal indexicals—difficulties that may well be insurmountable.

In chapter 7, I construct a semantics of tense in the spirit of Prior (1967, 1968), again exploring some of the metaphysical consequences of the view (in particular, showing that it is committed to a version of the A-theory of time that Prior himself advocated). I then argue that the Priorean semantical theory can easily avoid the difficulties with temporal indexicals that plague Reichenbachian theories. I then canvass a number of standard objections to Priorean semantics of tense and argue that those objections can be overcome.

In chapter 8, I take up the treatment of temporal anaphora in the A-theory and develop a theory of "E-type" temporal anaphora. The idea is that, rather than referring to time points or to past and future events, temporal anaphors are implicit when-clauses (or, more generally, implicit temporal conjunctions). I then extend this idea to a number of cases of complex temporal anaphora. Finally, I apply the theory to the refutation of McTaggart's paradox.

In chapter 9, I expand the investigation of the relative merits of the A-theory and the B-theory, drawing in particular on data from research into the acquisition of tense. I argue that the available evidence clearly leans in favor of the Priorean semantics and its attendant A-theory conception of time. Finally, I argue that, if one wants to take the phenomenology of time seriously, the revised version of the A-theory presented in chapters 7 and 8 comports quite nicely with at least some of the leading phenomenologies of time.

In chapter 10, I take up some of the philosophical and linguistic consequences of the theory, first pursuing the philosophical consequences for the nature of logic, epistemology, and memory and then pursuing some linguistic consequences—in particular the prospects for eliminating the linguistic notion of tense altogether.

It is admittedly a long and tortuous journey to get to the issues of indexicality and temporal anaphora, not to mention the relative merits of the A-theory and the B-theory, but once again careful groundwork and stage setting will be crucial to the arguments presented in the end. As I have already noted, some will want to jump ahead and see what the destination looks like. For the rest of us, the long march begins directly.

Chapter 1
The Nature of Language

1.1   I-Language vs. E-Language[1]

Chomsky (1986) distinguishes between two conceptions of the nature of language: *I-language* and *E-language*. An I-language is not a spoken or written corpus of sentences, but is rather a state of an internal system which is part of our biological endowment.[2] Thus, I-language representations are not to be confused with spoken or written natural language sentences. They are, rather, data structures in a kind of internal computational system with which humans are born and which they have co-opted for communication and for other purposes.[3]

From the E-language perspective, on the other hand, a natural language is a kind of social object the structure of which is purported to be established by convention (however 'convention' is to be understood),[4] and persons may acquire varying degrees of competence in their knowledge and use of that social object.

I gather that, on Chomsky's view, such social objects do not exist and would be of little scientific interest if they did exist.[5] To see why Chomsky's basic idea is right, consider the problem of trying to individuate such social objects. For example, simply consider the linguistic situation in Italy. We speak of "the Italian language," and we say it is distinct from Spanish, but why? In large measure, Castilian Spanish and Standard Italian are mutually intelligible when read or spoken slowly. Why don't we say that they are regional variants of the same language?

In various regions of Italy, various dialects are spoken. For example, a different dialect is spoken in Parma than in Venice. For all practical purposes, these dialects are no more mutually intelligible than Castilian Spanish and Standard Italian. Why do we say that both are dialects of Italian? Why not say that they are separate languages on equal footing with Standard Italian (and Castilian Spanish), not "merely" dialects?

In Italy, some dialects (e.g., Friulian and Sardinian) *are* recognized as official languages by the government. What makes those dialects special? What makes them languages in a way that the Venetian dialect isn't? The answer, of course, is that what counts as a distinct language is a political decision. (As Max Weinreich said, "a language is a dialect with an army and a navy.") Political identity precedes E-language identity.

But this isn't just an observation about the distinction between language and dialect; it also applies to the distinction between dialect and idiolect. My wife, who teaches where I teach and lives where I live, speaks slightly differently than I do. For example, she pronounces 'Mary', 'marry', and 'merry' differently. I pronounce them all the same. Do we speak the same dialect? How much divergence is necessary before we can say that we do?

This isn't a case of fuzzy boundaries, such as that between a couch and a chair. The problem is that sufficient divergence will depend upon factors that have nothing to do with what we are actually saying and everything to do with whether we feel disposed to identify with each other.

Nor is the problem resolved simply by throwing out talk of E-languages and E-dialects and reverting to talk about E-idiolects. What portion of the noises I make count as belonging to my idiolect? If I cough in the middle of a particular utterance, does the extra noise become part of my idiolect? How do we distinguish parts of my idiolect from simple errors? But suppose we had an error theory. If we wrote down everything I ever (correctly) uttered, would that exhaust my idiolect? Would everything I ever have said or ever will say exhaust my idiolect? Don't we have to consider what I might say or could say? But how do we make sense of that from the E-language perspective?

Or suppose that I speak differently at home and at school. Does it follow that I employ two idiolects? Since my speech varies slightly with every person I talk to, why not say that I have a different idiolect for each of my conversation partners? And since I speak to them differently at different times, ... It should be clear where this is going. Why not say that I employ a different idiolect every time I open my mouth? At that point, the concept of idiolect (and language) has effectively collapsed.[6]

Clearly there is no way to sort out any of these questions if we are thinking of language or idiolect in terms of some set of external utterances or inscriptions. We can make choices about what counts as an error or a possible utterance, but on the E-language perspective these choices are going to be stipulative or prescriptive. The difficulty is that there is no way we can stipulate everything that we need to. Consider the following two examples from Chomsky 1986:

(1)

John filed every letter without reading it.

(2)

What letter did John file without reading it?

Somehow, speakers of English—even those of us who never remember to say 'whom' rather than 'who' in dative case—know that if we delete the pronoun 'it' in these two sentences the effects on meaning are rather different:

(1')

John filed every letter without reading.

(2')

What letter did John file without reading?

Sentence (2') is ambiguous in a way that sentence (1') is not. Both (1') and (2') have the meaning in which the filing was done without some (arbitrary) reading taking place, but (2') also preserves the meaning of (2)—it can still be understood as asking what letter John filed without reading *it* (the filed letter). Who taught us *that*?

Facts like these are ubiquitous in natural language, and it would be impossible for any institution to prescribe or stipulate even a small subset of them. The Academie Française is supposed to dictate that a certain set of properties that cover the French lexicon and the pronunciation of the words in it. However, the Academie doesn't dictate as much as it thinks it does. At best it dictates a small range of superficial rules about French. All the while, it relies on shared tacit knowledge of I-language, which provides the substrate upon which those prescribed rules are parasitic. What the Academie has is a collection of proclamations about what the structure of French *should* be but which is not even sufficient to constitute a respectable candidate E-language.

In short, the only way out of these imbroglios is to give up talk of language and idiolect as a natural object or to think about the mechanism that explains the linguistic competence that each of us obviously has.[7] The only sensible way to do that is to suppose something along the lines suggested by Chomsky: that our linguistic competence is attributable to an internal computational system that is part of our biological endowment. That system and the representations encoded in it are objects that we can study and about which we can have theories. Anything else is just vaporware.

1.2   What Is I-Language *For?*

The question "What is I-language *for?*" has profound consequences for the theory of indexicals and for the theory of propositional attitudes advanced in subsequent chapters of this book. On the standard view—ordinarily presupposing an E-language picture of language—it is assumed that the purpose of language is communication, and hence it is assumed that a semantical theory (including the theory of indexicals and propositional attitudes) must respect the communicative function of language.

In the case of indexicals, for example, an utterance of 'I am hungry now' is taken to have a component to its meaning that holds at all times and for all speakers (i.e., that the speaker of the sentence is hungry at the time of its utterance). Allegedly, inserting anything more (e.g., the "nowness" of the indexical character of the utterance) into the meaning would throw off your communicative partners when you left messages on their answering machines. The communicative function of language thus requires that propositional content not vary from individual to individual or from time to time.

There is probably room to argue that the communicative function of language (if it exists) does not put such serious constraints on propositional content. However, it seems to me that the basic premise itself needs to be called into question. Specifically, once we suppose that the I-language perspective is correct, it immediately raises questions about why I-languages should be *for* communication—or, for that matter, why they should be *for* anything at all.[8]

The issue can be put in a general way. If one takes the E-language perspective that languages are established by human beings by convention, it is entirely sensible to suppose that languages can have a certain end. In this case the end is established by human intentions. Persons simply agree (perhaps tacitly) to follow certain linguistic conventions in order to further the end of communicating with one another.

But if we reject the E-language picture and adopt an I-language picture in which the language faculty is part of our biological endowment, human intentions simply don't enter into the equation. If an individual I-language is to have some sort of end, it can't be established by human convention; it must be established by biology. Here we are on very tricky terrain.

In the first place, teleological explanation in biology is a controversial doctrine. There is a strong temptation to appeal to evolutionary theory to establish the purpose of a biological system (for example, by arguing for selectional value of a faculty to which we want to attribute some purpose). But this requires some strong assumptions about evolutionary theory—in particular, it requires a gradualist approach to evolution. In the case of attributing a communicative end to language, it also assumes that we *have* a faculty dedicated to communication (as opposed to just an ad hoc bundle of abilities that we employ in order to communicate).

The issue about gradualism is, of course, familiar from recent writing on evolutionary theory. On one side, Stephen Jay Gould et al. hold that human evolution has been far from gradual and that in many cases organs that evolved for certain purposes were subsequently co-opted for quite different purposes.[9] Humans are not unique in this respect; evolution is typically of this character. Hence, for example, membranes that evolved for thermal regulation might be co-opted for the purpose of flight. In the context of the language faculty, the idea is that we cannot reason backward from the current ways in which we use the language faculty to the conclusion that the language faculty evolved for those purposes. And even if we could, there is no reason to suppose that the language faculty is thereby an optimal system for those purposes. Biology, as Chomsky and Lasnik (1993) have observed, is typically "'messy,' intricate, the result of evolutionary 'tinkering,' and shaped by accidental circumstances and by physical conditions that hold of complex systems with varied functions and elements." Perhaps, then, I-language is a very imperfect system for purposes of communication. More to the point, its handling of indexical expressions may not coincide with philosophical intuitions about how an optimal system of communication ought to be built.

On the other side of this issue, Pinker and Bloom (1990) have argued that evolution is in fact a much more gradual process and that it makes good sense to think of the language faculty as having evolved in response to the selectional advantage of communication. But even if we accept their arguments for gradualism and the thesis that the I-language faculty evolved in response to selectional pressures, it does not follow that I-language evolved for purposes of *communication*. For example, it is still possible that it evolved in order to serve as a medium of thought (see section 1.3 and appendix P1). Or, in view of the rich metrical theory found in various I-languages,[10] it could even have evolved for purposes of producing poetic sound patterns. Clearly there are advantages to having communicative abilities; however, there are advantages to having other abilities, and if one is to argue backward from the existence of I-language to some selectional advantage one must argue carefully that the main advantage is its communicative function and not some other function.

In summary: The language faculty (I-language) is not a product of human intentions but rather a product of human biology, so any end that we attribute to I-language must be biologically based. This means that an argument for the communicative function of language would require an evolutionary story about the selectional advantage of having a language faculty for purposes of communication. This strategy assumes a controversial view about the nature of evolutionary theory; further, it assumes that communication is the only (or the chief) function of I-language. Finally, even if we were to assume that I-language evolved for the express purpose of human communication, it is a very long distance to the conclusion that the propositional content of an utterance must contain only information that is stable among language users. Evolutionary tinkering may well have found an alternative strategy.

1.3   Is I-Language the Language of Thought?[11]

Although it is not crucial to the line of argumentation in this book, it turns out that equivalence between I-language and the language of thought would help us to cut some corners.

Just to be clear, we need to distinguish thought (or, better, the having of thoughts) from cognition in general. No one would suppose that all human cognition takes place in I-language, but that is not what is at issue. The question is this: When we have thoughts about the world, are those thoughts simply interpreted I-language tokens, or are they tokens to be found elsewhere in our cognitive architecture?

Because this could easily slide into a terminological dispute over what gets to be called "thought," I am perfectly willing to admit (for purposes of argument) that my definition is stipulative. My primary interest is in cognitive states that purport to be about the world, and for purposes of this investigation I am calling such states "thoughts." However, there is a fair bit of history on the side of defining thoughts in this way, beginning with Franz Brentano's claim that intentionality (aboutness) is the mark of the mental. But again, I am not advocating a broad equivalence of I-language and cognition; I am suggesting an equivalence between certain I-language representations and those cognitive states and thoughts that are about the world.

With this clarification, could I-language be the language of thought? Prima facie, one might suppose not, on the ground that even if there is a close connection between language and reality there must be some language of thought that mediates between I-language and the world. But why suppose this? Indeed, the postulation of an intermediary medium of thought strikes me as redundant and unmotivated at best.

The postulation of a third medium is redundant for this reason: If there is a mechanism that maps from I-language onto the language of thought (LOT), then either the LOT must be isomorphic to I-language (in which case it can do no more than I-language can) or the properties of the LOT are recoverable from I-language representations via some algorithm. In either case, I-language representations already carry all the information necessary for serving as the language of thought.

Once we move from the E-language conception of language to the I-language conception, most of the stock arguments against natural language being the language of thought collapse. For example, Jackendoff (1993) and Pinker (1994) raise several arguments that seem to leave the I-language-as-LOT hypothesis untouched. I'll consider these technical arguments in appendix P1, but some less formal arguments due to Pinker (ibid., p. 68ff.) are worth exploring here. For example, Pinker notes that "babies cannot think in words because they have not yet learned any," that "monkeys . . . cannot think in words because they are incapable of learning them," and that many human adults claim to do their best thinking without words. Clearly these arguments have consequences for any thesis that I-language is the language of thought. If human babies and chimps are thinking thoughts but have no I-language, that certainly undermines any identification between I-language and thought; likewise if human adults have thoughts which are nonlinguistic. But are such things possible?

One problem with babies is knowing precisely when they begin having genuine thoughts (in the sense specified above). There is no question that cognition is taking place in the womb, but when do babies have thoughts about states of affairs in the world? I know of no illuminating developmental studies on this question. It is one thing to find evidence of a concept of number, or of the permanence of objects, or of the ability to identify one's mother, but by what line of argument can it be shown that these are genuine representational thoughts?

And insofar as we are inclined to call these thoughts (and the more sophisticated and world-related the cognition the more apt we are to do so) it becomes less clear that babies don't have the relevant I-language representations. For example, linguistic comprehension precedes production by a good bit (as any parent knows). On the theory of I-language adopted here (from Chomsky 1995b), sentences are construed as ordered pairs of representations, ⟨PF, LF⟩, in which the PF representations interface with the "perceptual-articulatory" component and the LF representations interface with the "conceptual-intensional" system. It is entirely possible that the I-language system is intact in babies but that the interface of PF representations with the perceptual-articulatory component is not yet developed.

By the way, this possibility also undermines arguments about intelligent adults with no apparent linguistic abilities. Such individuals may well have full-blown linguistic abilities, which may well be servicing the conceptual-intensional system, yet be incapable of speech production and comprehension. The opposite may also be true: an individual may be producing and responding to well-formed natural language sentences, but if the LF representations are not being utilized as thoughts (that is, if they are causally inert in plans and actions) he or she will appear to have language but no thoughts. In effect, such an individual would have causally inert thought forms.

The case of animals raises more subtle issues. On the one hand, we want to say "Fido thinks his dish is empty," and presumably to say this is to ascribe a thought to Fido. It is certainly a cognitive state about the world. On the other hand, I-language is supposed to be unique to humans. So how can Fido's thought be an interpreted I-language representation? Could Fido (or at least chimps) have rudimentary forms of I-language? Here, I tend to be in Pinker's camp. The evidence suggests that nonhuman animals lack anything remotely like our language faculty. So how come they all think?

The question is vexing only if one supposes that nature provides only one way to solve a problem. For example, we know that various marine animals employ various methods of propelling themselves (contrast the squid with the manta ray), yet it is perfectly correct for us to say that they all swim. We also know that nature provides different ways for animals to be sexed male and female (our X-and-Y-chromosome strategy being a minority strategy), yet we are not blundering when we say "That is a male chicken" or "That is a female spider." The point is that the terms 'swim' and 'male' cover a broad class of phenomena as we move from species to species. What I want to suggest is that 'thinks' is a bit like this. We are perfectly within our rights to say that Fido is thinking, just as we are within our rights to say that Sam the squid swims and that Charlotte the spider is a female; we just have to keep in mind that Sam doesn't swim like we do, that Charlotte is sexed by different biological mechanisms than we are, and, crucially, that Fido thinks by different mechanisms than we do.

Fido may well have a language of thought. His language of thought may have some rudimentary syntax, and he may (as the Greek philosophers supposed) be capable of some inferential reasoning. But his language of thought isn't human I-language. It's that simple. It is entirely reasonable to suppose that Fido and other animals co-opt other cognitive systems (with relevant syntactic properties) to do their thinking. They may even have faculties that evolved for that express purpose. But humans appear to be different. It is entirely possible that we have co-opted I-language for the purpose of thinking (or perhaps it evolved for that purpose and has been co-opted for communication). In any case, the rudimentary thoughts of Fido and the chimps do not tell against our use of I-language for the kind of robust thinking of which we are capable.

In regard to adult humans who purport to have nonlinguistic thoughts, Pinker gives several anecdotal stories about famous creative individuals who claim some role for imagery in their thinking. Of course, for every such anecdote there is an anecdote that delivers just the opposite conclusion. One famous example, reported in Monk 1996, is the case of Bertrand Russell, who claimed to be incapable of thinking imagistically.[12] Clearly there are individual differences concerning our use of images in cognition and creative problem solving, but this doesn't entail individual differences in the language of thought.

Even if we concede for the sake of argument that there are mental images, and that these images are fundamentally pictorial and not text-based,[13] we still have to be on guard against a fallacious step in reasoning. It is surely true that images can be useful in our thinking. Does it follow that our thoughts are imagistic?

For example, maps are very useful in planning invasions and family vacations, but when we are deliberating whether to go north or south on Tuesday it does not follow that our thoughts are in any way composed of maps. Likewise, in working out an argument I may find it useful to doodle pictures on a piece of paper, but no one would suppose that I am having "doodlistic" thoughts. Why should we choose to identify thoughts and images when the images happen to be mental?

I may dream of a snake biting its tail, and this may inspire a thought about the structure of carbon-based molecules, but it does not follow that the dream and its attending image constituted a thought. The thought came later. This fact is actually evinced in Pinker's account of how Roger Shepard came up with his famous image-rotation experiments:

Early one morning, suspended between sleep and awakening in a state of lucid consciousness, Shepard experience a "spontaneous kinetic image of three-dimensional images majestically turning in space." *Within moments* and before fully awakening, Shepard had a clear idea for the design of an experiment. (Pinker 1994, p. 71; emphasis added)

I am perfectly willing to concede that the kinetic image helped Shepard come to have the thought that he did. *Something* must inspire us to have the thoughts that we do. We blunder, however, when we suppose that these inspirational images must be thoughts themselves.

In any case, we have known for nearly 400 years that images are very poor candidates for thoughts. Descartes observed that although we have thoughts about chiliagons (thousand-sided figures) we do not have images of them. Even among the British Empiricists, the equation of images with thoughts was unraveling by the time of Berkeley. It was he who observed that vague thoughts (say, about the concept of a triangle) are often associated with a very clear image (say, a red equilateral triangle), and that thoughts about particular individuals (say, a long-lost friend) can be associated with a very vague image.

Moreover, as Fodor (1975) observed, images appear to be too coarse-grained to serve as thoughts. I may have the thought that Santa Claus is bearded, and this may well be accompanied by an image of Santa; however, that image is the same image that accompanies my thought that Santa is red-cheeked. Here we have one image and two thoughts. Conclusion: the thoughts cannot be identified with images.

If images don't work, could something else besides language serve as the medium of thought? One idea, advanced by Johnson-Laird (1983), is that we might introduce nonlinguistic "mental models" to do the necessary work. Mental models can be as fine-grained as we please. The only problem with this family of strategies is that such models, while often presented in pictorial form, necessarily have a syntactic structure that is crucial to our interpretation of them (Rips 1986). Moreover, they are successful only insofar as they mimic the syntactic form we would use to express the thoughts they are intended to model. That is, our expression of a thought is conceptually prior to the construction of a model for the thought.

It is certainly an empirical question as to what the language of thought must look like, but there is a heavy presumption in favor of the I-language alternative. The nonlinguistic alternatives, such as images and mental models, fail to get out of the blocks, and once we are working with an I-language conception of language any intermediary language of thought is simply redundant.

Obviously there is a lot more to be said about the identification of I-language with the language of thought. I don't presume to have given knock-down evidence for the thesis here (or even in appendix P1). Rather, my goal has been to suggest its plausibility. For those who find the thesis plausible, some of the arguments in this book will unfold much more rapidly.

Chapter 2

The Form of the Semantic Theory

2.1   The Nature of Semantic Knowledge

One of the key assumptions of this work is the idea is that part of the job of semantics is to characterize the semantic *knowledge* that an agent has. "Semantic knowledge" is not intended to suggest a thesis limited to how an agent represents meaning to himself or herself. Rather, it is assumed that agents standardly have knowledge about things in the world (tables, chairs, etc.), and that a great deal of semantic knowledge is a species of this sort of knowledge. So, for example, a speaker of English might know that the word 'snow' refers to snow (the stuff in the world), and this bit of knowledge would be an example of genuine semantic knowledge.

Talk of "semantic knowledge" has a tendency to set off alarm bells among philosophers, no doubt because these philosophers take 'knowledge' to be referring to a Cartesian conception of knowledge[1]—knowledge that the agent could have completely independently of any environmental relations. That is not what is intended here. The idea is that one can perfectly well have knowledge of the external world (as noted above) and that one can know things that link expressions of the language with those things in the external world; semantic rules being cases in point.[2]

It will also be assumed that much of an agent's semantic knowledge is "tacit knowledge"—knowledge which the agent may not assent to having, but knowledge which nonetheless underwrites abilities which the agent has. This sort of knowledge has been proposed in syntactic theory, where it is argued that tacit knowledge of certain linguistic principles explains our linguistic competence.[3] Analogously, it will be assumed here that tacit knowledge of a number of semantic rules underlies our semantic abilities.

Various theories of tacit knowledge are possible (e.g., tacit knowledge as a disposition to act in a certain way), but here I shall be adopting the view that genuine tacit knowledge is in some sense represented by the knower in the form of a data structure—that is, that the representation is a semi-stable syntactic state in the agent's mind/brain.

Again, the claim is not that the object of semantic knowledge *is* the representation. Rather, it is that the object of semantic knowledge is related to the representation in an interesting way. So, for example, my knowledge that 'snow' refers to snow does not consist solely in my representation of snow, since the representation itself is a syntactic object. Rather, the object of my semantic knowledge is snow itself, since that is what my representation determines.

2.2 Why an Absolute Semantics?

So far, I have discussed semantic theory in very general terms and have left open the question of what form such a theory should take. In this section I will argue that semantic theory should take the form of an "absolute" truth theory, in the form of a truth-conditional semantics.

This general approach is controversial, but for the most part the controversy has been due to misunderstandings. The controversy has been fostered in part by a failure to articulate the difference between the goals of absolute truth-conditional semantics and the goals of alternative semantic theories. I will therefore begin by trying to get clear on how an absolute semantics differs from the other candidates, and why an absolute semantics is best suited for the kinds of concerns that arise in the semantics of natural language.

Let me begin by identifying three broad classes of semantic theories:

- structural semantics
- model-theoretic semantics
- absolute truth-conditional semantics.

As indicated above, I will be defending the third type of semantic theory. To see why, we need to take a closer look at the other two alternatives.

Structural Semantics
Structural semantic theories have been advocated by Katz (1972), Katz and Fodor (1963), Katz and Postal (1964), and Jackendoff (1972, 1987). The key idea behind all these proposals has been the notion that providing a semantics for a natural language expression requires that one provide a mapping of that expression onto some representational language (possibly the language of thought). For example, in Katz 1972, Katz and Fodor 1963, and Katz and Postal 1964 the idea is to map a given natural language expression onto a "semantic marker,"

which is in turn a symbol in a particular representational language. (Following Lewis 1972, we can call this language "Semantic Markerese"). In turn, Semantic Markerese is designed so that ambiguous expressions of a given natural language are disambiguated in Markerese. In addition, entailment relations and synonymy relations between natural language expressions are supposed to follow by virtue of the forms of their Semantic Markerese counterparts.

Lewis (1972) raised an important and widely accepted objection to structural semantics. According to Lewis, if we provide a mapping of English expressions onto the expressions of Markerese, the expressions of Markerese will still stand in need of interpretation. What we have at best is a mapping from one system of notation onto another, but what we wanted was some indication of what the system of notation is about.

Lewis's point can also be characterized as a point about the semantic knowledge that we have. We all come to know the reference of various English expressions, and it is natural to expect a semantic theory to characterize what it is that we have come to know. But notice what kind of knowledge is attributed to the speaker when all one has are mappings into Markerese. As Lepore (1983) notes, at best one gets theorems like (1).

(1)
'Fragola' in Italian translates into the language of Semantic Markerese as S.

We might even follow current fashion and render the expressions of Semantic Markerese as capitalized versions of their natural language counterparts, as in (1').

(1')
'Fragola' in Italian translates into the language of Semantic Markerese as FRAGOLA.

But clearly neither of these theorems characterizes what a speaker of Italian is saying when he or she says 'fragola'. That is, these theorems do not tell us that 'fragola' means strawberry.

This general point is not particularly contentious. Even advocates of structural semantics have essentially granted that the kind of semantic theory they are offering will not yield a connection between language and the world. What *is* contentious to the advocates of structural semantics is the question of whether there is any reason for a semantic theory to characterize such a language-world connection. Katz (1972, p. 183) has taken precisely this tack, arguing that it is not the business of semantics to "study the relations between objects of one sort or another and the expressions of a language that speak about them."

There is no point in debating the question of which enterprise gets the honorary title *semantics*. There may well be an important place for the type of enterprise advocated by Katz, Jackendoff, and others. My main concern is to note that such an enterprise will not address the sorts of concerns raised earlier in this chapter and hence cannot exhaust our interest in language. In particular, such an account cannot help us to characterize the very basic knowledge that underlies our ability to know what the expressions of our language are about.

Some readers may find this discussion old hat, but for all its familiarity it seems to me that the moral has been lost on many semanticists. As we shall see in the next section, precisely the same concerns can be raised against model-theoretic semantics.

Model-Theoretic Semantics

Many proponents of model-theoretic semantics have argued that it can overcome the limitations of the structural semantics—that model-theoretic semantics can successfully characterize the relation between language and the world.

The question, as we shall see, is whether a model-theoretic semantics does in fact provide us with language-world connections. Specifically, it has been observed by Lepore (1983), Higginbotham (1990), and others that model-theoretic semantics falls victim to the same considerations that have been raised against structured representation theories. Let's see why.

A model-theoretic semantics might characterize the content of an expression as in (2).

(2)
The content of the Italian word 'fragola' is the extension of 'fragola' in every possible world.

Alternatively, one might find 'fragola' characterized as in (3).

(3)
The content of the Italian word 'fragola' is that which 'fragola' is true of in every model.

But, as Higginbotham (1990) has stressed, a native speaker of English who knows only a bit of Italian syntax and the meanings of virtually no Italian words, could know both (2) and (3) while knowing essentially nothing about the content of 'fragola'. The kind of knowledge such a speaker would not have, but which would be crucial to understanding 'fragola,' is expressed by (4).

(4)
'fragola' refers to strawberries.

The point to be stressed here is that model-theoretic semantics fails in exactly the same way that structural semantics fails. What we expect a semantic theory to deliver is a characterization of the speaker's knowledge about the connection between language and the world. Structural semantics does not deliver this because it only gives us a mapping from one language onto some other system of representation. Model-theoretic semantics likewise fails, because it never makes the connection between language and the world; at best it gives us a mapping from expressions of a given language onto certain model-theoretic objects.

It might be objected that we can always specify an intended model, and that the actual world should be the intended model.[4] But Lepore (1983) has observed that this move will not work. If there is to be an intended model, then we should like to know how to identify it. But, on the face of it, this is no easy task (ibid., p. 184):

How much about a world do we need to know before we can distinguish it from all other worlds? Presumably a lot. There presumably is a class of worlds in which the number of trees in Canada is even and one in which the number is odd. So far are we from being able to single out the actual world from all others that we do not even know which class it falls in. But do we need to distinguish the actual world from all others to understand our language?

However, I think there is a way of specifying an intended model. What is needed is a recursive theory that will tell us that 'snow' is intended to refer to snow in the model, 'white' is to be true of white things in the model, and so on. Such an intended model must also specify the intended interpretation of complex expressions in the model—indeed an infinite number of them. There are theories that can do this; after all, that is precisely what T-theories do! In effect, talk of intended models amounts to a kind of hand waving at precisely the point where T-theories are required.

None of the above is to suggest that model-theoretic semantics is useless or flawed in any sense. What is suggested is that claims made on its behalf are often excessive. In particular, one must be wary of claims that a model-theoretic semantics can provide a theory of language-world connections.[5]

Absolute Truth-Conditional Semantics

On the theory I will be pursuing—that of Davidson (1967a)—a semantic theory is a system of rules that yields theorems of the following form:

(T)

s is true iff p.

Here s is an expression in the *object language* (i.e., the language about which the investigator is theorizing), and p is an expression in the *metalanguage* (the language the investigator is using to state the theory). The metalanguage might be English, or it might be some other language. Of course, since the theory is stated in it, the metalanguage has to be a language that the theorist already understands.

The schema above (sometimes called a T-schema) says that the sentence s is true if and only if it is the case that p. The phrase 'is true if and only if' is actually a very weak constraint. What it means is that either s and p are both true or they are both false.

For example, the system of rules might yield theorems like the following:

(i)
'Snow is white' is true iff snow is white.

(ii)
'Snow is white' is true iff grass is green.

Systems of rules (T-theories) that yield only theorems like (i) are said to be *interpretive*, because the expressions in the metalanguage successfully give the contents of the expressions in the object language. T-theories that yield theorems like (ii) are said to be *non-interpretive* T-theories.

Here I will be interested only in interpretive T-theories, i.e., those that deliver the contents of the object-language expressions. I assume that those theories are the ones that speakers exploit in the generation and comprehension of language. As it turns out, this assumption has some strong consequences for the origin and nature of our semantic knowledge. For example, it follows that we must have knowledge of a certain class of constraints on T-theories. If we did not, we would be unable to construct interpretive T-theories. Of course we must know more than just the rules of an interpretive T-theory. We must know that our theory is interpretive and that it can be exploited in the comprehension of language.[6] Larson and Segal (1995) argue that it follows that we must be "hard-wired" to construct interpretive T-theories and to exploit them in language comprehension.

For our current interests, the key idea in a T-theory is that one can have a theory that will provide the language-world connections for any expression of the language (or part of language) under study. Typically, this is accomplished via an axiomatic theory in which certain axioms give the referents of the terminal symbols of a sentential phrase marker and other rules show how the semantic values of the terminal symbols contribute to the semantic value of the nonterminal nodes of the phrase marker. It will be helpful to consider a concrete example of a T-theory. The following example from Larson and Segal 1995 will suit our purposes nicely in this regard.

Since we will be considering a relatively simple fragment of natural language, the syntax will be described by a context-free phrase-structure grammar, using rewriting rules of the form

A → B C

Roughly, this rule states that a node of category A may have the daughters B and C:

In this and subsequent fragments, we will proceed by specifying the syntax and then stating the semantic (interpretive) rules for the fragment.

Syntax

S → S1 and S2

S → S1 or S2

S → it is not the case that S1

S → NP VP

NP → Dick, Sally

VP → leaps, walks

Semantics   Here we introduce the predicate Val(A, B), which is to be read as "A is the semantic value of B." The theory will include two kinds of axioms: axioms that assign semantic values to the lexical items (i.e., words) and axioms that show how we can determine the semantic value of a mother node A, given the semantic values of its daughter nodes B and C. Examples of axioms for the lexical items are given in (5).[7]

(5)
a.
Val(x, Dick) iff x = Dick
Val(x, Sally) iff x = Sally
b.
Val(x, leaps) iff x leaps
Val(x, walks) iff x walks

Examples of axioms for the nonterminal nodes are given in (6) and (7).

(6)

a.

Val(T, [$_S$ NP VP]) iff for some x, Val(x, NP) and Val(x, VP)

b.

Val(x, [$_\alpha$ β]) iff Val(x, β) (where α ranges over categories, and β ranges over categories and lexical items)

(7)

a.

Val(T, [$_S$ S1 <u>and</u> S2]) iff it is both the case that Val(T, S1) and Val(T, S2)

b.

Val(T, [$_S$ S1 <u>or</u> S2]) iff either Val(T, S1) or Val(T, S2)

c.

Val(T, [$_S$ <u>it is not the case that</u> S1]) iff it is not the case that Val(T, S1)

For example, rule (6a) shows how the semantic value of the S node in the structure

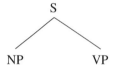

is determined by the semantic values of the NP and the VP. The rule says, in effect, that the semantic value of S will be true just in case there is something that is both the semantic value of the NP and the semantic value of the VP. Similar considerations apply to the rules in (7). For example, (7b) tells us that in the structure

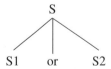

the semantic value of S will be the true just in case either the True is the semantic value of S1 or the True is the semantic value of S2.[8]

   The idea is that we can use these axioms to derive the truth conditions of a sentence of the object language. In order to carry out these derivations, we will need to introduce production rules like those shown in (8) and (9).

(8)

Production Rule (SoE)

$$\ldots \alpha \ldots$$
$$\alpha \text{ iff } \beta$$
_____

therefore $\ldots \beta \ldots$

(The basic idea of this rule is that we can substitute β for α at any step in a derivation, just in case α iff β holds.)

(9)

Production Rule (SoI)

$$\phi \text{ iff for some x, x} = \alpha \text{ and} \ldots x \ldots$$
_____

therefore ϕ iff $\ldots \alpha \ldots$

It is important to keep in mind that these are not logical rules, and that the steps in each derivation are much more tightly constrained than they would be if the full resources of logic were at our disposal. For example, we are not allowed to substitute logically equivalent expressions unless they have been generated in a previous step in the derivations.[9] These are simply rules for deriving T-theorems.

Given simple rules like (8) and (9), and the axioms above, one can "prove" T-theorems by recursive application of the axioms to the structural description of the object-language sentence. To see how this will work, consider a simple example: the derivation for the structural descriptions of the sentence 'Dick walks or it is not the case that Sally leaps':

Val (T, [$_S$[$_{S1}$[$_{NP}$ Dick][$_{VP}$ walks]] or [$_{S2}$ it is not the case that [$_{S3}$[$_{NP}$ Sally][$_{VP}$ leaps]]]]) iff . . .

(1)

either Val(T, [$_{S1}$[$_{NP}$ Dick][$_{VP}$ walks]]) or Val(T, [$_{S2}$ it is not the case that [$_{S3}$[$_{NP}$ Sally][$_{VP}$ leaps]]])

[instance of (7b)]

(2)

either Val(T, [$_{S1}$[$_{NP}$ Dick][$_{VP}$ walks]]) or it is not the case that Val(T, [$_{S3}$[$_{NP}$ Sally][$_{VP}$ leaps]])

[from (1) and (7c), by SoE]

(3)

either for some x, Val(x, [$_{NP}$ Dick]) and Val(x, [$_{VP}$ walks]) or it is not the case that for some x, Val(x, [$_{NP}$ Sally]) and Val(x,[$_{VP}$ leaps])

[from (2) and (6a), by applications of SoE]

(4)
either for some x, Val(x, <u>Dick</u>) and Val(x, <u>walks</u>) or it is not the case that for some x, Val(x, <u>Sally</u>) and Val(x, <u>leaps</u>)
[from (3) and (6b), by applications of SoE]

(5)
either for some x, x = Dick and x walks r it is not the case that for some x, x = Sally and x leaps
[from (4), (5a), and (5b), by applications of SoE]

(6)
either Dick walks or it is not the case that Sally leaps
[from (5) by SoI]

This fragment, obviously extremely simple, is introduced here to give some flavor of how theorems are derived in a T-theory. In the technical appendixes we will examine T-theories of greater complexity.

Of course, it is crucial to the project that we establish that a T-theory *can* deliver language–world connections. Crucially, the theorems of a truth-conditional semantics are also disquotational. That is, they express relations between expressions of the object language and the world. For example, (10) tells us that the English expression spelled s-n-o-w-#-i-s-#-w-h-i-t-e is true iff snow is white.

(10)
'snow is white' is true iff snow is white.

Thus, statements like (10) straddle language and the world, describing the relation between the two.

As Lepore and Loewer (1981, 1983) note, since T-theories are disquotational, they support reasoning that intuitively accompanies semantic knowledge. Consider how a disquotational T-theorem like (10') allows inferences from a fact about language to a fact about the world, and from a fact about the world to a fact about language.

(10')
'der Schnee ist weiβ' is true iff snow is white
'der Schnee ist weiβ' is true iff snow is white
'der Schnee ist weiβ' is true
therefore: snow is white

'der Schnee ist weiβ' is true iff snow is white
snow is white
therefore: 'der Schnee ist weiβ' is true

Not all theories have this feature, however. We saw above that structural semantics and model-theoretic semantics do not have this property. We can easily imagine other semantic theories that would not be disquotational, e.g., theories which issue theorems like (11).

(11)
'der Schnee ist weiß' is true iff 'snow is white' is true.

By itself, (11) does not tell us enough about the expression 'der Schnee ist weiß', for one could know (11) but not know the conditions under which it is true. Likewise with (12).

(12)
'der Schnee ist weiß' is true iff the English translation of 'der Schnee ist weiß' is true.

Also, it will not do to simply translate the object-language sentence into some uninterpreted language. So, for example, (13) would not be disquotational.

(13)
'snow is white' is true iff SNOW IS WHITE is true.

Examples like this simply fail to deliver the semantic values of expressions, because they are not disquotational.

As obvious as this feature of T-theories may appear, there are those who have suggested that T-theories lack the ability to make language-world connections. For example, Chierchia and McConnell-Ginet (1990, p. 82) appear to hold that such connections could not be delivered:

What a Tarski-style definition of truth does is to associate sentences with a description of the conditions under which they are true in a certain metalanguage. It thereby seems to shift the issue of meaning from the object language to the metalanguage without really telling us what meaning is.

However, it is not accurate to say that a T-theory consists in "associating" object-language expressions with metalanguage expressions. Rather, the idea is that the truth conditions are *stated* in the metalanguage. The contrast is equivalent to that between (14) and (15).

(14)
'snow is white' is true iff snow is white.

(15)
'snow is white' is associated with the metalanguage expression 'snow is white'.

Clearly the latter sort of claim is less informative than the former. Crucially, it fails to be disquotational, and therefore fails to provide a language-world connection. But, just as crucially, a T-theory delivers theorems like (14) rather than (15).

In addition to providing language-world connections, T-theories are *compositional*. As both Chomsky and Davidson have stressed, speakers typically have knowledge of the meanings of an infinite number of expressions. How can this be, given that we have finite memories? We presumably can't represent an infinite number of rules. The idea behind a compositional semantic theory is that it must be possible to state the agent's theory of meaning in terms of a finite number of axioms plus a finite number of rules for determining the meanings of longer expressions from the meanings of their parts. You know the meanings of a finite number of words, and you know some rules for combining words into meaningful expressions. The result would be knowledge of an infinite number of sentences from a finite base.

Put another way, instead of attributing knowledge of an infinite number of T-sentences of form shown in (16), we can attribute knowledge of axioms for each of the lexical entries, and then combinatorial axioms that show how the contents of the sentences can be derived from the contents of the parts.

(16)
a.
'the cat died' is true iff the cat died.
b.
'the cat that ate the rat died' is true iff the cat that ate the rat died.
c.
'the cat that ate the rat that lived in the house died' is true iff the cat that ate the rat that lived in the house died.
.
.
.

2.3   Modest vs. Robust Truth Theories

Dummett (1975; 1991, chapter 5) has argued that the theory I have sketched thus far would constitute a *modest*, rather than a *robust* semantic theory. The theory is modest because, though it might tell us something about the semantic knowledge that an agent has, it falls far short of telling us everything. For example, the kind of semantic theory envisioned above may tell us that 'snow' refers to snow, but it does not tell us about the knowledge we use to identify snow. According to Dummett, it therefore fails to explain the abilities that underlie our semantic competence.

One might reply that the abilities that underlie semantic competence are not part of semantics proper but rather part of some other and perhaps deeper psychological theory. However, this reply seems unhelpful, since our concern is not with drawing pre-theoretical boundaries around the various disciplines but rather with investigating the knowledge (semantic or otherwise) that underlies semantic competence.

Ultimately, however, there is no reason to take Dummett's point as an objection to T-theories. To think of it as an addendum to the overall project would be more useful. Sooner or later, semanticists will be interested in the psychological abilities that underwrite the knowledge that, for example, Val(x, <u>laughs</u>) iff x laughs. We might then regard T-theory axioms to be descriptions of semantic knowledge at a certain level of abstraction. For certain purposes, there will be no harm in our operating at this level of abstraction. For other purposes, important clues to the nature of semantic knowledge may be obscured at higher levels of abstraction.

What exactly would a robust axiom look like? Higginbotham (1989) has made some proposals in this regard, suggesting that such axioms would include the kind of information that recent research has proposed to be part of our lexical knowledge. For example, Higginbotham, following Hale and Keyser (1987), proposes the following "elucidation" of the meaning of the term 'cut':

a V that applies truly to situations e, involving a patient y and an agent x who, by means of some instrument z, effects in e a linear separation in the material integrity of y.

Thus, a robust T-theory axiom would incorporate the information that has been the subject of much recent work on the nature of the lexicon, both in linguistics (Hale and Keyser 1987, 1993; Grimshaw 1990; Pustejovsky 1995) and in natural language processing (Nirenberg and Raskin 1987; Pustejovsky and Bergler 1991; Boguraev and Briscoe 1989).[10]

The proper perspective, then, is not to view robust and modest semantic theories as competitors, but rather to see that they are theories of the same phenomenon at different levels of abstraction and idealization. Once they are viewed in this way, the insights gained from the investigation of the lexicon become a potentially powerful tool in the evaluation of competing T-theories, and ultimately in determining more precisely what the ontological commitments of such theories might be.

2.4 Psychological Evidence for the Nature of Semantic Knowledge

If we push our investigation no further than the construction of truth-conditional semantic theories, we may find that it soon stalls. Suppose that we have conflicting metaphysical intuitions; perhaps you have B-theory intuitions and I have intuitions that are consistent with the A-theory. With adequate ingenuity, it may be possible to construct several possible semantic theories for a given natural language phenomenon (by hypothesis, theories with different metaphysical consequences). Is there some way to pick between them? If we view semantics as the study of the knowledge that an agent has, it provides us a fair bit of leverage in adjudicating between candidate T-theories. The question becomes this: Which of the T-theories does the agent actually know?

Evans (1985b) has given an example of what sorts of considerations might become relevant. For the time being, let us think only about finite languages. In fact, let's imagine an agent whose linguistic competence is limited to twenty sentences.

We can imagine at least two T-theories for this language. The first, T1, introduces twenty rules, beginning with these six and continuing in obvious fashion:

(1)
[$_S$ Dick walks] is true iff Dick walks

(2)
[$_S$ Dick leaps] is true iff Dick leaps

(3)
[$_S$ Dick sings] is true iff Dick sings

(4)
[$_S$ Dick runs] is true iff Dick runs

(5)
[$_S$ Dick laughs] is true iff Dick laughs

(6)
[$_S$ Jane walks] is true iff Jane walks

In T2, on the other hand, there are only eleven rules. There is one rule for each of the names, and one for each of the properties, and one rule for the nonterminal node:

(1)
Val(x, Dick) iff x = Dick

(2)
Val(x, Jane) iff x = Jane

(3)
Val(x, Sally) iff x = Sally

(4)
Val(x, <u>Spot</u>) iff x = Spot

(5)
Val(x, <u>walks</u>) iff x walks

(6)
Val(x, <u>leaps</u>) iff x leaps

(7)
Val(x, <u>sings</u>) iff x sings

(8)
Val(x, <u>runs</u>) iff x runs

(9)
Val(x, <u>laughs</u>) iff x laughs

(10)
Val(T, [$_s$ NP VP]) iff, for some x, Val(x, NP) and Val(x, VP)

(11)
Val(x, [$_\alpha$ β]) iff Val(x, β) (where α ranges over categories, and β ranges over categories and lexical items)

Both T1 and T2 successfully yield interpretive T-theories for this speaker's language. Is there any reason to prefer one over the other? That is, is there any reason to suppose that the speaker knows either T1 or T2? According to Evans, there may well be empirical considerations favoring one of the proposals. For example, suppose that we had a record of the order in which the speaker acquired the language. Suppose, for example, at some point the speaker suddenly showed the ability to understand the following four new sentences:

Dick laughs.

Jane laughs.

Sally laughs.

Spot laughs.

On theory T1, this would have to be explained by the hypothesis that the speaker had suddenly learned four new and unrelated rules. On theory T2, the explanation would simply be that the speaker had acquired the semantic rule for the predicate 'laughs'.[11]

Likewise, consider losses of semantic competence. Suppose that a speaker suddenly loses the ability to understand the four expressions above. On T1, the explanation would have to be that the speaker had suddenly lost the tacit knowledge of four different and unrelated rules. On T2, the explanation would be that knowledge of a single rule had been lost.

Larson and Segal note that in theories like T2, which admit two kinds of rules (rules for referring expressions and rules for predicate expressions), it is entirely possible that there should be acquired language deficits that affect one class of rules and not the other. Indeed, not only do such cases seem to be possible; as Larson and Segal note, there in fact seem to be such cases on record. They point to a case study (Semenza and Zettin 1989) in which a subject suffered a severe head injury and subsequently lost the ability to deal with "purely referential nondescriptive semantic relations." In effect, the subject lost the ability to know rules of the form of (1)–(4) in T2.

Of course, as the linguistic theories under consideration become more complex, the possible psychological probes also become more interesting. A number of psycholinguistic probes have been proposed for elements ranging from clausal boundaries to the morphological constituents of words. Whether the specific probes offered thus far turn out to be fruitful, the important consideration for our purposes is the idea that we can, in principle, appeal to such considerations in grounding a particular version of semantic theory.

In sum, it appears that we can bring a number of considerations to bear on the question of what T-theory a speaker realizes. Specifically, we may find it useful to enlist data from other branches of the cognitive sciences, and following the hypothetical situations envisioned above, we may find relevant evidence in the interaction of semantic theory with the theory of language acquisition, and with the theory of acquired language deficits.

2.5   Do T-Theories Display Senses?

Much of the interest in absolute T-theories has stemmed from the suggestion, due to several authors,[12] that T-theories can deliver more than the truth conditions of expressions, but that they can deliver the truth conditions in a way that "shows" or "displays" the sense of expressions.

It has been argued since Frege that two expressions like 'Cicero' and 'Tully' have the same referent but have distinct senses, for they have different modes of presentation—that is, they present the referent of Cicero/Tully in different ways. Because 'Cicero' and 'Tully' have different senses, there is supposedly no irrationality in the beliefs of someone who believes both (17a) (a belief about Cicero under a certain mode of presentation) and (17b) (a belief about the same individual under a different mode of presentation).

(17)

a.

Cicero is bald.

b.

Tully is not bald.

    With respect to T-theories, the question naturally arises as to whether the theorems of such a theory deliver only the referents of expressions or the senses too. That is, does the right-hand side of a T-theory theorem simply give the reference of the expression on the left, or does it also give the reference in a way that shows or displays its sense? This question turns out to have important consequences. Indeed, some authors have suggested that the ability of T-theories to display senses is central to whether a T-theory can serve as a meaning theory. For example, Lepore and Loewer (1987) claim that there are certain adequacy conditions which a theory of truth must meet in order to function as a theory of meaning suitable for interpreting a language L. On their view, if a T-theory is to serve as a meaning theory, it must be the sort of T-theory that can display senses.

    But *can* T-theories display senses? According to Lepore and Loewer (1987, p. 104), an adequate T-theory for an agent (call her Arabella) will contain theorems (18) and (19) without containing theorems (20) and (21).

(18)

'Cicero is bald' is true iff Cicero is bald.

(19)

'Tully is bald' is true iff Tully is bald.

(20)

'Cicero is bald' is true iff Tully is bald.

(21)

'Tully is bald' is true iff Cicero is bald.

The reasoning is that Arabella may believe that Cicero is bald but not that Tully is bald, so a T-theory that generates (20) as a theorem will not correctly characterize Arabella's semantic competence. The danger of introducing (20) into a semantic theory for Arabella appears to be that it leads to a false belief attribution in the following fashion:

(a)

Arabella utters 'Cicero is bald'.

(b)
Arabella believes that 'Cicero is bald' is true (from (a) and certain assumptions
about Arabella's truthfulness, etc.).

(c)
Arabella believes that 'Cicero is bald' is true iff Tully is bald (by hypothesis).

(d)
Arabella believes that Tully is bald (from (b), (c), and assumptions about closure).

Notice that step (c) relies on the assumption that Arabella actually believes a
theorem of the T-theory.[13] This assumption is interesting, since it suggests that
Arabella (presumably not a semanticist) must have beliefs about theorems of a
particular kind of T-theory. Since it is implausible to suppose that Arabella (unless she is trained in semantics) has conscious knowledge of such matters, it appears to entail that Arabella must have some sort of "tacit" knowledge of (20)—a
possibility that is entirely consistent with the theory laid out this chapter.

Now we need to avoid a confusion—indeed, one to which I have been party.[14]
The idea is not that the T-theory will *state* the sense of the expressions. Clearly,
a T-theory cannot do that.[15] If we go by what is literally stated, (20) attributes
no more semantic knowledge to an agent than (18) does. Both are literally talking about the same individual.

But what is stated is not the same as what is displayed. Dummett (1973) and
Evans (1981) have argued that this distinction was made as far back as Frege,
and Dummett (1973, p. 227) has invoked Wittgenstein's distinction between saying and showing to elucidate the distinction:

... even when Frege is purporting to give the sense of a word or symbol, what he actually *states* is what the reference [is]: and, for anyone who has not clearly grasped the relation between sense and reference, this fact makes his hold on the notion of sense
precarious. The sense of an expression is the mode of presentation of the referent: in
saying what the reference is, we have to choose a particular way of saying this .... In a
case in which we are concerned to convey, or stipulate, the sense of the expression, we
shall choose that means of stating what the referent is which displays the sense: we might
here borrow a famous pair of terms from the *Tractatus*, and say that, for Frege, we *say*
what the referent of a word is, and thereby *show* what its sense is.

Of course, Wittgenstein's distinction between saying and showing is notoriously
difficult, so perhaps, rather than worry about Wittgenstein exegesis, I should
try to elucidate a similar sort of distinction within my framework.

In the beginning of this chapter, I made a distinction between the semantic
knowledge that an agent has and the way in which the agent represented that

knowledge. For example, an agent might know that 'snow' refers to snow, and that knowledge might be represented by a kind of data structure in the mind/brain.

Let's call the first sort of knowledge (e.g., that 'snow' refers to snow) first-order knowledge of meaning. Can an agent also have second-order knowledge of meaning (tacit or otherwise)? That is, can the agent not only know certain axioms of a T-theory but also (i) know that he knows the axioms and (ii) know that he is representing the knowledge in a way that displays a certain sense? It seems to me that the answer has to be yes.

We know that the way we package our claims can radically affect the way people behave. For example, whether I choose the name 'Cicero' or 'Tully' for my utterance may well affect the behavior of my interlocutor. Similar considerations apply to the way we tacitly represent semantic information. How we represent our semantical knowledge may well have consequences for our behavior.

It seems to follow that a correct T-theory not only must correctly characterize our semantic knowledge but must do it in a way that correctly characterizes our second-order knowledge of how the semantical knowledge is represented. This raises a number of interesting issues about tacit second-order knowledge and about the transparency of the way our T-theory axioms are represented. What seems beyond dispute is that there is such second-order knowledge. What remains to be investigated (another day) is the nature and reliability of this knowledge.

2.6   A Word on Predication

In chapter 4 we will consider some alternative axiomatizations. For now, it is worth noting that the axioms for the predicates given above—the VP axioms—are not what many people are accustomed to. That is, people working in semantics are accustomed to thinking of predicates as referring to either properties or to sets of individuals. In the latter case, we would expect to find axioms like (22).

(22)
Val(x, walks) iff x = {x: x walks}

That is not what is offered up here, and it is not the path taken elsewhere in this book. Nor need it be. Instead, I am supposing that in a sentence like 'Jane walks' the semantic value of 'walks' is Jane. Thus, the semantic value of the predicate will depend on the sentential context in which it appears.

We can think of this approach as incorporating an idea discussed by Carruthers (1989),[16] who attributes it to Wittgenstein's *Tractatus*. The core of this idea is that predicates do not refer to their extensions; rather, their senses specify rules of classification which are applied to the referent of the subject expression. The rule applies to that referent in virtue of some "property-token" possessed by the referent of the subject expression:

> ... the sense of a predicate is not ... a mode of thinking about a referent. It is rather a rule of classification, applying to the referent of the name in virtue of some property-token which that thing possesses. On such a view, to understand a predicate 'F' is to know the difference between things which are F and things which are not F, where this knowledge consists in the grasp of the rule of classification which constitutes the sense of 'F'. (Carruthers 1989, p. 170)

What is the advantage of this approach? The difficulty with directly referring to extensions is that only by virtue of our understanding the predicate are we able to identify the extension. And, indeed, no one really knows the extension of 'x walks'; the closest we can come to specifying that extension is by saying that "it is the set of all those things that walk"—in effect, that we must have some rule of classification which is prior to the set of things that walk.

It is worth noting, as Carruthers does, that *everyone* needs to appeal to some such nonreferring predicates, otherwise we run into the "third man" problem discussed in Plato's *Parmenides* dialogue and emphasized early in the twentieth century by Wittgenstein and by F. H. Bradley. Consider a standard semantical treatment of predicates as extensions. On such accounts, the referent of the subject and the referent of the predicate (the extension) must still be related by the relational predicate 'is-an-element-of'. But then we want to know if this predicate too must refer. If it does, then we have embarked on an infinite regress, for how is this new referent to be related to the two that are already on the table?

Finally, I should make it clear that the introduction of nonreferring predicates does not amount to abandoning referential semantics for procedural semantics. I am not *identifying* the semantic value of the predicate with a procedure or a rule of classification. That rule is in the background (after all, Carruthers is talking about the sense of the predicate, not its referent). I am still after a theory that delivers language-to-world connections. The point here is that properties and extensions (sets of objects) don't have to be part of that picture.

Chapter 3
Attitudes and Indexicals

Section 2.6 told a bit about what the picture need not include. However, a number of resources will have to be included if we are to tackle the semantics of tense. I will now begin adding those resources.

So far, my exposition of truth-conditional semantics has focused on very simple constructions. However, it is crucial to the program in this book that something be said about indexicals (at a minimum, about *temporal* indexicals). In particular, it is required that indexicals be handled in a nonstandard way; temporal indexicals can't be treated as referring expressions, and furthermore their indexical character *must* be reflected in the semantics. (More on this in a bit.)

Some things must also be said about propositional-attitude constructions. In later chapters I am going to argue that tense morphemes are indexical predicates that take interpreted logical forms (ILFs) as their arguments. Accordingly, I need to say something about the construction of ILFs and about their use in the treatment of propositional-attitude reports. As will be seen, the ILF theory of the attitudes leads to a certain shift in perspective in our understanding of what must be stable among language users for us to say that they are saying or thinking the same thing. This shift in perspective will serve us well when we turn to the problem of indexicals. Accordingly, my plan is to begin with propositional attitudes and then move on to the general question of the proper handling of indexicals.

3.1   Propositional Attitudes

One of the central problems in the semantics of natural language has been the problem of accounting for the semantics of "opaque" or "hyperintensional" environments. To illustrate the problem, consider the contrast between (1) and (2).

(1)
a.
Max met [$_{NP}$ Judy Garland].

b.

Max met [$_{NP}$ Frances Gumm].

(2)

a.

Max believed [$_S$ that Judy Garland was a fine actress].

b.

#Max believed [$_S$ that Frances Gumm was a fine actress].

If it is true that Judy Garland is Frances Gumm, then (1a) entails (1b). Indeed, as a general rule, co-referring terms can be substituted for each other without affecting the truth value of the sentence in which they occur. The examples in (2) constitute an exception to this general rule. (2a) may be true, but it needn't follow that (2b) is true. Let us say that opaque environments are precisely those environments where substitution of co-referring terms fails.

Part of our task in constructing a T-theory is to determine the "semantic values" of the constituents of natural language sentences. Ordinarily, semanticists would like to say that the semantic value of a referring expression is the thing that it refers to. But notice that the semanticist apparently cannot say this in the face of (2). 'Judy Garland' and 'Frances Gumm' both refer to the same individual; hence, the terms have the same semantic value; hence, we would expect that the terms should be intersubstitutable without semantic effect. However, as the examples in (2) show, that expectation is wrong.

The semantic value of referring expressions is not the only difficulty facing the semanticist. It is also unclear what semantic values should be assigned to the embedded clauses of belief reports. Consider (3), for example.

(3)

[$_S$ Galileo believed that [$_S$ the Earth moves]]

Intuitively, (3) expresses a relation between Galileo and some sort of object, but what sort of object? One possible proposal is that it expresses a relation between Galileo and the clause itself—in other words, between Galileo and (4).

(4)

[$_S$ the Earth moves]

But this does not seem plausible, since (4) does not carry as much information as the belief report intuitively does. For example, pointing at the moon, I might utter (5).

(5)

[$_S$ Galileo believed that [$_S$ that moves]]

But I might also utter (5) when pointing at the sun. The trouble is this: if the content of the belief attribution in both cases is simply the syntactic object in (6), then these two belief attributions are not distinguished in the semantics.

(6)

[$_S$ that moves]

There have been many responses to this problem in the literature of semantics over the last three decades. One response has been to argue that propositional-attitude reports like (3) express relations between agents and sets of possible worlds (for example, the set of all worlds in which the Earth moves).[1] Another response has been to argue that an attitude report like (3) expresses a relation between Galileo and a Russellian proposition consisting of the Earth itself and the property of moving.[2] There are, of course, variations on these two proposals.

In recent literature, however, a number of authors, including Higginbotham (1986a, 1991), Segal (1989), Larson and Ludlow (1993), and Larson and Segal (1995), have suggested an alternative proposal in which the semantic problems arising with propositional-attitude verbs might be resolved by taking such verbs to express relations between agents and interpreted logical forms (phrase markers whose nodes are paired with semantic values).

For example, the ILF for "The Earth moves" would be the syntactic phrase marker in (7) (abstracting from detail here), with semantic values assigned to each node of the tree. We might therefore represent the ILF as in (8), where each node is paired with its semantic value.

(7)

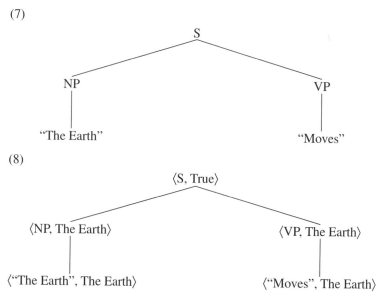

(8)

Such objects in effect represent a semantic value together with its linguistic "mode of presentation." Unlike the naive syntactic theory discussed above, ILF theories, by including the semantic values, can distinguish both of the beliefs reported as "Galileo said that that moves," because the two different acts of pointing pick out different semantic values (the moon in one case and the sun in the other). Thus, in the case where I point at the moon, we get the ILF in (9). In the case where I point at the sun, we get the ILF in (10).

(9)

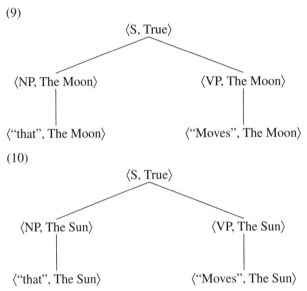

(10)

ILF theories thus provide an alternative to the treatments of propositional-attitude constructions that traditionally make use of possible-world semantics, Russellian propositions, or Fregean senses. Because they eschew these resources, ILF theories are more *austere*—they attempt to cover as much of the data (or more) with fewer theoretical resources. Furthermore, because of their austerity, they can be embedded in a truth-conditional semantics for natural language of the kind advocated in chapter 2.

My A-theory of tense will regard tenses as being predicates of proposition-like objects. Strictly speaking, however, propositions will not do—propositions, as ordinarily construed, are eternal; they don't change over time. Instead we will be looking for proposition-like objects that are not eternal—objects whose truth values can shift over time. Before the A-theory can be incorporated into a truth-conditional semantics, then, it will be necessary to introduce technical resources that will do the work that propositions are routinely designed to do yet will be non-eternal. Accordingly, I will be proposing that ILFs can serve as the arguments of tense in addition to being the objects of the attitudes. Clearly ILFs will play a central role in my semantics, so it is critical that I lay out the details of ILF formation carefully. (Hereafter I will indicate ILFs with structural descriptions enclosed in closed brackets ('[] ... []'); e.g. the ILF in (8) would be abbreviated as '[] [$_S$ The Earth moves] []').

Larson and Ludlow (1993) propose that the ILF theory consist of three parts: axioms for propositional-attitude verbs such as 'believes', 'thinks', and 'claims'; an axiom for VPs containing a complement clause; and a recursive definition of ILFs. The axioms for propositional-attitude verbs in (11) exploit the idea that these predicates are relational. Intuitively, x will be an agent and y will be an ILF.

(11)

a.

Val($\langle$x,y$\rangle$, believes, σ) iff x believes y.

b.

Val($\langle$x,y$\rangle$, thinks, σ) iff x thinks y.

c.

Val($\langle$x,y$\rangle$, claims, σ) iff x claims y.

Axiom (12) introduces ILFs in the interpretation of VPs of the general form [$_{VP}$ VS]—that is, VPs containing a clausal complement.

(12)

Val(x, [$_{VP}$ V S], σ) iff for some y, Val($\langle$x,y$\rangle$, V, σ) and y = []S[] w.r.t. σ.

Finally, there is a general inductive definition of the interpreted logical form of α with respect to a sequence σ.[3] ILFs are constructed "on the fly" by having the T-theory run through the complement clause, determining the semantic value of each node, and then constructing the corresponding ILF. A T-theorem for 'Smith believes Jones walks' would look like (13).

(13)

Val(T, [$_S$[$_{NP}$ Smith][$_{VP}$[$_V$ believes][$_S$[$_{NP}$ Jones][$_{VP}$[$_V$ Sings]]]]], σ) iff Smith believes [] [$_S$[$_{NP}$ Jones][$_{VP}$ [$_V$ walks]]] [] w.r.t. σ

Construction of the ILF ([][$_S$[$_{NP}$ Jones][$_{VP}$[$_V$ walks]]][]) proceeds as follows: The truth definition must be applied to the embedded clause to determine the semantic values of each node of the embedded p-marker. Recall that the embedded p-marker in this case is just as shown in (14).

(14)

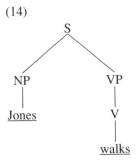

We can get the semantic value of each node from a derivation utilizing axioms like those employed in chapter 2.

Given the calculation of these semantic values, the ILF shown in (15) can be constructed.

(15)

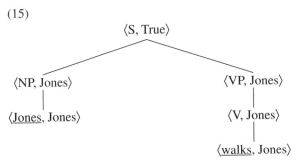

Finally, then, we have derived the theorem shown in (16).

(16)
Smith believes Jones walks is true iff Smith believes

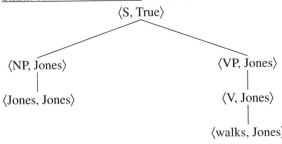

Overt propositional attitudes are not the only environments that exhibit intensionality effects, and it is quite natural to ask how ILF theories are to be extended to these other environments. Of course a complete story is a book in itself, but here I can at least show how the framework might handle so-called intensional transitive constructions.

These constructions involve intensional verbs, such as 'seeks', that do not take clausal complements yet nevertheless show intensionality effects. Consider (17)–(19).

(17)
John wants a donkey.

(18)
John seeks a donkey.

(19)
John looks for a donkey.

Of course, everything turns on whether the clause in these cases is really missing, and ever since the Middle Ages linguists and philosophers have toyed with the idea that there might actually be an implicit clause in these sentences.[4]

One way to make sense of the hidden clause analysis within the framework outlined here is to suppose that the LF representations of these sentences actually have a hidden clause in them—perhaps something along the lines of (17')–(19').

(17')
John wants [PRO (to have) a donkey].

(18')
John seeks a donkey [PRO (to find) a donkey].

(19')
John looks for [PRO (to find) a donkey].

The evidence for the hidden clause includes an adverb-attachment ambiguity, which is most evident in cases like (17). Consider (20).

(20)
John wants a donkey tomorrow.

Intuitively it is not the wanting which is to take place tomorrow, but the having. This is naturally accounted for if we assume an implicit clause, as in (17'), and allow an additional adjunction site for the adverb:

(20')
John wants [[PRO (to have) a donkey] tomorrow].

Of course an analysis of this form makes a very strong claim upon our syntactic theory, and this claim has to be argued through on standard syntactic grounds.[5] But if the syntactic claim can be sustained, then it is possible to unburden the semantics of the need for heavy machinery to handle these intensional environments.

In short, they can be assimilated to propositional attitudes and subjected to an ILF analysis.

I do not introduce this analysis of intensional transitive verbs merely to show how one can achieve semantical austerity and still treat attitude constructions. In chapter 8, I will explore a similar sort of strategy for the semantics of tense, introducing implicit clauses in support of a particular theory of tense. Once again the implicit clauses will have to obey the constraints of current syntactic theory, but provided they can, I hope I have shown here that the move is quite legitimate, if not yet entirely commonplace.

Questions about ILFs

The ILF theory sketched in this section has led to a number of misunderstandings. One of these has to do with the relation between an ILF and the agent to whom an attitude is ascribed.

As was noted in chapter 1, we routinely ascribe beliefs to dogs and other creatures that do not have language—certainly not an I-language similar to what humans have. A number of individuals have supposed that an ILF is intended to mirror the structure of some object in the mind/brain of the ascribee; as Segal (1989) and Larson and Ludlow (1993) argue, this supposition is mistaken. I may say "Fido believes his dish is empty," employing an ILF with English words, but I do not thereby suppose that there are English lexical items located somewhere in Fido's language of thought. I do not even suppose that what is happening in Fido's language of thought must be "similar" to the ILF that I have constructed.[6] For all I know, Fido may have a language of thought that is radically different from my own.

When I say "Fido believes his dish is empty" I am saying that Fido believes a particular ILF with English expressions in it. If we were interested only in modest T-theories this would be the end of the discussion, but we might want to know more about the psychological abilities which underlie our use of the term 'believes'. Exactly what is going on if 'believe' isn't supposed to express a relation between an ILF and something that is going on in Fido's head? How do we go about elucidating the robust background theory that underlies our understanding of 'believes'? As we saw earlier, the elucidation of a verb like 'cuts' is nontrivial. As we will see, 'believes' is even more complex.

Since we can faithfully ascribe attitudes to creatures without I-language, it is crucial that ILFs not be understood as describing episodes in the creature's language of thought but rather as providing information for the benefit of a hearer who wants to construct a theory of the creature's mental life. Put another way, the emphasis should be on the relation between the ascription and the hearer rather than on the relation between the ascription and the agent to whom the attitude is ascribed.

Larson and Ludlow (1993) make a preliminary sketch of how that could be possible, suggesting that a system governing belief ascriptions (and our ability to use the phrase 'x believes y') will involve at least the following three components:

- the tacit theory of belief
- the tacit theory of the goals of belief ascription
- the tacit theory of belief-ascription logistics.

The preliminary sketch proceeded as follows: Consider a speaker S, who wishes to ascribe an attitude to an agent A for the benefit of a hearer H. In order for S to succeed, S and H must share a theory of what beliefs are, for it is the shared ontology of beliefs that will guide the way in which beliefs are ascribed. S must also have tacit knowledge of the goals of belief ascription. That is, S must have a theory that allows him or her to determine what features of A's belief will assist H in the relevant way. Finally, S must have a tacit theory that allows him or her to deliver the kind of ascription that will be helpful to H.

The common-sense theory of belief will state the properties that speakers tacitly ascribe to beliefs, including their relations to other components of thought and to action. The theory of the goals of belief ascription will state the theory a speaker deploys in determining a hearer's interest. In almost every case, the goal of a speaker S is to cause a hearer H to form a certain theory about the belief structure of an agent A.

Finally, the theory of belief-ascription logistics will state which expressions must be used in a given context to achieve specific belief-ascription goals. This theory interacts with ILFs directly and incorporates the knowledge required for determining which ILF should be used in reporting a given attitude. For example, depending upon H's interests, it is sometimes the referential component of an ILF and sometimes the syntactic component that will be important to the goals of ascription.

We can identify several rules of thumb in characterizing which component of an ILF will be relevant in a given attitude report.[7] For example, if H is interested in information that A has about the world (for example, the distance from Earth to Venus), then the objectual component of the ILF will be of primary importance to the goals of belief ascription. H will therefore be indifferent to the choice between "the Morning Star" and "the Evening Star" in an attitude ascription concerning Venus. By contrast, if H is interested in explaining or predicting A's behavior (for example, whether A will assent to an utterance of "The Morning

Star is the Evening Star," or whether A will act in a way compatible with the knowledge that the Morning Star is the Evening Star), then H may well be interested in the syntactic expressions that S uses to characterize A's belief.

In cases of the latter kind, where prediction or explanation of behavior is the goal, Larson and Ludlow envision the speaker's choice of syntactic constituents in an ILF to involve a two-stage process with respect to the hearer H.

In the first stage, S determines the way in which H models A's belief structure. Then S "negotiates" with H the expressions to be used in speaking of the components of that model. Both steps involve complex subprocesses. For example, in inferring H's model of A's belief structure, S would appear to draw at least on all of the following:

• S's knowledge of H's interests
• general principles of common-sense psychology that S supposes that H believes
• knowledge which S knows H to have about A.

Suppose that S knows H to be interested in the behavior of A—for example, in whether A will train her telescope on a particular region of the dawn sky. Then, by general principles of common-sense psychology, which S supposes H to share, S may infer that H will deploy a fine-grained model of A's psychology—one that distinguishes Morning Star beliefs from Evening Star beliefs. S may also rely upon information supplied directly by H or some other source. For example, S may learn that H knows that A is unaware that the Morning Star is the Evening Star.

In the second stage of selecting an ILF, S and H must agree on expressions used to speak of the components of H's model of A's belief structure. Expressions used in attitude ascriptions will be tacitly "negotiated" by participants in the discourse, following quite general principles holding of discourses of all kinds. The general process by which discourse participants negotiate a way to speak of objects (sometimes called "entrainment" by psychologists) is currently a subject of research in psycholinguistics. (See Brennan and Clarke 1992 for a discussion.) Ultimately, this work must be extended to the study of how states of mind come to be described and of why subtle differences in expression will have great consequences for the truth of an attitude ascription.

All this is preliminary, though it may be a serviceable enough treatment of what lies beneath the surface of our use of the verb 'believes' (and of related propositional-attitude verbs). But notice what a powerful resource this collection of abilities can be: these abilities allow us to keep track of a single belief in many formal guises. For example, Larson and Ludlow (1993) examined cases in which ILFs with different structures (indeed different objectual contents) might be used to characterize "the same" belief or report—for example, when I hear

A and B utter sentences of different structure and I say that A said what B said.[8] The robust theory of 'believes' tries to elucidate the ability to keep track of a single belief under the guises of different that-clauses. A similar sort of ability will have to be employed in the theory of indexicals.

3.2   Indexicals

One of the most vexing issues for semantical theory has been the question of how to treat indexical expressions like 'I', 'you', 'this', 'that', 'here', and 'now'. All these expressions appear to be referring expressions, but they refer in a very context-sensitive way. 'I' as uttered by me picks out a rather different individual than 'I' as uttered by you.

Clearly, there is some stable meaning to an indexical like 'I' (e.g., "the utterer of the sentence") that allows us to determine who is being spoken of in different contexts. This part of the meaning of 'I' might be called the "character" of the indexical (Kaplan 1977) or the "role" (Perry 1977). Whether we choose to call it the character, the role, or something else, the big question is whether this extra element is to be considered part of the semantics of indexical expressions.

The received view has been that character/role is not part of the semantics proper—that it is not part of the propositional content of an utterance. This view is associated notoriously with Kaplan and Perry, but also with theorists working within absolute truth-conditional semantics. For example, Larson and Segal, despite holding that T-theories can otherwise display senses, hold that the character/role of a demonstrative does not make it into the theorems of a T-theory.

Specifically, Larson and Segal propose that T-theories be "conditionalized" so that the extra meaning we associate with the character of an indexical must be fixed outside of the T-theory biconditional proper. As an illustration, consider the case where Katherine Hepburn utters (21) and Cary Grant, gesturing at Ms. Hepburn, utters (22).

(21)
I need a haircut.

(22)
She needs a haircut.

On the proposal of Larson and Segal (1995, p. 220), the conditionalized T-theorems for these two utterances will be (21') and (22'), respectively.

(21')
If u is an utterance of $[_S[_{NP}$ I] $[_{VP}$ need a haircut]] and x is the utterer of u, then u is true iff x needs a haircut.

(22')

If u is an utterance of [$_S$[$_{NP}$ She] [$_{VP}$ needs a haircut]] and x is the object demonstrated by the utterer of u, then u is true iff x needs a haircut.

Notice that in (21') and (22') the truth conditions themselves are identical. Consistent with the basic Kaplan-Perry line, Larson and Segal (p. 220) argue as follows:

What are the actual truth conditions of the particular utterances ([21]) and ([22])? In both cases the RHSs of the conditionals is "x needs a haircut." Who is x? it is Katherine Hepburn, the utterer of ([21]) and the object demonstrated by the utterer of ([22]). As far as our theory is concerned, it is this object x that enters into the truth conditions. No particular way of specifying that object is given, no descriptive content enters into the truth conditions.

Why this eagerness to keep character/role out of the semantics? Part of the answer to this question lies in Perry's (1977) critique of Frege's theory of demonstratives. The objection is that for a Fregean semantical theory (and, by extension, for any semantic theory with similar goals) there is simply nothing that can describe the sense of an indexical like 'I'. Even if we are prepared to believe that there are distinct senses that can explain the difference in cognitive significance between 'Cicero' and 'Tully', there is nothing that is going to do all the work that we expect the character/role of an indexical to do.

The root problem is illustrated by a famous passage from Frege (1956, p. 296):

If someone wants to say the same today as he expressed yesterday using the word 'today', he must replace this word by 'yesterday'. Although the thought is the same, the verbal expression must be different so that the sense, which would otherwise be affected by the differing times of utterance, is readjusted. The case is the same with words like 'here' and 'there'. In all such cases the mere wording, as it is given in writing, is not the complete expression of the thought, but the knowledge of certain accompanying conditions of utterance, which are used as means of expressing the thought, are needed for its correct apprehension. The pointing of fingers, hand movements, glances may belong here too. The same utterance containing the word 'I' will express different thoughts in the mouths of different men, of which some may be true, others false.

As Perry notes, if Frege is going to identify the sense of a sentence with a thought he is in trouble. Roughly, if the sense of the indexical is to be identified either with its character/role or with some sort of descriptive content, then a sentence containing 'today' and a sentence containing 'yesterday' will have to have different senses and hence express different thoughts. No descriptive content is going to be able to reflect the distinct senses of 'yesterday' and 'today' while preserving the consequence that 'yesterday was fine' expresses the thought that 'today is fine' expressed the day before.

Something has to give. Either Frege must give up the identification of senses with thoughts (in which case the semantical machinery seems incapable of giving the semantics of our thoughts) or Frege must give up the idea that the two utterances express the same thought. But then we run into trouble with our ability to communicate what we thought. Can it really be that we can't express today what we thought yesterday?

Another problem with trying to keep character/role in the semantics has to do with the embedding of demonstratives in modals. As Kaplan (1977) has argued, if the character of a demonstrative makes it into the truth conditions, what are we to say about examples like (23)?

(23)
You are the person I'm addressing with this utterance.

We surely don't want it to be a consequence that (24) is true, for (24) appears to be necessarily true whereas (23) is not.

(24)
The person I'm addressing with this utterance is the person I'm addressing with this utterance.

Clearly there are counterfactual environments where another person is my addressee. Someone else might have been standing before me. But (24) does not appear to allow this possibility.

Still, despite these powerful objections, the conclusion seems unsatisfactory. Recall this familiar story: In a house of mirrors, someone might point at a man who is about to be attacked by a dog, saying 'He is being attacked by a dog', and I may assent to this judgement, not realizing that I am about to be attacked. Intuitively, someone who says 'You are about to be attacked by a dog' is saying something more than the first speaker. To say that this extra information lies outside the province of semantics seems to be surrendering all too quickly. Speaking directly to the import of Kaplan's modality argument, Higginbotham (1995, p. 248) argues that "the quirks of modality should not ... be allowed to undermine the thesis that what we say and think is literally and robustly expressed by the words that we use."

Have we surrendered prematurely? I tend to think that we have. Let me begin with the modality argument. One solution would be to argue that this talk of evaluating the sentence in a counterfactual environment really amounts to a shorthand way of saying that we evaluate a modalized proposition that asserts the possibility that I am not addressing you:

(25)

It could have been that you are not the person I'm addressing with this utterance.

It is arguable that this is all it means to evaluate a proposition in a counterfactual situation. We can't, after all, travel to other possible worlds to evaluate (23). (I will return to this issue in chapters 4 and 6; for now I merely want to mark this as a possible way out.)

But why does (25) help? Don't we get the same difficulties when we unpack 'you' as before? Consider (26).

(26)

It could have been that the person I'm addressing with this utterance is not the person I'm addressing with this utterance.

We must move with caution here. We have a definite description ('the person I'm addressing with this utterance') and we have a modal ('it could have been that'), and we need to be on guard for the possibility that the description has taken wide scope over the modal.

No conundrums need arise in (26) if we take the description to have scope over the modal, as in (26').

(26')

[the x: person I'm addressing with this utterance x] It could have been that x is not the person I'm addressing with this utterance.

In sum, the strategy would be to show that "counterfactual evaluation" is in fact parasitic on our ability to evaluate corresponding modal sentences (in the actual world, not some other world). That is, to evaluate 'I am speaking' in a counterfactual situation would be nothing more than evaluating 'I might not have been speaking' in the *actual* situation. Our grasp of other possible worlds would then be posterior to our grasp of the relevant modalized sentences. If that is right, then we would merely need to show that such modal sentences admit of scope ambiguities, and to show that there is no problem if the descriptions can have wide scope with respect to these modals (as in (26')).

Perhaps there are ways to answer the modal arguments of Kaplan, but what of Perry's arguments for banishing character/role from the semantics? Despite the elegance of Perry's critique of Frege, Evans (1981) has argued that it falls short:

... there is no headlong collision between Frege's suggestion that grasping the same thought on different days may require different things of us, and the fundamental criterion of difference of thoughts which rests upon the principle that it is not possible coherently to take different attitudes towards the same thought. For that principle, properly stated, precludes the possibility of coherently taking different attitudes towards the same thought *at the same time.*

On Evans's interpretation of Frege, we needn't think of thoughts as holding at slices of time; we can think of them as enduring. Thus, our ability to grasp them as we move about in the world requires that we have an ability to keep track of them from different vantage points:

> Frege's idea is that the same epistemic state may require different things of us at different times; the changing circumstances force us to change in order to keep hold of a constant reference and a constant thought—we must run to keep still. From this point of view, the acceptance on $d2$ of 'Yesterday was fine', given an acceptance on $d1$ of 'Today is fine' can manifest the *persistence* of a belief in just the way in which acceptance of difference utterances of the sentence 'The sun sets in the West' can.

This idea, whether or not it is properly attributed to Frege,[9] is appealing for a number of reasons. Thoughts, after all, are supposed to be persistent, and our ability to grasp them must therefore be quite dynamic. The idea can be reframed as follows: There is the objectual content of a thought—what the truth conditions literally state. Then there is the way in which the truth conditions are represented. In chapter 2, I spoke of such representations as displaying the sense of the utterance or thought. It would be an error to suppose that the sense is to be *identified* with a single representation at a particular time. On the contrary, a single thought having a single sense must be represented in different ways from different spatio-temporal perspectives. If this idea is applied to T-theorems, the way a theorem is represented can display a sense; however, it cannot be identified with the sense, for that sense must be displayed in different ways at different times.[10]

What would underlie the ability to keep track of senses? Here we might opt for an extension of the underlying theory of 'believes' that was offered in Larson and Ludlow 1993 and discussed in the previous section. On the Larson-Ludlow proposal, the idea was to explain our ability to know when two that-clauses attribute the same belief or count as saying the same thing. In that case, the puzzle was to show how using different words in an ILF presented to different hearers could count as having attributed the same attitude to an agent. The answer was found in a rich theory underlying the use of 'believes'—a theory that took account of the hearer's interests, the speaker's goals, shared knowledge about the structure of the agent's beliefs, and so on.

The relation between that analysis of propositional attitudes and Evans's proposal for indexicals should now be obvious. Indeed, since attitude reports routinely include indexicals, what is called for is some amplification of the ILF theory that can explain how we keep track of when two indexical utterances (beliefs) say (mean) the same thing.

Clearly, much of the Larson-Ludlow machinery will be useful here. What we will need to do is expand on the tacit theory of belief-ascription logistics, which held that our ability to ascribe beliefs involved, among other things,

- S's knowledge of H's interests,
- general principles of common-sense psychology that S supposes H to believe,

and

- knowledge that S knows H to have about A.

It seems that we need not only a theory of the hearer's interests but also a theory of the hearer's spatiotemporal perspective. When reporting what the agent said or thought, I need to know where the hearer is relative to the agent. If on Wednesday an agent says 'It is fine today', when I report this to a hearer on Thursday I will want to report the same statement but relative to the hearer's temporal position. Thus we get 'A said that it was fine yesterday'. Roughly, then, we will want the theory to keep track of the following:

- S's knowledge of H's spatiotemporal position
- S's knowledge of H's and A's relative positions
- H's knowledge that S knows A's spatiotemporal position (with standard assumptions about common knowledge).

What goes for attitude reports and indirect discourse goes for determining when two indexical I-language tokenings express the same thought. These tokenings, after all, are also reports of a certain kind, since they are tokenings of an I-language sentence to oneself. The twist is that in such cases the agent, the "speaker," and the "hearer" are all the same individual. The puzzles that arise here do so because the tokenings take place at different times and at different places. Accordingly, we must adjust to the new temporal position, just as though the original tokening had been made by another person.

Clearly a lot of work must be done to elucidate the exact nature of these "tracking" abilities. Evans (1982) has made a start, but realistically this picture must be fleshed out by a full-scale psychological research program—at least if we are interested in the robust underlying theory. In the meantime, what would the modest semantical theory look like?

It seems to me that there are two possibilities. The first is that we simply introduce the descriptive information into the T-theorems, thus obtaining theorems like (21″) and (22″) for (21) and (22).

(21″)
If u is an utterance of $[_S[_{NP}$ I] $[_{VP}$ need a haircut]] then u is true iff the utterer of u needs a haircut.

(22")

If u is an utterance of [$_S$[$_{NP}$ She] [$_{VP}$ needs a haircut]] then u is true iff and the object demonstrated by the utterer of u needs a haircut.

As we will see in chapter 6, there are serious limitations to this sort of approach. For now I just want to put the strategy on the table.

Alternatively, we can simply disquotationally enter the indexical expression into the right-hand side of a biconditional. For example, we might have axioms and theorems like (27) and (28).

(27)

Val(x, 'I') iff x = I

(28)

Val(T, 'I walk') iff I walk

Admittedly, this idea *appears* naive. Wouldn't we get absurd results when interpreting the utterances of others? For example, if Smith says "I walk," it is no good for me to have a T-theory that interprets that utterance as saying that I walk. But that is precisely where the above sort of axiom seems to lead.

Likewise, if someone sends me an e-mail on Tuesday saying "Smith went to the dentist today," if I only read the e-mail today (several days later) it is no good for me to interpret this as saying that Smith went to the dentist today. Thus, axioms like (29) for temporal indexicals presumably are also out of court.

(29)

Val(x, 'today') iff x is true today

On the other hand, perhaps this objection is given far more weight than it is due. In the first place, if we are talking about I-language, and if (as I suggested in section 1.3) the primary use of I-language is not communication but thought, then axioms like (27) and (29) are suited to a broad range of I-language tokenings. Such axioms are also entirely suitable for the interpretation of any speech we produce. The only drawback for such axioms appears to be associated with using them in interpreting the utterances of others.

But even as applied to the interpretation of others it is far from clear that these sorts of axioms are inadequate. For example, one strand of thinking would be that when we interpret others we try to "simulate" their thoughts.[11] That is, perhaps when we interpret another's utterance we try to "project ourselves into" that person's egocentric space. If that is how we interpret others, then of course we want the axioms to reflect the egocentric perspective of the speaker. Anything less would get in the way of our ability to simulate, and hence understand, our interlocutor.

A less radical solution is also available. Perhaps, when we interpret the remarks of another, we amend the axioms of our T-theory to account for the position of the speaker. Accordingly, we might have conditionalized axioms like (30), where 'Val(X, Y, Z)' says that X is the semantic value of Y as uttered by Z.

(30)
if s is my interlocutor, then Val(x, "here", s) iff x is there (near s)

This sort of paraphrase might allow us to track the indexical utterances of others from different spatial and temporal vantage points, just as we did in determining when two tokenings expressed the same thing.[12]

I shall return to these strategies when we take up the issue of temporal indexicals in chapters 6 and 7. For now, I merely want to suggest the plausibility of these strategies and to propose that they might help us to avoid the prima facie unattractive solution of banishing so-called character/role from the semantics.

There is now an entrenched tradition in the philosophy of language that would have us face problems in semantics by bracketing them off and trying to cast them out of semantics and into psychology. (Such exorcisms usually are accompanied by charges of "sloppy thinking" directed at those who see close connections between these disciplines.) Wettstein 1986 and Kaplan 1990 are canonical examples of this phenomenon, but I too have been caught up in the game (see Ludlow 1989). This sort of divide-and-wall-off strategy is almost never successful in the natural sciences,[13] and it is hard to see why it should be successful here (where we are at least knee deep in natural science). Artificial disciplinary boundaries simply do not solve problems.

In sum, it seems to me unwise to try and divorce semantics from the theory of meaning (in the robust sense of a theory that also incorporates cognitive significance). As will be seen in the next chapter, I think it is equally unwise (if not impossible) to try and divorce semantics from metaphysics.

Chapter 4
Drawing Metaphysical Consequences from a T-Theory

The idea that the study of language can provide insights into metaphysics has a long pedigree in the history of philosophy. It seems to have been operative as far back as the pre-Socratic philosopher Parmenides,[1] and it has been common in twentieth-century philosophy.

A number of linguists have also flirted with the idea that the study of natural language might have strong consequences for metaphysics. Perhaps the most notorious example, noted in the preface to this volume, is the case of Whorf (1956), who attempted to draw conclusions about the Hopis' metaphysics of time from their temporal language. There are also a number of more recent, if more tentative, claims about the link between *semantics* and metaphysics. Bach (1981, 1986), for example, has spoken of the relation between semantics and the "metaphysics of English," and has specifically addressed the question of what metaphysical consequences are entailed by the semantics of tense. But although Bach offers slogans like "No semantics without metaphysics!" (1986, p, 575), he later retreats with remarks like the following:

I've now said a little (but perhaps more than enough) about some of the kinds of things we seem to need in our ontology for English and a little bit (not near enough) about how we might get them into a semantics for English. It would be immoral of me as a linguist (I'm stealing a phrase from Montague) to make claims one way or the other about whether or not these sorts of things correspond to real things in the real world, perceptual or conceptual categories that are independent of language, or nothing at all. (ibid., p. 592)

It is, of course, a central assumption of the present work that it is far from immoral to draw metaphysical consequences from a semantic theory (so long as it is an "absolute" theory), whether one is a linguist or a philosopher. Yet this assumption, if it is to be helpful, must be clarified. Although philosophers and linguists have long pressed for a connection between language and metaphysics, they have not always been clear about what sort of connection there is supposed to be, much less why there should be such a connection.

Therefore, we need to get clear on how language and metaphysics are supposed to hang together. There are two questions to consider:

• Just what kinds of metaphysical conclusions can be drawn from the kind of semantic theory outlined in chapters 2 and 3, and how can we identify the specific metaphysical commitments of the theory?
• Can such a semantic theory be revised to avoid metaphysical commitments?

4.1   The Nature of the Metaphysical Commitment

One standard procedure in semantic theory has been to define the domain of relevant objects in advance of stating the theory. However, it is arguable that such a procedure simply papers over the most interesting and contentious issues. A number of questions can often be raised about what a semantic theory of such and such form actually commits us to. To simply stipulate a domain in advance requires that the most interesting questions have already been answered.[2]

I have suggested that metaphysical consequences can be drawn from semantic theory, but I have said little about *what* features of the semantic theory give rise to metaphysical commitments. The short answer to the question is that we will be committed to whatever objects serve as a semantic values in a correct T-theory for natural language.

To be more precise, let us suppose, on the basis of considerations laid out in chapter 2, that there is a correct T-theory that describes (at a certain level of abstraction) the semantic knowledge that an agent has. The axioms and theorems of that T-theory will introduce certain semantic values—implicitly quantifying over those semantic values. For example, (1) is shorthand for (1'), where the metalinguistic quantification over semantic values is made explicit.

(1)
Val (x, snow) iff x = snow

(1')
For all x, Val (x, snow) iff x = snow

Because the quantification in (1') is not vacuous, (1') commits us to the existence of snow. So far, nothing says that a true semantic theory must employ (1'); however, any theory that does employ it will have a clear metaphysical commitment.

A fairly straightforward claim can be made about the ontological commitments of semantic theories of the form discussed in this book. It is, with apologies to Quine (1953), that *to be is to be a semantic value*.

4.2   Sample Cases

Consider how two distinct semantic theories might introduce different kinds of objects as semantic values, and might hence have different ontological commitments.

The Commitment to Properties

Consider, for example, the adjective 'red' and the two ways of giving the semantics for the adjective shown in (2) and (3).

(2)
Val(x, red) iff x = the property of being red

(3)
Val(x, red) iff x is red

In the first case there is reference to the property redness—a kind of abstract object. In the second case (discussed in section 2.6) it appears that reference to redness has been circumvented. Even if axiom (3) is employed in giving the truth conditions for a true sentence of English, there is merely a commitment to one or more objects that happen to be red.[3] The difference between (2) and (3) reflects the intuitive difference between axioms that introduce reference and those that introduce something more akin to predication. (2) refers, in the sense that it identifies a specific semantic value for 'red'. (3), on the other hand, does not refer to a particular property; rather, it predicates something of those values that satisfy 'red'.

For example, the technical fragments introduced in the appendixes avoid reference to properties and sets. From a technical point of view, there would be no barrier to introducing the axioms shown in (4) instead.[4]

(4)
a.
Val(x, dog, σ) iff x = property of being a dog
Val(x, cat, σ) iff x = property of being a cat
Val(x, man, σ) iff x = property of being a man
Val(x, woman, σ) iff x = property of being a woman
b.
Val(x, barks, σ) iff x = the property of barking
Val(x, walks, σ) iff x = the property of walking
c.
Val(x, sees, σ) iff x = the seeing relation
Val(x, likes, σ) iff x = the likes relation

The nonterminal axioms would then have to be modified accordingly:

(5)

a. Val(T, [$_S$ NP VP], σ) iff for some x, p, Val(x, NP, σ) and Val(p, VP, σ) and x has p

b. Val(p, [$_{VP}$ V NP], σ) iff for some r, z, Val(r, V, σ) and Val(z, NP, σ), and p is the property of bearing r to z

The substitution of rules like these into the fragment would yield theorems like (6).

(6)

[$_S$ [$_{NP}$ Smith][$_{VP}$ [$_V$ sees][$_{NP}$ Jones]] is true iff Smith has the property of bearing the seeing relation to Jones

This alternative axiomatization would have the same empirical coverage as the axiomatization introduced in chapter 2, but it would have profoundly different metaphysical commitments. The chief difference would, of course, be its commitment to properties and relations.

Often the choice between alternative axiomatizations is argued on a priori metaphysical grounds. Of course, it is also possible to argue for one position or the other on linguistic grounds. The question is, just how far can we get with a priori metaphysics alone?

On the one hand, there are independent reasons for supposing that properties ought to exist. Wright (1983) has pointed to cases of apparent pronominal reference to properties in examples like (7).

(7)

A: At least John is honest.

B: Yes, he certainly is *that*.

And Chierchia (1984) has noted that we appear to routinely quantify over properties in examples like (8) and in reasoning like (9).

(8)

John is everything his mother wanted him to be.

(9)

John is everything that Mary is.

Mary is intelligent.

John is intelligent.

But none of these arguments is particularly compelling. In the first place, the argument from anaphora is weak. Pronominal reference usually allows us to use plural anaphors to pick up reference to several objects, as in (10).

(10)

A: Baccalà is delicious and so is polenta.

B: OK, I'll try them.

But similar plural anaphors are not available for alleged property reference.[5] Consider (11).

(11)

A: John is tall and honest.

B: #Yes, he certainly is them/those.

The alleged quantification over properties in (8) is also suspect, as one cannot continue the utterance in the usual way by listing the things we are supposedly quantifying over. Compare (12) with (13).

(12)

I tried everything my mother asked me to try: the chicken, the beef, the tuna surprise, ...

(13)

#John is everything his mother wanted him to be: kindness, thriftiness, the property of being a Republican, ...

It is simply no good to list the properties, but those are the things that we are supposed to be quantifying over. There is something very wrong with the idea that we are quantifying over properties here.

Similar considerations undermine the argument from inferences like those in (9). We may well have second-order quantification in such examples, but there is no apparent quantification over properties.

If the usual arguments for and against properties are not persuasive, perhaps we can gain some leverage by seeing what constraints the semantic theory might place on our choice.

Larson and Segal have given an example of a linguistic argument that might decide between an analysis like that in chapter 2 and the property analysis. According to them, the property analysis encounters difficulties when one attempts to develop an account of "coordination constructions" (e.g., 'Smith walked and swam'). For example, one can extend the fragment L1 to handle constructions such as those in (14).

(14)

$\text{Val}(x, [_s \text{ VP1 } \underline{\text{and}} \text{ VP2}], \sigma)$ iff $\text{Val}(x, \text{VP1}, \sigma)$ and $\text{Val}(x, \text{VP2}, \sigma)$

On the other hand, if the semantic values of sentences are to be rendered as properties, the account becomes much more complex—perhaps, following Larson and Segal, along the lines of (15).

(15)

Val(p, [$_s$ VP1 <u>and</u> VP2], σ) iff Val(p1, VP1, σ) and Val(p2, VP2, σ)

As Larson and Segal note, this will require the introduction of some kind of property-combining mechanism. But what sort of mechanism? Intuitively, what is wanted here is a rule that will take properties and combine them into new properties that are exemplified only by those objects that had the original two properties. But how is this mechanism to work, and how is it to be integrated into the axioms of the T-theory in an intelligible way? The answer is far from clear.

We may not even need to consider cases like conjunction; the property analysis may not get off the ground, in view of the kinds of constraints we would like to put on T-theories. We want to say that an agent "knows" the axioms of a T-theory, but what does it mean to know an axiom like (16)?

(16)

Val(x, 'red') iff x = redness

Redness, if there is such a thing, is an abstract object well outside space and time. Our knowledge of such things (if such knowledge is possible) is, of necessity, mediated by other sorts of knowledge that we have—for example, our knowledge of the meaning of 'red', and, by extension, our having a rule of classification that allows us to identify red things. Strictly speaking, knowing that x is red is more fundamental than knowing what redness is.

But if knowing that x is red is more fundamental than knowing what redness is, one has to wonder what work the property is doing here. It isn't needed to account for our semantical knowledge, that is for sure; hence, there can be no purely semantical motivation for positing such properties. Perhaps there are other motivations (say, in physical theory), but it seems to me that properties are very poor candidates for admission into our ontology.[6]

Keep in mind that our goal here is not to argue against property theory, but rather to show how the question is reframed on this approach to metaphysics— it becomes a question of simultaneously solving the constraints of semantical theory and constraints imposed by our metaphysical intuitions. Neither set of constraints is a priori privileged; the resulting theory must satisfy both. A similar situation holds when we move from the investigation of predication to the role of names within the semantical theory.

Names

I said earlier in this chapter that *to be is to be a semantic value*. Although the claim is straightforward, in this formulation it is also a claim with some *very* strong consequences. Just how strong the thesis is becomes clear when we consider an axiom like (17).

(17)

Val (x, <u>Pegasus</u>) iff x = Pegasus

If our true semantic theory includes an axiom like (17), we are committed to an ontology that includes Pegasus.[7] Presumably (Meinong 1904), Pegasus is a kind of nonexistent object. We may well recoil from this sort of commitment, but we must observe that inconsistencies in the theory of Meinongian objects have been exorcised in recent years—for example, in Parsons 1980, in Routley 1980, in Zalta 1983, and in Zalta 1988. Thus, in evaluating such proposals, what we have to go on are our metaphysical intuitions and whatever purchase semantical theory can give us.

As far as the semantical theory is concerned, nothing says that T-theories that correctly characterize an agent's semantic knowledge must employ axioms like (17). Indeed, under a number of plausible circumstances, the agent's semantic knowledge may diverge from (17) significantly. In particular, if we attend to *robust* T-theories when trying to ascertain our ontological commitments, then a careful study of the agent's knowledge may deflect concerns about nonexistent objects.

One possibility is that closer investigation will show that the lexical entry for 'Pegasus' is much more complex than is reflected by (17). This would not be an unusual state of affairs. Recent work on the lexicon suggests that words are in fact highly structured objects. For example, if the lexical entry were to encode the rich structure of a Russellian description, the metaphysical commitments would doubtless be much more austere. For example, the entry for the word we pronounce "pɛgəsəs" would be the following: on a naive Russellian picture 'N: [the x: x is white, x is winged,...]'. For a richly structured lexical entry like this, there would not even be a single semantic axiom. Rather, the axioms for 'the', 'white', 'winged', etc., would come into play.

The problems inherent in descriptive theories of names are well known,[8] of course, but perhaps not decisive. For example, much of Kripke's (1980) argument turns on our metaphysical intuitions about rigidity. But we have already seen in section 3.5 that there may be ways to accommodate rigidity without giving up on the cognitive content of a term.[9]

For example, following a suggestion made by Dummett (1973), we might let the description take wide scope over any modal operators in the sentence. Despite Kripke's protestations in the preface to *Naming and Necessity* (1980), one probably can go some distance towards "capturing" the relevant rigidity intuitions in this way. Clearly, Kripke's characterization of such a stipulation as "unaccountable!" (ibid., p. 13) overstates the case. At worst, the stipulation is unaccounted for, not unaccountable (just as many other scope and movement restrictions in generative grammar are not yet accounted for). That something is not accounted for by current theory is the norm in empirical inquiry. It is something to investigate, not something to despair over.

Nor does one necessarily have to bow to Kripke's argument that rigidity effects are apparent in (18) (which contains no modals) and that hence apparent rigidity cannot be accounted for by scope.

(18)
Aristotle was fond of dogs.

According to Kripke, (18) can be considered under various counterfactual situations, as it surely can. But here the unargued assumption is that when we consider (18) under various counterfactual situations the descriptive content of the name must remain constant. We need to consider what it means to evaluate a sentence under other counterfactual situations. There is no a priori reason why a proper evaluation cannot include a correlative shift in the descriptive content of the name.[10]

Of course, this gambit against Kripke requires a particular perspective towards rigidity and trans-world identity. The idea would be that we do not simply rigidly designate an individual, but rather that trans-world individuals are constructed from descriptive "manifestations" in various worlds. The individual is synthesized, as it were, from these manifestations. Theories of trans-world identity in this vein have been proposed by Hintikka (1969b, 1972). Smith (1983) has drawn an interesting parallel between technical efforts like Hintikka's and Kantian/Husserlian theories of how individuals are "constituted."

This discussion is not intended to be anything like a serious defense of the descriptive theory of names. That would take another work at least as lengthy and detailed as this one. Rather, the point is to illustrate the shift in perspective that follows if we are allowing epistemology, semantics, and metaphysics to be connected in an interesting way. The precise nature of our commitment will not turn solely on a priori argumentation about the plausibility of such objects or our intuitions about rigidity; it will also turn on a careful elucidation of the agent's lexicon and of the corresponding semantic knowledge. The point is that within this framework the question of names is not closed; indeed, it is very much open. There is still much interesting work to be done.

Events

It is well known that Davidson (1967b) argued for the existence of events on the basis of the logical form of action sentences. Roughly, the reasoning went as follows. One can easily make the inference from (19) to (20).

(19)
John ate the chips gracefully.

(20)
John ate the chips.

Davidson proposed that this inference was a logical inference, and that the inference could be made formally once the underlying logical form of 'John ate the chips gracefully' was revealed. Davidson suggested that its logical form should be as in (21).

(21)
$(\exists e)[ate(John, the\ chips, e)\ \&\ graceful(e)]$

Roughly, (21) can be understood as saying that there was an event e which was an eating of the chips by John, and e was graceful. The conclusion (20) follows by simple conjunction reduction. Davidson took this to be one piece of evidence for the existence of events.

But notice that it is not even necessary that there be explicit event quantification in the object language. What matters is whether there is quantification over events in the metalanguage. For example, in the fragment introduced in appendix T2 we have semantic rules like (22).

(22)
a.
$Val(T, [_s NP\ VP], \sigma)$ iff, for some e, $Val(e, VP, \sigma)$, and for some x, x is the agent of e and $Val(x, NP, \sigma)$
b.
$Val(e, [_{VP} V\ NP], \sigma)$ iff $Val(e, V, \sigma)$ and for some y, y is the theme of e and $Val(y, NP, \sigma)$
c.
$Val(e, [_{VP} V\ ADV], \sigma)$ iff $Val(e, V, \sigma)$ and $Val(e, ADV, \sigma)$

The crucial quantification for our purposes is the metalinguistic quantification over the e position. If these axioms are correct, and if at least some of the action sentences we utter are true, then we are committed to the existence of events.

It might be argued that we are indeed committed to something when we quantify into the e position, but that is a far cry from saying that we are committed to the existence of events. It is certainly true that we are not committed to events simply because the variables happened to be labeled with little e's. What we do know, however, even from simple axioms like the above, is that we are quantifying over things (whatever we may choose to call them) that have agents (cf. (22a)) and themes (cf. (22b)), and of which adverbs like 'intentionally' and 'slowly' are true. These certainly sound like candidates for events to me.[11]

Notice too that, if this approach is right, much of what we know about the structure of events (or whatever we choose to call them) will not be deduced from a priori intuitions about the nature of events (whether they have parts, whether they can have multiple agents, and so on); rather, it will flow from the constraints imposed by the demands of constructing the T-theory. The demands of semantic theory will help to elucidate the nature of ontology.

4.3   Can a T-Theory Avoid Having Metaphysical Consequences?

In the preceding section I suggested that ontological commitment might be tied to the semantic values introduced by the semantic theory. In support of this suggestion, it can be noted that there is, after all, implicit quantification over semantic values in the axioms of the semantic theory. If there is quantification over semantic values, then there must be an ontological commitment to those values.

However, it has been argued that one can neutralize the ontological commitments entailed by quantification by treating the quantifiers as *substitutional* quantifiers. The basic idea is that a sentence like (23) will be true just in case (23') (where $\frown$ is a concatenation symbol) is true.

(23)
A dog barked.

(23')
For some term t, t$\frown$'is a dog' is true and t$\frown$'barked' is true.

Since there is a term (say, 'Lassie') that when concatenated with 'is a dog' and 'barked' results in a true sentence, (23') must be true. Notice that this is accomplished without ever quantifying over actual dogs.

It has been proposed that this device might be useful in a number of contexts, including the philosophy of mathematics (Gottlieb 1980), the semantics of intentional constructions like 'John seeks a unicorn' (Ioup 1977), and the treatment of classes and attributes (Sellars 1963).

The question, then, is whether utilizing substitutional quantification can eliminate the ontological commitment in natural language semantics. In this section, we shall see that it cannot.

A number of objections have been raised against substitutional quantification in connection with its compatibility with truth-conditional semantics and the Davidsonian program.[12] I will not be addressing this concern; rather, I will be addressing the independent issue of whether substitutional quantification can free us from ontological commitment when doing semantics.

The most notorious statement of the view that substitutional quantification does not embody a genuine concept of existence is found on p. 106 of Quine 1969:

... substitutional quantification gives no acceptable version of existence properly so-called, not if objectual quantification does. Substitutional quantification makes good sense, explicable in terms of truth and substitution, no matter what substitution class we take— even that whose sole member is the left-hand parenthesis. To conclude that entities are being assumed that trivially, and that far out, is simply to drop ontological questions.

Against Quine, Parsons (1971a, p. 232) has argued that substitutional quantification in fact "has a genuine claim to express a concept of existence." Parsons (ibid., p. 233) responds to the above argument from Quine by arguing that there are two formal features of the category of singular terms that make substitutional quantification with respect to singular terms far less trivial than substitutional quantification with respect to the left parenthesis:

First [substitutional quantification] admits identity with the property of substitutivity *salva veritate*. Second, it has infinitely many members that are distinguishable by the identity relation. This has the consequence that '$(\forall x)Fx$' is stronger than any conjunction that can be formed of sentences of the form 'Ft', while '$(\exists x)Fx$' is weaker than any disjunction of such sentences.

After considering the specific case of introducing a predicative theory of classes, Parsons (ibid., pp. 234–235) concludes that the substitutional quantifier will in fact have certain ontological commitments:

... in the case where the terms involved have a nontrivial equivalence relation with infinitely many equivalence classes, substitutional quantification gives rise to a genuine "doctrine of being" to be set alongside Quine's and others. It parallels certain idealistic theories of the existence of physical things, such as the account of perception in Husserl's *Ideen*.

What does Parsons have in mind here? Parallels to Husserl are generally problematic, since there is wide variation in the interpretation of his work.[13] By some accounts Husserl is an idealist; by other accounts he is a realist; by still others (e.g. Hall 1982) he is neither. On each account, however, the theory of object perception is highly complex.

There is, however, a section in chapter 1 of *Ideas* (1972) in which Husserl suggests a deep connection between syntactical forms and *Stoffen* (sometimes translated as 'matter', sometimes as 'elements'). One possible interpretation of

Parsons's suggestion might be that certain syntactic positions of a sentence (for example, the subject or noun phrase position) might show a privileged connection to *Stoffen*. The word 'connection' is used loosely here, since it suggests some sort of chasm between the syntactic object and *Stoffen* when in fact these forms are better thought of as playing an active role in organizing the world.

These are, as Dummett is fond of saying, "deep waters," and some might add that the waters also are murky. Nevertheless, there are clearly many candidate notions of existence in the idealist tradition and elsewhere, and in at least some parts of the tradition, existence or being is closely tied to certain kinds of privileged syntactic representations. It stands to reason that not all syntactic forms are so privileged, and that the positions into which we quantify substitutionally (noun phrase or subject positions) may well be privileged. A reconstruction of certain idealist conceptions of being could easily involve resources like substitutional quantification. In short, the move to substitutional quantification does not necessarily eliminate ontological commitment in the sense that we are interested in.[14]

Fundamentally, in view of the kind of deflationary metaphysical investigation being proposed here, it should not appear particularly bold or surprising that our metaphysical commitments are tied to our use of quantification over semantic values in the metalanguage. A move to substitutional quantification would hardly undercut this project. In fact, one might ask whether it is not precisely the best way of thinking about metalinguistic quantification within this program.

The discussion in this chapter has been in the service of seeing how we can "read" metaphysical consequences off a T-theory (and seeing that if we have a genuine T-theory we cannot avoid these consequences). But so far the discussion has concerned the metaphysical commitments imposed on us by our use of NPs and basic predicates. In the next few chapters I will extend this general strategy to two more complex T-theories that have incorporated different approaches to the semantics of tense and which, accordingly, have very different metaphysical commitments.

Chapter 5

The B-Theory Semantics

Having sketched the basic semantic framework and shown how metaphysical commitments can arise within that framework, I will now turn to the semantics of tense and begin to explore in a general way a class of semantical theories that are consistent with the B-theory metaphysics. I will begin with what is essentially the received view: the Reichenbachian theory of tense, which I call the *B-theory semantics*.

5.1 The Basic Theory

Here I will utilize the resources of event quantification to develop a specific semantic theory for temporal discourse that is consistent with B-series metaphysics. Recall the criteria that Gale (1967) gave for that metaphysical picture of time:

- The A-series is reducible to the B-series.
- Temporal becoming is psychological.
- The B-series is objective. All events are equally real.
- Change is analyzable solely in terms of B-series relations (earlier-than, later-than).

A first attempt at a semantical theory consistent with this picture would be to give "tenseless truth conditions" for tensed sentences. That is, we want the right-hand sides of the T-theorems to utilize only B-theory resources (e.g., the B-series time line and the before/after relation), and we want the right-hand sides to be free of A-series predicates (including 'past' and 'future' as well as temporal indexicals). This idea could be executed somewhat as in (1), where we take the tense operators to be quantifying over arbitrary future and past times.[1]

(1)
a.
An utterance of 'Fred is hungry' at time t, is true iff Fred is hungry at time t

b.

An utterance of 'Fred was hungry' at time t, is true iff Fred is hungry at time t' earlier than t

c.

An utterance of 'Fred will be hungry' at time t, is true iff Fred is hungry at time t' later than t

We might carry that general idea over into our Val notation as in (1'), where Val(A,B,C) says that A is the semantic value of B relative to the utterance time C.

(1')

a.

Val(e, PAST, t) iff e is temporally before t

b.

Val(e, PRES, t) iff e temporally overlaps t

c.

Val(e, FUT, t) iff e is temporally after t

Ironically, the simple semantics just sketched is often the one that is some-times imputed to Prior. Whatever the merits of the analysis, it pretty clearly is not one that Prior could countenance; it is replete with quantification over past and future times.

The main problem for a semantics of tense like the one I have just sketched is that it is suitable only for simple tenses, such as past, present, and future. When we get to more complex tenses, such as the future perfect, matters become much more involved. For example, we will need a semantics for sentences like (2).

(2)

Smith will have swum in the lake.

Clearly, the event of Smith's swimming is not past, nor is it merely future. What is suggested is that at some future point the event of Smith's swimming will be past. Two other complex tenses that will have to be dealt with are the present perfect and the past perfect. Is there anything we can do to accommo-date these?

One promising B-theory strategy is to borrow from the work of Reichenbach (1947) and from its use in grammatical theory by a legion of linguists in vari-ous traditions, including Åqvist (1976), Guenthner (1979), Hinrichs (1986, 1988), Hornstein (1990), and Giorgi and Pianesi (1997). The central idea in Reichenbach's proposal was that accounting for complex tenses requires that we make reference to three distinct temporal points (or, on some formulations, events): S, R, and E, where S is the speech time, E is the time of the event, and R is a (possibly independent) reference time. As an illustration of the relationship among these points, consider the case of the future perfect in (2) again. Intuitively, (2) says that the time of Smith's swimming (E) is later than the speech time (S) but earlier than some established reference time (R).

Thinking of a schematic time line ($\leftrightarrow$) on which points to the left are earlier than points to the right, we have the following standard Reichenbachian analysis of the tenses[2]:

present: $\leftarrow$E/R/S$\rightarrow$

past: $\leftarrow$E/R—S$\rightarrow$

future: $\leftarrow$S—E/R$\rightarrow$

pluperfect: $\leftarrow$E—R—S$\rightarrow$

future perfect: $\leftarrow$S—E—R$\rightarrow$

future in future: $\leftarrow$S—R—E$\rightarrow$

future in past: $\leftarrow$R—S—E$\rightarrow$ or $\leftarrow$R—E—S$\rightarrow$

We can introduce Reichenbach's proposal into a truth-conditional semantics in the following fashion.[3] We begin by augmenting the Val predicate to be a six-place predicate Val(A, B, S, R, E, σ) asserting that A is the semantic value of B at time of utterance S, reference time R, event time E, and assignment σ. Axioms would include the nonterminal axioms shown in (3) to cover the case of simple sentences with intransitive verbs and would include the axioms shown in (4) for the tense morphemes.

(3)

a.

Val(T, [$_{IP}$ NP I'], S, R, E) iff for some x, e, Val(e, I', S, R, E) and at(e, E) and for some x, x is the agent of e and Val(x, NP, S, R, E)

b.

Val(e, [$_{I'}$ I VP], S, R, E) iff Val(e, I, S, R, E) and Val(e, VP, S, R, E)

c.

Val(e, [$_{VP}$ V], S, R, E) iff Val(e, V, S, R, E)

(4)

a.

Val(e, PAST, S, R, E, σ) iff R/E is earlier than S

b.

Val(e, PRES, S, R, E, σ) iff S, R, and E temporally overlap

c.

Val(e, FUT, S, R, E, σ) iff S is earlier than R/E

d.

Val(e, PRES PERFECT, S, R, E, σ) iff E is earlier than S/R

e.

Val(e, PAST PERFECT, S, R, E, σ) iff E is earlier than R and R is earlier than S

f.

Val(e, FUT PERFECT, S, R, E, σ) iff S is earlier than E and E is earlier than R

g.

Val(e, FUT IN PAST, S, R, E, σ) iff R is earlier than S and R is earlier than E

Clearly it would be desirable to axiomatize the semantic theory in such a way that the complex tenses could be derived from the simpler ones. For example, one might introduce an axiom for 'had' that when used in conjunction with a past-tense morpheme would yield the past perfect, as in (5).

(5)

a.

Val(e, had, S, R, E, σ) iff E is earlier than R, and At(e,E)

b.

Val(e, will, S, R, E, σ) iff S is earlier than E, and At(e,E)

Consider again the case of 'Smith will have swum in the lake'. In combination, the axioms given in (5) state that S is earlier than E and E is earlier than R—in other words, when combined they yield the future perfect.[4]

This Reichenbachian analysis of tense also leads to several natural analyses of temporal adverbs such as 'yesterday', 'today', and 'tomorrow'. For example, they can be construed as fixing the time of the reference event. We might introduce the auxiliary axioms shown in (6).

(6)

a.

Val(e, yesterday, S, R, E, σ) iff R is the day before S

b.

Val(e, today, S, R, E, σ) iff R is the same day as S

c.

Val(e, tomorrow, S, R, E, σ) iff R is the day after S

Following the suggestions of numerous authors in this framework, we can likewise incorporate temporal connectives such as 'before' and 'after' as in (7).[5]

(7)

a.

Val(T,[$_{IP}$ IP1 <u>before</u> IP2], S, R, E, σ) iff Val(T, IP1, S, R1, E1, σ) and Val(T, IP2, S, R2, E2, σ) and E1 is earlier than E2

b.

Val(T,[$_{IP}$ IP1 <u>after</u> IP2], S, R, E, σ) iff Val(T, IP1, S, R1, E1, σ) and Val(T, IP2, S, R2, E2, σ) and E1 is later than E2

c.

Val(T,[$_{IP}$ IP1 <u>when</u> IP2], S, R, E, σ) iff Val(T, IP1, S, R1, E1, σ) and Val(T, IP2, S, R2, E2, σ) and E1 temporally overlaps E2[6]

The crucial thing to see in the exposition thus far is that the truth conditions have been restricted to events or times and to a linear before/after relation holding between them. In this sense the theory reflects a genuine B-theory approach to time. Can the approach be extended far enough?

5.2   Extending the Theory

The B-theory axioms offered so far only hint at how various B-theory semantics of tense have been developed. The research in this area is vast, and to survey the entire literature here would be impracticable. There are, however, a few constructions that bear comment, if only because they have figured in disputes over A-theory and B-theory approaches to tense.

Aspect

First, it is necessary to see how a theory of aspect can be incorporated into this framework, and to see how it will interact with the rest of the theory. Here the standard move (see, e.g., Comrie 1976; Parsons 1991; Kamp and Reyle 1993) has been to regard aspect as a predicate of events. For example, Parsons introduces the predicates CUL (for "culminates") and PROG (for "in progress") to account for the perfective and the imperfective aspect, respectively. This idea can be incorporated in a straightforward way with the introduction of axioms like those in (8).

(8)

Val(e, <u>PROG</u>, S, R, E, σ) iff in-progress-at(e, E)

Val(e, <u>CUL</u>, S, R, E, σ) iff culminates-at(e, E)

This allows a single event variable to have both temporal and aspectual properties predicated of it. For example, with the axioms I have introduced thus far, the derivation of a T-theorem such as (9) will be possible for 'Smith swam yesterday'.[7]

(9)

Val(T, [$_{IP}$[$_{NP}$ Smith][$_I$[$_I$[$_{TNS}$ PAST][$_{ASP}$ CUL]][$_{VP}$[$_V$ swims][$_{ADV}$ yesterday]]]], S, R, E, σ) iff for some e, S is later than R/E, and At(e,E) and culminates-at(e, E) and e is a swimming by Smith, and R is the day before S, and Smith is the agent of e

Other sorts of aspectual predicates can be added in similar fashion. Syntactically, they can be housed in the Infl (I) node[8]; semantically, they can be regarded as predicates that take the event variable as their argument.

Tensed Nominals

The second extension one can make has to do with the fact that not only verbs but also noun phrases have been argued to have argument positions for times. For example, Enç (1986, 1987) has observed that in (10) there is good reason to suppose that 'hostages' means something like "everyone who was a hostage during time t."

(10)

The hostages came to the White House.

The way to incorporate this idea in the Reichenbachian framework being sketched here is to have the lexical axiom for the noun to introduce a kind of reference event of its own.[9] For example, we might try (11).

(11)

Val(x, hostage, R') iff there is an e', e' an event of x being a hostage, and At(e', R')

There are puzzles surrounding the proper treatment of such cases (see the Enç references for discussion), but no puzzles that appear to pose special problems for the introduction of this idea into an absolute semantics like the one being sketched in this chapter.

Sequence of Tense

Also of considerable interest is the "sequence of tense" phenomenon discussed by Smith (1975, 1978), Ladusaw (1977), Dowty (1982), Stowell (1994), Enç (1987), Higginbotham (1995), Hornstein (1990), Abusch (1997), Giorgi and Pianesi (1997), and many others. The basic idea is that in certain embedded environments the reference time gets shifted further into the past. Consider (12).

(12)
Mary said that Biff was ill.

There are two readings to this sentence. In one, Biff's illness overlaps with Mary's remarks; in the other, Mary reported that Biff had been ill. The puzzle lies in trying to account for both readings.

To get the shifted reading, one general strategy has been to take the internal event (the event of Biff being ill) as being past relative to the matrix event (the event of Mary speaking). As Higginbotham (1995) spells out the idea, we want to say that the event of Mary speaking is past relative to the utterance event as in (13) (where $<$ expresses the relation of temporal precedence, u is the utterance event, and Φ is the content of Mary's utterance), and the event of which Mary is speaking is previous to this event e.

(13)
$(\exists e)[\text{say}(\text{Mary}, \Phi, e) \text{ and } e < u]$

(14)
$(\exists e')[\text{ill}(\text{Biff}, e') \text{ and } e < e']$

Putting (13) and (14) together, and using '[|. . .|]' to indicate an ILF, Higginbotham proposes the analysis shown in (15) for the shifted reading of (12).

(15)
$(\exists e)[\text{say}(\text{Mary}, [|(\exists e')[\text{ill}(\text{Biff}, e') \text{ and } e < e']|], e), \text{ and } e < u]$

The puzzle for this analysis then becomes how to account for the nonshifted reading. On Higginbotham's proposal (1995, p. 235) "the appearance of the past tense in a complement clause can be an appearance merely; cross-reference takes place as in the first case, but the tense of the complement is present, not past." That is, 'was ill' only *appears* to be past-tense morphology in these cases—thus, the relation between e and e' is not temporal precedence but overlap. The result is shown in (16).

(16)
$(\exists e)[\text{say}(\text{Mary}, [|(\exists e')[\text{ill}(\text{Biff}, e') \text{ and } e' \text{ includes } e]|], e), \text{ and } e < u]$

Of course, if this solution is available, then so too is the option of having the internal reference variable R pick out some arbitrary past reference event. In the case of (12), the identified event might be past relative to Mary's utterance or the speaker's utterance or it might be contemporaneous with either of these events; all that is specified for sure is that R is past relative to S and that E is past relative to S. The relations between E and R would remain undetermined.

This idea, subsequently characterized as the "independent theory of embedded tenses,"[10] was initially suggested by Smith (1975) and Ladusaw (1977) and was worked out formally by Dowty (1982). If the approach is right,[11] then it is really a mistake to talk about genuine "ambiguity" in cases of sequence of tense. What we are witnessing is simply the phenomenon of having multiple internal reference events available for R—something much closer to vagueness than to ambiguity.

If this story works for SOT cases, how can it be extended to so-called double access readings in cases like 'Biff said Mary is pregnant'? In this case, Mary had to be pregnant at the time of Biff's utterance; and she must remain pregnant at the utterance time S, when the sentence is spoken. How is this to be represented with B-theory resources? Presumably one wants to invoke some sort of reference to an interval that includes both the time of Biff's utterance and the speaker's time S.

Of course, here we are ignoring the really interesting empirical questions—questions concerning which environments admit DAR readings and concerning the mechanism by which reference to the relevant interval arises.[12] My interest here is not to solve these problems, but to give a sample of some of the possible responses within the Reichenbachian framework. The idea is to illustrate the kinds of theoretical resources that are in the Reichenbachian toolbox. As we will see, the A-theorist has a rather more restricted set of tools available, and some of the solutions to these puzzles must be different.

This has been a very superficial whirlwind tour of B-theory approaches to the problem of the sequence of tense. Clearly there are a number of resources at the disposal of the B-theorist (reference events, possible relative orderings, etc.), so one might suppose that a solution is within grasp even if difficulties remain in each of these areas. But if the B-theorist encounters difficulties here, one naturally supposes that the A-theorist (who does not have recourse to reference events, to the relative ordering of events, or to any other B-theory resources) will be in much greater difficulty. I will return to this issue in chapter 7.

5.3   Metaphysical Commitments of the Theory

As I noted in section 5.1, this semantic theory for tense is tied to a certain metaphysical picture of time. If we take the metaphysical consequences of semantic theory seriously, then we shall be committed to a metaphysics in which future and past temporal points can be referred to and in which they are, in some sense, just as real as the present.

This is so, for, as argued in chapter 4, we will at minimum be committed to those entities that we quantify over, and metalinguistic quantification over times is ubiquitous here. If this wasn't obvious, it is perhaps worth noting that each of the axioms that contain variables for utterance, reference, and event times (S, R, and E) is bound by implicit metalinguistic quantifiers. More important, in the above T-theory ((3)–(7)) it is supposed that the values assigned to these variables stand in certain temporal relations to one another (earlier-than, later-than, etc.). Thus, it seems that this semantic theory is committed not only to the existence of times but also to their standing in certain temporal relations to one another (however those relations are ultimately to be cashed out).

Perhaps, however, the values of R, S, and E need not be supposed to be time points. It is possible, with minor adjustments, to employ events alone. In fact, the only portion of our truth definition that appears committed to the idea that R, S, and E are time points is the clause 'At(e,E)' in the axioms in (3). Revised axioms, making use of only events, could be written along the lines of (3').

(3')
a.
Val(T, [$_{IP}$ NP I'], S, R, E) iff for some x, e, Val(e, I', S, R, E) and e = E and for some x, x is the agent of e and Val(x, NP, S, R, E)
b.
Val(e, [$_{I'}$ I VP], S, R, E) iff Val(e, I, S, R, E) and Val(e, VP, S, R, E)
c.
Val(e, [$_{VP}$ V], S, R, E) iff Val(e, V, S, R, E)

In this case the commitment is only to the existence of events that stand in certain temporal relations to one another. Times could be introduced, of course, but they would consist of sets of temporally overlapping events.[13]

Quite apart from the obvious commitments to either events or temporal points (or both), there may well be other metaphysical commitments lurking in a full development of the theory. One interesting example, discussed in Parsons 1991, concerns the metaphysical commitments of the axiom I introduced for the progressive. The core issue, perhaps first noted by Aristotle, concerns the so-called imperfective paradox. It appears possible for there to be an event of my drawing a circle that in some sense is in progress but which is never completed (perhaps I am run over by a bus before I finish the circle). However, it seems that on the proposal given in (8) there *is* a circle such that there was an in-progress event of my drawing it. Can there be incomplete objects? Can there be incomplete events? Parsons (1991) is inclined to answer in the affirmative. There are alternative strategies (some of which Parsons discusses), but it is interesting to note that, depending on how the theory is axiomatized, we may well be committed to more than vanilla-flavored events and temporal points.

For now, I will have to set aside these tantalizing metaphysical questions and focus on the relative merits of the B-theory and the A-theory. My survey of the B-theory semantics of tense has been brief, but perhaps it has been detailed enough to support an examination of the basic philosophical presuppositions of the B-theory (and hence, as will be seen in the next chapter, detailed enough for us to see just how and where the B-theory founders).

Chapter 6

Problems with the B-Theory Semantics

A number of objections to the B-theory have been raised in the philosophical literature, some of which are genuinely semantical in character. Chief among the problems cited is the worry that the B-theorist is unable to account for the indexical character of temporal discourse. As we will see, however, indexicality is not the only semantical problem. There is also the long-standing question of how the B-theorist is to treat constructions that refer to linguistic tokens (constructions like 'There is no language' and 'There were no utterances').

These semantical objections may or may not be solvable in isolation. (I seriously doubt that the indexicality objection is solvable.) However, when the objections are combined they form a serious dilemma from which there is no escape.

My basic line of argument will be the following: The B-theorist can't solve the problem of indexicality, and in any case the most promising theory offered by the B-theorist is one that, if adopted, makes it impossible to provide semantics for sentences about linguistic tokens.

After taking up the problems individually, I will show how together they lead to the B-theorist's dilemma.

6.1 Problems with the Indexical Nature of Temporal Discourse[1]

Let us return to the case discussed in the introduction, in which I know that my fifth anniversary is (this) March 12 but do not know that today is March 12. As the example was set up in the introduction, I initially think out loud "My fifth anniversary is March 12. I should think about buying my wife an anniversary present." I then take out a calendar to find today's date and discover to my horror that today is March 12. I subsequently shout "My fifth anniversary is today!" As in the introduction, we have the following two distinct utterances (or I-language tokenings) on the table.

(1)
My fifth anniversary is (this) March 12.

(2)
My fifth anniversary is today.

And, arguably, (1) and (2) do not express the same semantical knowledge. (They certainly express different kinds of knowledge.)

The semantical difference between propositions like (1) and (2) seems to evaporate in the semantical theory I introduced in chapter 5. In that theory, the axioms utilized for (1) and (2) would be (1') and (2').

(1')
Val(e, March 12, S, R, E, σ) iff R = March 12

(2')
Val(e, today, S, R, E, σ) iff R = S

And since March 12 is identical to the time of utterance S, these two axioms deliver the same evaluation for 'March 12' and 'today'.

Short of disquotationally introducing 'today' into the right-hand sides of the truth conditions, it appears that the axiom is going to fall short in characterizing the semantic knowledge that the agent has. But if we try to add 'today' into the right-hand side, we have sold out the B-theory and admitted that A-theory resources are required to give the semantics for temporal discourse.

A related difficulty has to do with (3), uttered after a dreaded visit to the dentist's office.

(3)
I'm glad that's over with.

About precisely what am I glad? By hypothesis, 'that' refers to the event of my going to the dentist, and 'over with' means past (and culminated). On the standard B-theory analysis, this amounts to my saying that I am glad that my visit to the dentist's office culminated at some time earlier than S, the time of the utterance. If my utterance was at 5 o'clock, this amounts to my saying that I'm glad the visit culminated before 5 o'clock. But is that really what I'm glad about?

Even if one *can* pack some missing ingredient into the RHSs of the axioms, there is the danger that the missing ingredient will undermine the B-theory program. The missing element on the RHS has to be something that a B-theory metaphysics can countenance. What could that be?

These are not trivial problems. Although they have been largely ignored in the linguistics literature, they have exercised some of the leading advocates of B-theory metaphysics.

What is the best response for the B-theorist here? The leading B-theory strategy, based on suggestions by Reichenbach (1947), Kneale (1949), and Smart (1963, 1966), has been to invoke the idea of "token-reflexive" truth conditions, in which the missing ingredient is an explicit reference to the token itself. For example, Reichenbach (p. 284) suggests that "'now' means the same as 'the time at which this token is uttered'." The token-reflexive part is the part where there is talk of "*this* token." By making reference to the very tokening of a sentence like 'I am hungry now', one can situate it relative to one's own temporal position. Notice that this is a much richer story than the story that survives in the contemporary Reichenbachian theories of tense surveyed in chapter 5.

In the example of my fifth anniversary, the difference in the respective treatments of 'today' amounts to the difference between (4) and (5).

(4)

An utterance (tokening) u at S of 'My fifth anniversary is today' is true iff my anniversary is at S (March 12).

(5)

This utterance (tokening) u at S of 'My fifth anniversary is today' is true iff my anniversary is the day of S—the time of this very utterance.

The treatment in (5) is the one that Reichenbach seems to have (informally) proposed. The treatment in (4) appears to be the one adopted by contemporary linguists who have executed Reichenbach's general program for the semantics of tense in natural language.[2] But clearly (4) is too austere. Reichenbach correctly saw that one needs to say more.

Generalizing the token-reflexive strategy, Smart (1966, pp. 133–134) proposed treating the basic tenses in a similar way[3]:

Let us replace the words "is past" by the words "*is* earlier than this utterance." (Note the transition to the tenseless "is.") Similarly, let us replace "is present" and "now" by "*is* simultaneous with this utterance," and "is future" by "*is* later than this utterance." ... Notice that I am here talking of self-referential *utterances*, not self-referential *sentences*. (The same sentence can be uttered on many occasions.) We can, following Reichenbach, call the utterance itself a "token," and this sort of reflexivity "token-reflexivity." Tenses can also be eliminated, since such a sentence as "he will run" can be replaced by "he *runs* at some future time (with tenseless "runs") and hence by "he *runs* later than this utterance." Similarly, "he runs" means "he *runs* (tenseless) simultaneous with this utterance." and "he ran" means "he *runs* (tenseless) earlier than this utterance." All the jobs which can be done by tenses can be done by means of the tenseless way of talking and the self-referential utterance "this utterance."

This is all very well (or let us suppose that it is for now), but theorems like (5) have to be generated with the help of axioms in the T-theory. Precisely where does the reference to the utterance (tokening) enter into the picture? As Yourgrau (1987, note 21) has observed, there are serious difficulties involved in trying to construct a general theory that can introduce the needed demonstration of the utterance event.

To see Yourgrau's point, consider an attempt to construct a general theory that allows demonstration of the utterance event. We might start by saying that the reflexive clause enters into the RHS as in (6).

(6)
Val(e, <u>today</u>, S, R, E, σ) iff R is the same day as this very utterance (I-language tokening)

So the RHS of the axiom introduces a reference to the utterance itself (or the I-language tokening itself). But this is not acceptable. If one learns the axiom in (6), one has to learn it as a general rule. If that is the case, then what is the force of the demonstrative in 'this very utterance'? If it is a genuine demonstrative, then it should pick out the same utterance (tokening) of (6). If it isn't a genuine demonstrative, then it is not clear how the token-reflexive theorem can be generated.

This looks like a kind of a technical objection, but in fact it points to a very deep problem with the token-reflexive response. Specifically, when the B-theorist attempts to smuggle an indexical expression (such as 'this utterance') into the RHS of a theorem, the B-theorist is breaking from the usual path of keeping the literal truth conditions free of such elements. If the use of the indexical on the RHS is to make any sense at all, it appears that 'this' has to be treated as an indexical predicate of the sort that was discussed in section 3.2. But if indexical predicates are possible in this case, why not allow them in the case of temporal indexicals? Still more perplexing for the B-theorist, the indexical element in 'this utterance' looks an awful lot like a temporal indexical predicate. It certainly isn't spatial; nothing in the perceptual environment is being demonstrated. It looks for all the world as if the extra indexical element just means *now*, and as if the expression 'this utterance' means something akin to 'the utterance happening now'!

I don't know if these difficulties can be overcome, but a pattern is beginning to emerge. The B-theorist can ladle more expressive content into the RHS of the truth conditions of a tensed sentence, but the theory begins to capture the indexical character of a tensed expression only at the point where the added content looks strikingly as if it contains an indexical predicate. If this is right, then it suggests that the B-theorist simply cannot do justice to the content of tensed language. But even if this pattern can be broken and the problem of indexical character can be solved by means of a strategy like the token-reflexive theory, the token-reflexive solution leads directly to an even more intractable puzzle about sentences imputing that there are no utterances or linguistic tokens.

6.2 "There Are No Utterances"

In the previous section we saw that the best chance the B-theorist has of capturing indexical content is by utilizing token-reflexive truth conditions. The resulting semantical picture for the B-theorist is something like (7).

(7)

a.

This utterance of 'Fred is hungry' at time t is true iff Fred is hungry at t—the time of this very utterance.

b.

This utterance of 'Fred was hungry' at time t is true iff Fred is hungry at time t' earlier than t—the time of this very utterance.

c.

This utterance of 'Fred will be hungry' at time t is true iff Fred is hungry at time t' later than t—the time of this very utterance.

The token-reflexive strategy is designed to allow B-theorists to both have and eat their cake. That is, the theory is designed to allow B-theorists to situate events in their past/present/future without invoking A-theory resources. Unfortunately, the B-theorist does not get to eat or to keep this cake.

The theorems in (7) tell us that a specific utterance $u*$ of 'Fred is hungry' is true iff Fred is hungry at the very time that $u*$ is uttered. This is the device by which (assuming I am the speaker) the proposal can situate events relative to *my* temporal position. Furthermore, the B-theorist argues that theorems like those in (7) give tenseless truth conditions (i.e., B-theory truth conditions) because the RHS of the biconditional is effectively "detensed"—only B-series resources are called upon.[4]

In the previous section I noted that there is already some slippage in the B-theorist position, since the RHS of the theorem is not completely purged of indexical character. But, whether these truth conditions are really tenseless or not, it is most likely the case that they simply fail to give the correct truth conditions in a broad class of cases. If reference to an utterance is required, then there will be cases where this extra requirement—this extra bit of content—throws a monkey wrench into the semantics.

The basic problem is not unique to token-reflexive treatments of temporal language. Casteñada (1967, p. 87) showed that it also arose in treatments of indexicals like 'I':

Reichenbach, for instance, claims that the word "I" means the same as "the person who utters this token." This claim is, however, false. A statement formulated through a normal use of the sentence "I am uttering nothing" is contingent: if a person utters this sentence he falsifies the corresponding statement, but surely the statement might, even in such a case, have been true. On the other hand, the statements formulated by "The person uttering this token is uttering nothing" are self-contradictory: even if no one asserts them, they simply cannot be true.

Smith (1993) and Craig (1996a) have subsequently argued that this argument applies mutatis mutandis to the token-reflexive analysis of temporal expressions. Token-reflexive truth-conditions of this form founder in cases like (8).

(8)
There is no spoken language.

According to Smith and Craig, on the token-reflexive theory the truth conditions of (8) appear to come out as in (9).

(9)
This utterance at time t of 'There is no spoken language' is true iff there is no spoken language at t—the time of this very utterance.

Statement (8) is clearly false, but statement (9) allegedly incorrectly entails that the sentence 'There is no spoken language' is *necessarily* false.[5] This appears to be a technical objection, but Smith (1993) and Craig (1996a) have argued that there is no way to maneuver around it and that, as a consequence, the objection ultimately undermines the plausibility of the token-reflexive tenseless theory of time. For example, one might hold that it is not crucial that one fix the relevant time by uttering a sentence, since it is equally possible to give the truth conditions as in (10).

(10)
This tokening (verbal or mental) at time t of 'There is no spoken language' is true iff there is no spoken language at t—the time of this very tokening.

But (10) will apparently fail when we consider sentences like 'There are no mental or verbal tokens of language', which, though clearly false, do not appear to be necessarily false. This objection can be generalized to any proposed vehicle for the tokening of a sentence: written, spoken, thought, intuited, etc.

Appeals to possible utterances of certain sentence types[6] will not help either, for a possible past-tense utterance by me will not be enough to situate an event in *my* past. It is no comfort to me that my dentist visit lies in the past relative to a possible utterance by me at some time. I have to know that the event lies in the past relative to the time I am tokening my thought/expression of relief.

Similar considerations apply to past-tense sentences like (11).

(11)
There was a time in which there was no spoken language (were no tokens).

The worry is that (11) seems to entail that there is some time in the past in which (8) holds. But if the truth conditions of (8) are as in (9), how is this possible? Statement (9) suggests that (8) can be true only if there is an utterance of a particular token, but that would be to undermine the very thing that (8) is asserting.

Here it is natural to note the similarity between examples like (9) and similar cases from Kaplan (1977, 1979) (e.g., 'I am here now'). If we want to follow Kaplan's strategy, then we want to remove talk of the utterance event from the literal truth conditions. Perhaps the most natural way to do this in our framework would be to invoke the Larson-Segal mechanism of conditionalized T-theorems discussed in section 3.2 of the present book.[7] As applied here, the idea would be to conditionalize (8) as shown in (12).

(12)
If u is utterance at time t of 'There is no spoken language', then u is true iff there is no spoken language at t.

This fixes the evaluation to the time of utterance of the token, but it keeps the quantification outside of the T-theorem. It also avoids the need to introduce potential (possible but unactual) utterances.[8]

Crucially, the truth conditions delivered in (12) do not make (9) a necessary truth. In similar fashion, the past-tense version ('There was no spoken language') would receive the truth conditions in (13).

(13)
If u is utterance at time t of 'There was no spoken language', then u is true iff there is a time t' earlier than t such that there is no spoken language at t'.

Though the problem of reference to utterances can thus be resolved, notice that we resolved it by stripping the reference to the utterance event from the RHSs of the truth conditions. But we thereby undid the very move that allowed us to account for the indexicality of utterances like 'My fifth anniversary is today'! This is the B-theorist's dilemma.

6.3   The B-Theorist's Dilemma

The strategy the B-theorist used in solving the problem of sentences like 'There is no language' was to say that the utterance that anchored the time S did not make it into the truth conditions proper. But the most promising solution we have for the problem of temporal indexicals—the token-reflexive theory—crucially relies upon the assumption that the utterance anchoring S *does* make it into the truth conditions. Hence, the B-theorist faces a rather nasty dilemma: either remove talk of the utterance event from the truth conditions (in which case the most promising answer to the problem of temporal indexicals has to be abandoned) or allow such talk (in which case utterances which claim that there is no language end up being necessarily false).

The options here are limited. Higginbotham (1995) has attempted to take the second horn of the dilemma, holding that talk of the utterance (tokening) must make it into the truth conditions but that some of the information need not make it into the truth conditions if we evaluate the sentence under counterfactual situations. We can, according to Higginbotham, allow "modal discards"; that is, we can allow information to be discarded when the sentence is evaluated in other possible worlds.

The general idea behind using discards is the following: The truth conditions for 'There is no language' are precisely those given in (8); however, if we evaluate that very same sentence in certain possible worlds (in particular the worlds in which there is no language), the truth conditions are the leaner ones that we get in (12).

The idea of modal discards may have merit in some cases (the less charitable might say that the mechanism amounts to discarding the counterexamples), but it is hard to see that it helps with the B-theorist's dilemma. Consider (14).

(14)
If there were currently no language I would be relieved.

Suppose that w is the actual world and w' is the world in which I am relieved that there is no language. The sense of relief I feel in world w' cannot stem from there being no language at some time t, which happens to be the time of my utterance of (14) in world w (the actual world). Why would I care about that in w'!

Even if we could find a way to make the modal discard solution work, we have to keep in mind that a number of other problems which we set aside earlier still nag the general token-reflexive theory (with or without modal discards). There remains the problem of the indexical character in 'this utterance', and there remains the problem of generalizing the theory (and incorporating it into a finitely axiomatized T-theory). Quite frankly, the second horn of the B-theorist's dilemma is not a very appealing option.

As far as I can see, the only remaining option for the B-theorist is to take the first horn of the dilemma and try to argue that we don't need to keep the indexical character in the truth conditions at all—that our knowledge of indexical character is extra-semantical knowledge. The strategy would be to say that we have tensed thoughts (for example, that my anniversary is today), but that we needn't have an A-theory semantics and an A-theory metaphysics. This, as I understand it, is the move advocated by Mellor (1981). In short: if we need tense, we can keep it in the realm of psychology (belief) and out of the realm of truth-conditional semantics and metaphysics.

In earlier chapters I argued that metaphysics, semantics, and psychology are not easily separated. This may be a good time to revisit that claim—particularly now that we know what is at stake.

6.4   On Mellor's Way Out

Mellor (1981, chapter 5) concedes that tense is indispensable, and that indeed we rely on it to explain our actions (for example, my acting the way I do when I discover that *today* is March 12). But Mellor holds that it is enough that my *beliefs* be tensed. On his view, a commitment to tensed beliefs entails nothing about there being tensed truth conditions for my tensed utterances, and certainly nothing about reality's being tensed.

The flaw in this line of reasoning is that beliefs too must have a semantics, so it is hard to see why alleged problems that occur at the level of language do not likewise occur at the level of belief.[9] That is, if there is some contradiction inherent in having temporal indexicals in our semantics for natural language, why is there no contradiction if we allow them in our semantics for belief? Indeed, if the considerations in section 1.3 above are on the right track, then the language of thought (i.e., the language in which our beliefs are couched) is simply I-language to begin with! One can hardly say that I-language is untensed and that the language of thought is tensed if I-language *is* the language of thought.

Even if we reject the identity of I-language and the language of thought, it seems to me that Mellor's strategy is fatally flawed. In the first place, we have been supposing that a semantical theory is a theory of the speaker's knowledge of meaning. If that is right—if the speaker's knowledge is part of the picture—and if knowledge and belief are tensed, then it is very difficult to see how tense (and indexicality in general) is going to be expunged from the semantical theory.

Mellor clearly is forced to adopt a picture of semantical theory that cannot allow notions such as knowledge of truth conditions, but just how adequate can such a semantical theory be? It certainly can't serve as a theory of meaning; it would fail to deliver truth conditions in a way that displayed the senses of the sentences of the language, and therefore it would fail one of the minimum criteria of adequacy for a semantical theory as discussed in chapters 2 and 3.

Quite apart from these considerations (Mellor, after all, may not be interested in the possibility that a T-theory may be able to serve as a theory of meaning), what would it mean to say that we have tensed beliefs but a B-theory semantics and metaphysics? If the world contains only B-theory resources, then precisely how do we avoid having a B-theory psychology?

The illusion of a possible way out here is fostered by thinking that there could be psychological concepts that are, as it were, disembodied—cut off from the actual world in important ways. How can a psychological property (call it *foo*) that bears no relation to tense in the actual world have anything to do with tense?

It is no good to say that our abstract property foo is tensed because it is grounded in our time consciousness or temporal perception. That merely keeps the question one step removed. Then we must ask what it is about time consciousness and temporal perception that makes them tensed. Why do we call consciousness or perception *tensed* if it does not correspond to something tensed in the actual world?

The weakness in such appeals to psychology can be characterized in a general way. Impressed by the ability of psychology to explain isolated cases where we are deceived (sticks that appear bent when seen in water, etc.), we ask psychology to account for catastrophic mismatches between our philosophical theory of the world and the way we perceive the world to be. But psychology cannot shoulder this burden. As Burge (1986) has argued, psychological states (particularly perceptual states) are individuated in part by relations to the external world.[10] In this case, that means that if the world is not tensed then it is difficult to see how our perception of the world could be tensed.[11]

But if psychology cannot supply the missing tensed component, there is no avenue of retreat for the B-theorist. If tense is to be expunged from the semantics, then it cannot be retrieved elsewhere. Here we have a clear case where both semantics and psychology place demands on our metaphysics, and a B-theory metaphysics appears unable to meet the demand. Can the A-theory alternative fare any better? This question will be addressed in the next chapter.

Chapter 7
The A-Theory Semantics

7.1 The Appeal of the A-Theory Semantics

The intuitive appeal of the A-theory semantics comes from its ability to handle the indexical nature of temporal discourse. Unfettered by the burden of delivering tenseless truth conditions, the A-theory can use indexical predicates in the metalanguage to deliver tensed truth conditions that preserve the indexical character of temporal phenomena.

Consider, for example, the temporal morpheme PAST. On the B-theory, that expression referred to (or quantified over) past events or times. In chapter 6 we saw the limitations of such a strategy. What is the alternative? The idea is that, on the basis of the discussion of indexicals in section 3.2, the A-theory can treat PAST as an indexical predicate that holds of a proposition-like object, effectively displaying the indexical sense of the past-tense morpheme on the right-hand side of the T-theory axiom:

(1)
a.
Val(x, PAST) iff x was true
b.
Val(x, PRES) iff x is true
c.
Val(x, FUT) iff x will be true

We can handle temporal adverbs in a similar fashion, taking them as predicates of proposition-like objects rather than as referring to times or events:

(2)
a.
Val(x, yesterday) iff x was true yesterday

b.

Val(x, <u>today</u>) iff x is true today

c.

Val(x, <u>tomorrow</u>) iff x will be true tomorrow

d.

Val(x, <u>now</u>) iff x is true now

There may also be ways to reduce these axioms to a handful of indexical predicates, or even one. For example, 'tomorrow' might receive truth conditions like Val(x, <u>tomorrow</u>) iff x is one day after today. In turn, 'today' might be defined by use of the indexical predicate 'now'.[1] Nor is it necessary that this decomposition take place in the truth conditions—it might just as well occur in the lexicon. The crucial point is that there must be at least one A-theory predicate to situate the described situation in the speaker's egocentric space.

To illustrate, let me return to the case, discussed in chapter 6, when I say "I'm glad that's over with" after a visit to the dentist. What I am glad about is that my visit to the dentist culminated in the recent past—i.e., that it is no longer in my present. We don't need to invoke token-reflexives or any other such devices to get this result; it falls out directly from the axioms introduced thus far. The two theorems shown in (3) display rather different senses, and reflect semantical knowledge of substantially different character.

(3)

a.

Val(T, [$_S$ PAST[($\exists$e)(e is the event of my having a root canal and e culminates]]) iff [][($\exists$e)(e is the event of my having a root canal and e culminates)][] was true

b.

If u is an utterance, at t, of [$_S$ PAST[($\exists$e)(e is the event of my having a root canal and e culminates)]], then Val(T, u) iff ($\exists$e)(e is the event of my having a root canal and e culminates and e < t)

When I am glad that my visit to the dentist is over, what I'm glad about is something that has the truth conditions shown in (3a), since those truth conditions effectively display the indexical character of the described state of affairs and situate it in *my* past.[2] I may be entirely indifferent to whether something that has the truth conditions shown in (3b) should obtain.

Now, it is certainly the case that A-theory axioms like those in (1) and (2) are "modest" axioms in the sense discussed in section 2.3, and it is fair to ask what the deeper analysis—the elucidation—of the axioms for these temporal indexicals is going to look like. That is, when we say that a proposition was true or will be true, exactly what are we getting at?

As Dummett (1969) has argued, a semantic theory that accounts for an agent's semantic knowledge must show how portions of the language are learned from the evidence available to the language learner. But now consider how we learn to use past-tense expressions such as (4).

(4)
Dinosaurs roamed the Earth.

We do not evaluate this sentence by imagining some time earlier than now and determining whether at that time (4) is true. Rather, we evaluate (4) by right now conducting the sort of investigation that is appropriate for past-tense statements like (4). (For example, we might study fossil records.) Likewise for any other past-tense statement. We have certain procedures for determining whether a past-tense proposition is true, and these procedures do not involve the evaluation of a proposition at some time past; rather, we simply evaluate the proposition in a particular way—a way which is independent of how we evaluate present-tense and future-tense propositions.

Consider the future-tense proposition (5).

(5)
The economy will recover in the third quarter.

Clearly we do not evaluate such a proposition by picking some time in the third quarter and determining whether it is true at that time that the economy is recovering. Rather, we evaluate it by studying the currently available economic data. Crucially, our evaluation of (5) can proceed without our ever attending to a corresponding present-tense proposition at some future time index.

If this picture of the underlying robust theory is correct, then it immediately leads to a second advantage for the A-theory proposal under discussion—in fact, a striking epistemological advantage. The B-theorist is in the untenable position of asserting that there is actually reference to past and future times and/or events. However, this flies in the face of everything we know about reference. We are in neither a perceptual relation nor a causal relation with future events, and our causal connection with most past events is tenuous at best. In regard to times, the idea that there could be reference to such abstract objects surely requires major adjustments to current epistemological thinking.

It is no good to take the standard dodge and argue that the B-theorist is using 'reference' in a loose and nonphilosophical sense. Past and future events and times are quantified over with impunity in the B-theory fragment; they serve as semantic values in the theory, and, as we saw in chapter 4, there is no escaping the ontological commitment to semantic values. In short, there is no escaping the metaphysical commitment to these entities, and with that commitment comes a heavy epistemological burden that the B-theorist simply must own up to.

So far, I have been talking about the A-theory (and its advantages) at a pretty abstract level. Perhaps it is time to go into a little more detail about the semantics.

7.2   The Basic A-Theory Semantics

A-theory semantics of tense are correctly associated with the work of Prior (1967, 1968), but Prior's position is still widely misunderstood. Ordinarily it is supposed that Prior took 'past', 'present', and 'future' to be quantifiers over past, present, and future times. For example, it is ordinarily supposed that on Prior's theory 'PAST[S]' means that S was true at some time earlier than now. But Prior never gave such a semantics for his tense logic, nor could he. He didn't believe in future or past events. He endorsed a kind of presentism similar to that discussed in the introduction to this book.

The source of the confusion may be that Prior never actually gave a semantics for his tense logic. I will now do so, in a way that is consistent with Priorean metaphysics. My basic strategy will be to develop a semantics in which the tenses are indexical predicates that take proposition-like objects as their arguments.

In chapter 5 we saw how the resources of event quantification and truth-conditional semantics could be exploited as a framework for a Reichenbachian semantics for tense. In this section, we shall make use of some resources introduced in chapter 3—namely, interpreted logical forms. The idea will be that tense can be construed as a predicate that takes ILFs as its arguments. For example, we can take the basic tense morphemes to have the simple axioms in (6), and we can have the nonterminal axiom for '[$_s$ TNS S1]' introduce the propositional object (in this case, an ILF).

(6)

a.

Val(x, PAST) iff x was true

b.

Val(x, FUT) iff x will be true

c.

Val(x, FUT) iff x will be true

d.

Val(T, [$_s$ TNS S1]) iff, for some x, Val(x, TNS) and x = []S1[]

Of course, this analysis assumes a certain picture about the syntactic form of these constructions—specifically that there is a level of representation at which

the tense morphemes take clausal scope. Presumably these tense operators orig-
inated in S-internal position (e.g., at infl) and adjoined to S at LF, so the representations we will be considering are assumed to be LF representations in the
sense discussed in appendix T1.

It is sometimes argued that the complex tenses fall out naturally from the nesting of the primitive tense expressions 'PAST', 'PRES', and 'FUT'. For example, it is natural to suppose that the future perfect could be construed as having
the syntax (7), that the past perfect would receive the analysis (8), and that the
present perfect would receive the analysis (9).

(7)
$[_S \text{FUT}[_S \text{PAST}[S]]]$

(8)
$[_S \text{PAST}[_S \text{PAST}[S]]]$

(9)
$[_S \text{PRES}[_S \text{PAST}[S]]]$

If both the auxiliary 'had' and the past-tense morpheme rise and take clausal
scope, the result is the LF in (10).

(10)
$[_S \text{had} [_S \text{PAST} [_S \text{Smith goes}]]]$

As we will see a bit later, this proposal turns out to be inadequate. It seems that
some form of temporal anaphora is necessary to account for genuine cases of
past perfect, future perfect, etc. The additional resources necessary for temporal anaphora will be introduced in chapter 8.

If we like, we can treat temporal connectives such as 'before' and 'when' disquotationally, as in (11).[3]

(11)
a.
Val(T, $[_S$ S1 <u>when</u> S2]) iff Val(T, S1) when Val(T, S2)
b.
Val(T, $[_S$ S1 <u>before</u> S2]) iff Val(T, S1) before Val(T, S2)
c.
Val(T, $[_S$ S1 <u>after</u> S2]) iff Val(T, S1) after Val(T, S2)

Temporal adverbs, such as 'yesterday', are simply predicates taking ILFs as
arguments, as in (12).

(12)

a.

Val(T, [$_S$ ADV(temp) S1]) iff there is an x, such that Val(x, ADV) and x = []S1[]

b.

Val(x, <u>yesterday</u>) iff x was true yesterday

This is just an initial gloss of an A-theory semantics. (I will flesh out the details in chapter 8 and in appendix T5.) Before developing the theory further, I need to deal with a number of objections that have been raised in the literature of semantics.

7.3   Some Objections to the A-Theory Semantics

In this section I will canvass some of the semantical arguments against the A-theory semantics of tense in preparation for answering them in chapter 8. The arguments to be considered involve some alleged problems surrounding the nature of temporal anaphora and some alleged difficulties with the handling of nested temporal operators.

Embedded Tenses and Nested Temporal Modifiers

Hinrichs (1981) and Dowty (1982), considering earlier operator theories of tense (principally that of Montague (1974)), observed that there are potential difficulties with a simple sentence like (13) and its two possible LFs, (14) and (15).

(13)

Smith left yesterday.

(14)

[$_S$ PAST [$_S$ yesterday [$_S$ Smith leaves]]]

(15)

[$_S$ yesterday [$_S$ PAST [$_S$ Smith leaves]]]

On a theory in which tenses are taken to be quantifiers, the LF in (14) is interpreted as asserting that in the past it was true that Smith departed on the previous day. This obviously does not yield the correct truth conditions. On the other hand, (15) will be interpreted as saying that yesterday it was true that Smith had left—clearly not consistent with our understanding of (13).

The appearance of a problem here stems from the questionable assumption that tense morphemes and temporal adverbials are nested and therefore must take scope over one another. But there is really no reason to suppose this. As

Dowty (1982) notes, it is equally plausible to suppose that the adverb and tense morphemes should be sister nodes, as in the following structure:

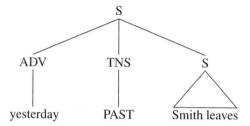

The axiom for this structure can be written as (16).[4]

(16)

Val(T, [$_S$ ADV TNS S1]) iff, for some x, Val(x, ADV), Val(x, TNS), and x = []S1[]

The Unconstrained Nature of the A-Theory

Another important objection to the A-theory has been that it is "unconstrained," meaning that the device in Prior's logic of nesting temporal operators seems to wildly overgenerate the set of possible tenses.[5] To see this, suppose that the nesting of tenses, as in FUT[PAST[S]], could provide an account of the present perfect. (As we will see, it doesn't even do that, but let us set this concern aside for the moment.) If tenses can be nested in this way to generate new complex tenses, then why can't we nest them arbitrarily deep? For example, why is there no tense corresponding to PAST[PAST[PAST[S]]] or to PAST[FUT[PAST[S]]]?

This is of genuine concern if we are interested in an account of tense that goes some way towards explaining linguistic competence. It is altogether too easy to construct theories that overgenerate the set of possible sentences. What we would like to have is a theory that is constrained enough to generate the sentences of our language and *only* those sentences.

Unfortunately, despite the apparent unconstrained nature of the theory and its propensity to overgenerate the possible natural language sentences, the theory appears to undergenerate too: it is allegedly unable to account for a broad class of temporal phenomena. In particular, it has no apparent resources to account for temporal anaphora.

The Apparent Need for Temporal Reference

At last we come to the central semantical objection to Priorean theories of tense.

In the introduction we considered the example shown here as (17) (Partee 1973, 1984).

(17)
I turned off the stove.

Clearly, (17) does not merely mean that at some time in the past I turned off the stove. Without a doubt there have been many such episodes in my past. According to Partee, (17) is informative because there is implicit reference to (or quantification over) some specific time or reference event. I might equally well have uttered 'I turned off the stove then', with 'then' serving as a temporal anaphor referring to some segment of time or event in the past.

Similar considerations apply to (18) (Partee 1973).

(18)
Smith did not turn off the stove.

If we think of negation and the past-tense morpheme as simple sentential operators, then there are two possible relative scopes for sentence (18):

(19)
[not [PAST [Smith turns off the stove]]]

(20)
[PAST[not [Smith turns off the stove]]]

But neither of these gets the truth conditions right if we are utilizing the semantics we supplied for theory A. The problem is that (19) would be given the truth conditions that it is not the case that [][$_s$ Smith turns off the stove][] was true—in other words, that he has never turned off the stove. (20) would be assigned the truth conditions that [][$_s$ it is not the case that Smith turns off the stove][] was true (which could have been satisfied by any past time when Smith refrained from touching the stove). Clearly neither of these truth conditions is what we are after. Rather, there is the sense in (18) that Smith failed to turn the stove off at some crucial time—for example, when he left the house this morning.

This problem seems to lie at the heart of another objection to Priorean theories: their alleged inability to account for complex tenses. The objection is that, for example, [PAST[PAST[S]]] simply collapses into the simple past. Recall that in chapter 5 we called the minimum unit of time a "chronon." Then, at best, [PAST[S]] is true iff S was true at least one chronon ago. But then [PAST[PAST[S]]] is true iff S was true more than one chronon ago. But this doesn't seem to capture what we intended to say by a past-perfect sentence like 'I had left'.

One might try to get around this difficulty by talking about degrees of pastness; however, as was noted above, this move fails. 'I had left' might be talking about an event at any arbitrary distance in the past. Plus, there is the strong intuition that there really is a reference event here—that we could very well continue 'I had left...' with '...when Smith arrived'. How is *that* to be cashed out on a Priorean theory if there is no way to avail ourselves of temporal reference? Before we look for solutions, we need to canvass one more objection to the A-theory—this one a philosophical objection.

7.4   The McTaggart Paradox: Is the A-Theory Contradictory?

One of the earliest and most influential critiques of the A-theory is McTaggart's (1908, 1927). Arguing for the unreality of time, McTaggart begins with the observation that certain pairs of properties are such that it would be inconsistent for one object to have both properties. For example, although a table can be both round and red, it cannot be both round and square, for roundness and squareness are inconsistent properties. Likewise, according to McTaggart, it would be inconsistent for something to be both past and future. Thus, for most cases, when we affirm the truth of (21) we have stated something that is inconsistent if not contradictory.[6]

(21)

future(ϕ) & past(ϕ)

But according to McTaggart this is exactly what the A-theory entails: an event E will at some point be past, at some point present, and at some point future.[7] Thus, we have the conjunction (22).

(22)

future(E) & past(E) & present(E)

The initial reaction to this part of the argument is often that it is absurd. Surely one is not saying that E is always future and always past and always present; rather, one is asserting that E *has been* future, that it *will be* past, and that it is currently present. As intuitive as this answer may seem, McTaggart (1927) argues that it is illegitimate:

> ... what is meant by "has been" and "will be"? And what is meant by "is," when, as here, it is used with a temporal meaning, and not simply for predication? When we say that X has been Y, we are asserting X to be Y at a moment of past time. When we say that X will be Y, we are asserting X to be Y at a moment of future time. When we say that X is Y (in the temporal sense of "is"), we are asserting X to be Y at a moment of present time.

According McTaggart's line of analysis, the problem with the step to propositions like 'X is Y at a moment of past time' is that no moment of time is intrinsically past, present, or future. As a result, if it is now true that X is past at a moment of future time, it will also hold at some time later than now that X is past at a moment of past time. Thus, again there is a contradiction.

One might try to escape the contradiction by suggesting that (23) and (24) are never true simultaneously but that (23) will be true and (24) has been true.

(23)
X is past at a moment of past time.

(24)
X is past at a moment of future time.

However, McTaggart suggests that this merely starts us upon an infinite (and vicious) regress.

But there are other problems that seem to stem from the rejection of the B-theory.

The A-theory and the Myth of Passage

According to Williams (1951), there is a deep conceptual problem in any assumption that time "passes" or "flows." Despite the natural appeal of metaphors that make reference to "change," change itself takes place in time. Thus, whether one regards time as a movement of an event along a time line or whether one thinks of the future approaching us and flowing past us like a river, the metaphor fails miserably.

Williams's objection is aimed at a conception of the A-theory in which a particular event is future, then present, and then past, and in which the event is thought of as undergoing a kind of change.

This general objection was anticipated by a number of adherents to the A-theory. Broad (1938), for example, argued that one need not recoil from such objections once one gets clear on the true nature of temporal becoming. The traditional philosophical notion of temporal becoming is that it is a species of qualitative change. For example, it might be thought that there is a particular event (say, World War II) that was future, then was present, and finally became past. But Broad thinks that this is a confused way to think about temporal becoming.

If temporal becoming is reduced to qualitative change, Broad notes, this change must take place at a certain rate (or must at least take place in time). And if it takes place at a certain rate, it can hardly be maintained that one has given a sensible analysis of temporal becoming—one has done so by appealing to the temporal notion of change.

According to Broad, events don't change from future to present to past in the same way that water changes from hot to tepid to cold. Rather, when an event becomes present it becomes *absolutely*. Accordingly, World War II was not an event that was future, then present, then past; it simply became *absolutely*.

Whatever the merits of Broad's suggestion, it is clear that the proposal as it stands does not go far enough—at least not far enough to answer Williams's concerns. If "become absolutely" simply means "pop into existence," then this sort of becoming must also take place in time. Initially, a thing fails to exist; then it comes into existence; then it ceases to exist. The problem is perhaps not as obvious as in the case of a fire poker which is initially hot, then warm, and then cool, but it is nevertheless a problem of the same general character. Broad may have something else in mind by his use of the phrase "become absolutely," but what it might be is difficult to see.

Prior's Defense of the A-Theory

Here, then, is the problem. The A-theory is allegedly committed to a notion of change in the temporal state of events. Mellor (1981, p. 90) describes the commitment as follows:

Change [for the A-theorist] is basically the changing tense (A-series location) of things and events moving from future to past.... The reality of the clock hand's movement consists ultimately in the events of its passing the figures '1' and '2' becoming successively present and then past; and similarly for all other changes.

Clearly it will not do to introduce accounts that tacitly appeal to change of this form. But what is the alternative? One possible solution is to simply maintain that some propositions are past, some are present, and some are future, and that is that. When we say that an object or an event underwent a temporal change, we are simply saying that a proposition describing the object was future but is now past. That is, we are saying that the proposition has the properties *was future*, and *is past*, and that further analysis is impossible.

This is essentially the proposal put forward by Prior (1968), who argued that for something to change is just for it to fit the schema (C).

(C)
It was the case that *p*, and is not now the case that *p*.

Problems arise only if we slide from this schema to taking its accompanying metaphor seriously. "The flow of time," Prior argued (ibid., pp. 11–12),

is merely metaphorical, not only because what is meant by it isn't a genuine movement, but further because what is meant by it isn't a genuine change; but the force of the metaphor can still be explained—we use the metaphor because what we call the flow of time does fit the above formula.

Constructing McTaggart-type arguments against this version of the A-theory is going to be very delicate. Consider the following part of the McTaggart argument, as I formulated it above:

... an event E will at some point be past, at some point present, and at some point future. Thus, we have the conjunction ... future(E) & past(E) & present(E).

On the Priorean version of the A-theory this premise is flatly false, since E did not go from being future to being present to being past; that simply isn't what change comes to. Responding to the claim that we are forced to an infinite regress, Prior (1967, pp. 5–6) suggests that McTaggart has drawn a "perverse conclusion":

We are presented, to begin with (in step 1), with at statement which is plainly wrong (that every event *is* past, present, and future). This is corrected to something which is plainly right (that every event either *is* future and *will be* present and past, or *has been* future and *is* present and *will be* past, or *has been* future and present and *is* past). This is then expanded (in step 2) to something which, in the meaning intended, is wrong. It is then corrected to something a little more complicated which is right. This is then expanded (in step 3) to something which is wrong, and we are told that if we correct this in the obvious way, we shall have to expand it into something which is again wrong, and if we are not happy to stop there, or at any similar point, we shall have to go on *ad infinitum*. Even if we are somehow compelled to move forward in this way, we only get contradictions half the time, and it is not obvious why we should get these rather than their running mates as the correct stopping-points. But why do we have to make the wrong moves in any case? At least after the first few times, when we've seen the trouble it gets us into, why not pass to the correct version immediately?

Swapping talk of propositions for talk of events, the solution, roughly, is to say that certain propositions have been future, certain propositions will be past, and let the matter rest there. There is no point in saying that there must be a time at which a certain proposition was future or at which a certain proposition will be past. To take that step is to blunder into a confused way of thinking about tense.

This general answer may not set well with certain readers, for there is a natural pull (at least among the philosophically trained) to suppose that 'has been future' must be reducible to the more primitive form 'is future' and a particular time index. But there is no logical reason we are forced to such an analysis.

Mellor (1981) argues that Prior cannot simply sweep away the "stopping points" that give rise to contradiction; that, in effect, Prior's having to move off these stopping points shows that he is trapped in a vicious regress. This is a very subtle issue, and I want to set it aside for now, since we need to equip ourselves with a better grasp of the A-theory and the technical execution of that theory before we can properly tackle the question. I will return to the problem in section 8.5.

Presentism

If we follow Prior's solution to the A-series paradoxes, what conception of time does the above proposal leave us with? How can we think about the A-theory metaphysics once we have abandoned the notion of time as change from future to present to past? One plausible answer is that, borrowing a phrase from Dummett, we are "immersed in time":

What the realist would like to do is to stand in thought outside the whole temporal process and describe the world from a point which has no temporal position at all, but surveys all temporal positions in a single glance: from this standpoint—the standpoint of the description which the realist wants to give—the different points of time have a relation of temporal precedence between themselves, but no temporal relation to the standpoint of the description—i.e., they are not being considered as past, present, or as future. The anti-realist takes more seriously the fact that we are immersed in time: being so immersed, we cannot frame any description of the world as it would appear to one who was not in time, but we can only describe it as it is, i.e., as it is now. (Dummett 1969, p. 369)

Notice that this version of the A-theory shares a number of features with the anti-realist position of Dummett. On both pictures we reject the reality of the future and the past (construed as future and past events). We nevertheless have a notion of temporality, albeit one that does not countenance a dynamic conception of temporality as change. Notice also that we have come to this conclusion via a rather different route than Dummett did. For him, the unreality of the past followed from the rejection of bivalence in semantical theory.[8] Here we have found our way to the conclusion in our effort to find a consistent version of the A-theory. Our path did not involve the rejection of bivalence.

All this having been said, we still have to rescue the A-theory of time. In particular it remains for us to show that the A-theory semantics is able to handle temporal anaphora. We take up this issue in the next chapter.

Chapter 8

Temporal Anaphora without B-Series Resources

The main predicament for applying Priorean theories of tense to natural language is that somehow one needs to make sense of temporal anaphora without appealing to future and past events, times, etc. Can this be done? On the face of it, this demand looks impossible for a true Priorean theory to meet. The A-series approach denies us access to past and future events, as well as to past and future times. In effect, it denies us the resources that are the building blocks of all current research into tense. How can we have temporal anaphora to events in the future and the past if there are no such events?

One of my goals in this chapter is to do the impossible—to build a semantics of tense that utilizes only A-series resources. More specifically, I shall try to construct a semantics for tense that satisfies the following conditions:

- It provides an account of temporal anaphora without reference to past and future events or times
- It provides a way to build complex tenses without the usual resources (reference events, etc.).

8.1   E-Type Temporal Anaphora

Basic Strategy
The basic strategy will be to treat temporal anaphors as a species of E-type temporal anaphora. The difference between these cases and E-type pronominal anaphora will be that pronominal anaphors stand proxy for descriptions, whereas temporal anaphors stand proxy for temporal conjunctions (e.g., when-clauses) that might be extracted from previous discourse. For an example, consider (1).

(1)
I turned off the stove then.

Following Partee (1973), one might hold that 'then' *refers* to a moment or period of time; however, this is not necessary. It is possible that 'then' is standing proxy for a temporal conjunction. For example, in (2) 'then' could be standing proxy for 'when I left the house', or 'when you told me to'.

(2)
$[_S [_S$ not $[_S$ PAST $[_S$ I turn off the stove] $[_S$ when . . .]]]]

Spinning out the strategy a bit, the idea will be that by having general propositions as the bearers of tense we can avoid commitment to such B-series resources as times and past and future events. Temporal anaphora can be achieved by the introduction of when-clauses (or, more generally, temporal conjunctions), which express general propositions about the world.

If this gambit is to work, 'when' cannot mean "at the same time"; it must be taken as a kind of primitive, just as the PAST, PRES, and FUT morphemes are. That is, 'when' must be understood as being more fundamental than the B-series conception of simultaneity. (More on this in a bit.)

Philosophical Preliminaries

Singular vs. General Propositions   The basic idea here is that we shall want to distinguish propositions that are about some object from general propositions that, strictly speaking, are not about anyone or anything.[1] For example, we might suppose that the utterance 'He is tall', accompanied by a demonstration of some individual, would express a singular proposition about that individual. In contrast, the utterance 'No one lives forever', which is obviously not about anyone, would express a general claim about the world.

Other cases are disputed. Does an utterance of a sentence with a definite description (for example, 'The tallest man in the room is tired') express a singular proposition, or a general proposition? According to Russell (1910–11), the answer would be that it expresses a general proposition—not a proposition about some particular individual, but rather a general claim about the world (e.g., that there is one tallest man in the room and that he is tall). Others have argued that such sentences in fact express singular propositions. How this and other cases fall out is not really important to the current discussion; I just want to introduce the distinction for later use.

Reference vs. Denotation   A great deal of semantic literature uses the terms 'denotation' and 'reference' interchangeably. This is unfortunate, for it ignores some very important considerations—considerations that were central in the dispute between Russell (1905) and Strawson (1950).

One useful way to understand the distinction between referring and denoting—exploited by Evans (1982), by Neale (1990), and by Ludlow and Neale (1991)—is to consider Russell's theory of psychology. Russell (1910–11) distinguished knowledge by acquaintance from knowledge by description, arguing that to have knowledge by acquaintance of a certain object, one must be directly acquainted with the object. Alternatively, to have knowledge by description of a certain object one need not be acquainted with the object; one need only know the object as the unique satisfier of a certain description.

On Russell's view, these two species of knowledge are in fact quite different. A belief about some object known by acquaintance is a belief in a singular proposition which has that object as a constituent. For example, my belief that my neighbor Jones is tall is a singular proposition having Jones as a constituent. It is a belief *about* Jones. On the other hand, I might believe that the thief who stole my computer is tall, and the thief may even be Jones, but unless I know that Jones is the thief, or unless I saw him stealing my computer, my belief will not be a singular proposition but rather a general proposition. It will not be a belief *about* Jones (or anyone else); rather, the object of my belief will be a general proposition about the world (essentially, that the world is such that there is a unique thief of my computer and that he or she is tall).

The same point can be extended easily to the semantics of natural language. Applied here, the question is whether there is a semantic difference between a sentence containing a description that uniquely determines some individual (e.g., 'the third planet') and a sentence containing a referring expression (e.g., 'Earth'). Of course, there have been important discussions as to whether descriptions cannot at times be referring expressions as well,[2] and claims to the effect that a number of names are in fact descriptions in disguise,[3] but these discussions need not detain us here. The important point is that genuine descriptions and genuine referring expressions are two entirely different things. The distinction is introduced here because it will play an important role in our investigation of the two alternative models for tense. On the one hand, there will be theories that will introduce reference to specific times or events. Obvious reasons for the introduction of temporal reference include expressions like (3)–(5).

(3)
I didn't know that <u>yesterday</u>.

(4)
I leave on <u>the 15th of December</u>.

(5)
I'll leave at <u>7 o'clock</u>.

On the other hand, the particular version of A-theory semantics I will be developing will do without reference to future time and events. It will have to account for what appears to be temporal reference by claiming that (3)–(5) merely *appear* to contain genuine referring expressions.

The problem (for theories of tense that cannot avail themselves of temporal reference) is compounded by the widespread occurrence of temporal anaphora, as illustrated in (6)–(8).

(6)
I didn't know that <u>then</u>.

(7)
I'll leave <u>when Smith does</u>.

(8)
I left <u>before Smith did</u>.

If anaphors are simply referring expressions, theories that prohibit temporal reference are in a difficult position. However, there is an alternative: Temporal anaphors might be "E-type."

E-Type Anaphors   One of the more hotly debated questions in the recent literature of semantics has been the status of unbound, anaphoric pronouns. Bound pronouns are in the scope of an operator, and they behave like bound variables in first-order logic. Sentences (9) and (10) contain bound pronouns.

(9)
[Every dog]$_i$ has its$_i$ day.

(10)
[No man]$_i$ hates his$_i$ dog.

Unbound anaphoric pronouns, on the other hand, are pronouns that do not (superficially) appear to be bound variables yet nevertheless appear to get their content from some antecedent noun phrase. Consider (11) and (12).

(11)
[A dog]$_i$ came into the room. It$_i$ bit me.

(12)
[Some dogs]$_i$ came into the room. They$_i$ barked.

Evans (1977) offered several reasons for supposing that examples (11) and (12) cannot be construed as genuine cases of bound variable anaphora. His most telling argument was that if the quantified noun phrase in (12), for example, bound the pronoun 'they$_i$', the truth conditions would simply come out wrong. Consider (13).

(13)
[Some x: dogs x](x came into the room & x barked)

Notice that (13) does not have the same truth conditions that (12) has, for (12) implies that all the dogs barked whereas (13) merely states that the intersection of the entering dogs and the barkers is nonzero.

Another difficulty with the bound-variable analysis is that it asserts the possibility of an operator's binding something outside of its scope. One test for this would be whether a quantifier like 'no x' can bind a variable in the same circumstances. For example, it is pretty clear that the operator cannot bind the co-indexed variable in (14), so one wonders why operators like those in (13) should be exceptional in this regard.

(14)
[No dogs]$_i$ came into the room. They$_i$ barked.

One possible alternative analysis of these anaphoric pronouns would be that they are actually referring expressions, and that they refer to whatever object has been raised to salience by the previous discourse. A view like this has been proposed by Lewis (1979, p. 243):

I may say 'A cat is on the lawn' under circumstances in which it is apparent to all parties to the conversation that there is some one particular cat that is responsible for the truth of what I say, and for my saying it. Perhaps I am looking out of the window, and you rightly presume that I said what I did because I saw a cat; and further (since I spoke in the singular) that I saw only one. What I said was an existential quantification; hence strictly speaking, it involves no reference to any particular cat. Nevertheless it raises the salience of the cat that made me say it.... Thus although indefinite descriptions—that is, idioms of existential quantification—are not themselves referring expressions, they may raise the salience of particular individuals in such a way as to pave the way for referring expressions that follow.

One objection to this view, discussed in detail by Heim (1982), suggests that certain facts undermine Lewis's idea that pronouns refer to objects raised to salience. As examples, Heim considers (15) and (16), where # indicates infelicity.

(15)
a.
John has a spouse; she is very nice.
b.
John is married; #she is very nice.

(16)

a.

I dropped ten marbles and found them all except one; it must be under the desk.

b.

I dropped ten marbles and found only nine; #it must be under the desk.

Similar examples are noted by Geach (1962), who considers the contrast between pairs like (17a) and (17b), and by Evans (1977), who notes the contrast between (18a) and (18b).

(17)

a.

Every man who owns a donkey beats it.

b.

#Every donkey owner beats it.

(18)

a.

John owns a donkey. It is brown.

b.

#John is a donkey owner. It is brown.

According to Heim, (15a) and (15b) are truth-conditionally equivalent, and an utterance of either would, on Lewis's theory, result in John's wife's being raised to salience. Heim concludes that the two occurrences of the pronoun 'she' should therefore be equally felicitous if salience were the relevant notion.[4]

In any case, it seems fairly clear that the raised-to-salience picture cannot be universally true, since there are numerous cases in which we would want to say that a pronoun is anaphoric on some expression yet we would have no way of identifying an object—that is, we have no singular object-dependent thought. A sentence like (19) would be a clear case of this.

(19)

A man came in. He tripped over the chair.

One attractive alternative is that pronouns stand proxy for definite descriptions. The idea that unbound anaphoric pronouns might stand proxy for definite descriptions has been proposed by Evans (1977), Parsons (1978), Cooper (1979), Davies (1981a), and Neale (1990).[5] The basic idea is that the pronoun in (19) may stand proxy for the underlined definite description in (20).

(20)

A man came in. The man who came in tripped over the chair.[6]

One of the key advantages of such an analysis would be that it avoids the unwelcome conclusion that the anaphoric pronoun is either a bound variable or a referring expression. More to the point, the theory allows that one might understand a sentence containing an anaphoric pronoun without there being some object that is the referent of the pronoun.

This is just a surface gloss of the theory of descriptive pronouns, of course. There have been a number of important objections to it, and the theory has been subsequently developed in a variety of interesting ways. For now, it is enough that we place the relevant machinery on the table so that we can explore ways in which it might be incorporated into the theory of temporal anaphora developed later in this chapter.

De Re/De Dicto Distinction   We will also need to make use of the celebrated de re/de dicto distinction. Repeating our earlier example from Quine, a sentence like (21) is ambiguous between a de re reading (21') and a de dicto reading (21").

(21)
The number of planets is necessarily odd.

(21')
de re: [the number of planets]$_i$ necessarily[e_i is odd]

(21")
de dicto: necessarily[the number of planets is odd]

The received view of these constructions is that the de re/de dicto distinction is a reflex of a scope ambiguity, with the de re reading corresponding to a case of quantifying into an intensional environment and the de dicto reading corresponding to a case of quantification within the scope of an intensional operator. We can generalize this idea as in (22), where a DP is a determiner phrase (or, if one prefers, a quantified noun phrase) and e_i is a variable bound by the DP.

(22)
de re: [DP]$_i$[Operator[... e_i ...]]
de dicto: Operator [[DP]$_i$[... e_i ...]]

8.2 Development of the Theory

I begin by introducing what can be called "absolute tense," which is not to be confused with the tense of a natural language utterance (the reason being that all natural language utterances may well be accompanied by possibly implicit when-clauses).

Let us take the absolute tense morphemes to be PAST, PRES, and FUT as they are applied to a sentence (clause) in isolation. Thus we have the following syntax for the occurrence of these morphemes (basically as in Prior's scheme):

(23)
Absolute Present: PRES[S]
Absolute Past: PAST[S]
Absolute Future: FUT[S]

Relative Tense introduces the implicit when-clause. It parallels the introduction of the reference event/time in Reichenbachian theories as shown in (24)–(26).

(24)
Relative Present
on Reichenbach analysis: E,R (simultaneous)
syntax on this analysis: [S] when [...]

(25)
Relative Past
on Reichenbach analysis: E——R
syntax on this analysis: [S] before [...]

(26)
Relative Future
on Reichenbach analysis: R——E
syntax on this analysis: [S] after [...]

Complex Tenses
To get a handle on complex tenses in natural language, we need to make some conjectures about the structure of tensed sentences. Let us begin with two working hypotheses:

(H1)
All natural language sentences have (possibly implicit) when-clauses.

(H2)
The structure of an implicit when-clause is the same as an explicit when-clause.

The basic intuition driving (H2) is that if we are to posit implicit tensed clauses our theory must be as constrained as possible. Ideally, we do not want to be in the position of proposing new grammatical rules or principles to account for the behavior of these clauses. If there really are implicit when-clauses, then prima facie we should expect them to be internally structured just like explicit when-clauses—the principle exception being that they are unpronounced.

If (H2) holds, we can extrapolate the structure of implicit when-clauses by making some observations about their explicit counterparts. Two observations are particularly germane here:

(O1)
All explicit when-clauses are tensed.

(O2)
All explicit when-clauses are coordinated with the tense of the matrix clause.

To illustrate (O1), we would never find an explicit construction of the form 'I left the room when John to be hungry'. When-clauses are never infinitival (at least in English). To illustrate (O2), for example, we don't find an English sentence like 'I will have left the room when John had arrived'. The lead tenses ('will' and 'had') fail to match in this case.

By (H2), it follows that *implicit* when-clauses will have these properties too. Accordingly, the logical form of these constructions (at a certain level of abstraction) will be as follows:

Pluperfect
on Reichenbach analysis: E——R——S
LF on A-theory analysis: PAST[S] before PAST[. . .]

Future perfect
on Reichenbach analysis: S——E——R
LF on A-theory analysis: FUT[S] before FUT[. . .]

Future in future
on Reichenbach analysis: S——R——E
LF on A-theory analysis: FUT[S] after FUT[. . .]

Future in past
on Reichenbach analysis: R——E——S or R——S——E or
LF on A-theory analysis: PAST[S] when PAST[. . .]

By (H1) it should follow that past, present, and future tenses in natural language do not consist merely of the simple PAST, PRES, and FUT morphemes but should be more complex constructions:

Past
on Reichenbach analysis: E,R——S
LF on A-theory analysis: PAST[S] when PAST[. . .]

Present
on Reichenbach analysis: S,E,R
LF on A-theory: PRES[S] when/as PRES[. . .]

Future
on Reichenbach analysis: S——E,R
LF on A-theory: FUT[S] when FUT[. . .]

The T-theory axioms for the absolute tenses are the following:

(T1)
Val(x, PAST, σ) iff x was true

(T2)
Val(x, PRES, σ) iff x is true

(T3)
Val(x, FUT, σ) iff x will be true

The axiom for the tense phrase is as follows:

(TP)
Val(T, [$_{TP}$ TNS S], σ) iff, for some x,
Val(x, TNS, σ) and x = []S[]

The semantics of the temporal connectives are as follows[7]:

(W1)
Val(T, [$_S$ TP1 <u>when</u> TP2] , σ) iff Val(T, TP1, σ) when Val(T, TP2, σ)

(W2)
Val(T, [$_S$ TP1 <u>before</u> TP2] , σ) iff Val(T, TP1, σ) before Val(T, TP2, σ)

(W3)
Val(T, [$_S$ TP1 <u>after</u> TP2] , σ) iff Val(T, TP1, σ) after Val(T, TP2, σ)

Example:
'I had eaten' is true iff [][($\exists$e)(eating(e) & agent(I, e))][] was true before
[] [. . .] [] was true.

Finally, we will want to incorporate a theory of aspect into the broader theory. I have no quarrel with talk about events; I am merely concerned that events not be the bearers of tense. Events may well be the bearers of aspectual properties (although later we will see that there are reasons for avoiding this view).

In event-based approaches to semantics (see, e.g., Parsons 1991; Higginbotham 1989; Schein 1993), sentences like (27) are argued to have the logical form shown in (28).

(27)

A man kicked Bill.

(28)

(∃e)(kicking(e) & [an x: man x]agent(x, e) & patient(Bill, e) & past(e))

Clearly this analysis presents problems for the A-theorist, since it argues that there is an event which is past. Is there some way to avoid this consequence of the introduction of events?

Recall the discussion of the de dicto/de re distinction earlier in this chapter. Event descriptions will be innocuous so long as they remain safely within the scope of TNS. The situation is parallel to that of modals. Depending upon the relative scope of an existential quantifier and the modal, we might find ourselves committed to some unwelcome entities. Consider (29).

(29)

A unicorn may have eaten my vegetables.

On the innocent interpretation of this example, the existential quantifier remains safely within the scope of the modal, as in (30).

(30)

possibly[(∃x)(x is a unicorn & x ate my vegetables)]

In the problematic case, illustrated in (31), the existential quantifier takes wide scope over the modal; the result is an ontological commitment to unicorns.

(31)

(∃x: x is a unicorn)possibly[x ate my vegetables]

Similar considerations apply to the introduction of quantification over events in cases like (27). The innocent case finds the event quantification safely within the scope of the past-tense operator:

(32)

PAST[(∃e)(kicking(e) & [an x: man x]agent(x, e) & patient(Bill, e))]

The case to be avoided (for the Priorean) is (28), where the event quantifier has scope outside of the temporal operator. However, so long as we exercise care, we can safely incorporate most of standard aspectual theories. Some modifications are necessary, however. Consider the following possible properties of events (Parsons 1991):

(33)

PROG(e,t): e in progress at t

(34)
CUL(e,t): e culminates at t

Can we get rid of the time references here? Easily. Suppose we adopt (35) and (36). (The PROG relation is actually redundant in the event semantics used here, and we will not need it in the following analyses.)

(35)
PROG(e): e in progress

(36)
CUL(e): e culminates

We then have available the analyses (37)–(42), where the PRES and PROG morphemes are omitted as redundant in these particular analyses.

(37)
Smith is drawing a circle.
$(\exists e)$(drawing(e) & agent(Smith, e) & theme(circle, e)) when [...]

(38)
Smith was drawing a circle.
PAST[$(\exists e)$(drawing(e) & agent(Smith, e) & theme(circle, e))] when PAST[...]

(39)
Smith drew a circle.
PAST[$(\exists e)$(drawing(e) & agent(Smith, e) & theme(circle, e) & CUL(e))] when PAST[...]

(40)
Smith had been drawing a circle.
PAST[$(\exists e)$(drawing(e) & agent(Smith, e) & theme(circle, e))] before PAST[...]

(41)
Smith had drawn a circle.
PAST[$(\exists e)$(drawing(e) & agent(Smith, e) & theme(circle, e) & CUL(e))] before PAST[...]]

(42)
Smith will have drawn a circle.
FUT[$(\exists e)$(drawing(e) & agent(Smith, e) & theme(circle, e) & CUL(e))] before FUT[...]]

Notice from the analyses in (39), (41) and (42) that we don't need to link the culmination time to the "reference time."

Aktionsarten can be incorporated in the usual ways. States, achievements, accomplishments, and actions can be distinguished by internal predicates of events. For example, we can introduce "HOLD(e)" for states. If states are distinct from the progressive, we can distinguish "PROG(e)" from "HOLD(e)." Actions will admit "CUL(e)," achievement verbs like 'win' will have "RESULT(e)," and so on.

There are, however, some reasons for supposing that aspect should be treated not as a predicate of events but rather as a predicate of proposition-like objects. Chief among these is the imperfective paradox, which was discussed briefly in chapter 5. Consider (43).

(43)
John is drawing a circle.

The "paradox" is that on the event semantics just given there will be an existential quantification over circles (There is a circle x, such that John is drawing x), yet (43) can be true even if there is no circle (say, if John is run over by a truck after he completes only a 15-degree arc). Unless we are prepared to follow Parsons (1991) and introduce "incomplete objects," our event semantics will give incorrect truth conditions for certain utterances of (43).

Notice that a tense-like analysis of the progressive actually can foil the imperfective paradox. If I take tense to be a property of sentences or of proposition-like entities, the analysis of (43) may run as shown in (43'), and the semantics of PROG may be given by the axiom (43*).

(43')
PROG[John draws a circle]

(43*)
Val(x, PROG) iff x is in the process of becoming true

Thus, if we go this route, (43') is true iff 'John draws a circle' is in the process of becoming true. The existential quantifier remains buried safely in the scope of the PROG operator.

Recall that one of the central objections to a Priorean semantics of tense is that it is unconstrained. If complex tenses are derived by nesting tense morphemes, then there is potentially no limit to the number of possible tenses. That objection certainly doesn't apply to this version of a Priorean semantics, for the simple reason that tense morphemes aren't nested at all!

The result is a highly constrained view of possible tenses, based upon the possible combinations of PAST, FUT, and the temporal connectives. (Here I assume that there is no genuine present tense.)

matrix	conj-clause	conjunction	tense
PAST	PAST	when	Past
FUT	FUT	when	Future
PAST	PAST	before	Past Perfect
FUT	FUT	before	Future Perfect
PAST	PAST	after	Future in Past
FUT	FUT	after	Future in Future

The picture is going to be a bit richer than this, since everything turns on the available constructions in the system of explicit temporal conjunctions. For example, are there some cases where matrix and when-clause tenses can be mixed (say, to get future shifted reading of Future in the Past)? It all depends on whether the explicit system of temporal conjunctions will also allow us such mixing. For example, do we have the following paradigm?

matrix	conj-clause	conjunction	tense
PAST	FUT	after	Future in Past

e.g.: 'John was leaving after the party next week'

It is arguable that this case is really talking about a past intention of John's (that he was intending to leave after the party next week), but whatever is going on in the explicit case, that is essentially what accounts for the apparent future shifted reading of 'John was leaving'.

The tense system merely recapitulates the structures made available by the system of explicit temporal conjunctions, and inherits the constraints on that system. That, in effect, is what constrains the tense system on this theory.

Temporal Adverbs Again

If there are going to be difficulties in executing this version of a A-theory semantics, they are doubtless going to come in the analysis of temporal adverbs. Matters begin easily enough. As noted above, temporal adverbs like 'yesterday' and 'tomorrow' can be treated disquotationally. At worst, we might run into a proliferation of such adverbs and there might be some concern about a finite axiomatization for them—but these worries stem from adverbs like 'three days ago' and 'four days ago', and it is pretty clear that we can come up with ways of decomposing these without slipping into talk of B-series relations.[8]

One might object that these "adverbs," even when treated disquotationally, are referring expressions. For example, whether we wish to call 'yesterday' indexical or not, and whether we think we can display its sense or not, some would say that it *still* refers to a day. That is, it refers to a time in the past, and hence (the argument would go) we do not escape the need for the B-theory conception of the past.

The flaw in this objection is that it simply begs the critical question by assuming that 'yesterday', 'tomorrow', etc. refer to days (or to anything else). On the theory being developed here, these adverbs are treated as predicates (i.e., with axioms like Val(x, yesterday) iff x was true yesterday (or, alternatively, one day ago), and not axioms like Val(x, yesterday) iff x = yesterday). On the assumptions made explicit in section 2.6, predicates are not referring expressions on this theory.

If this is right, a similar sort of disquotational treatment should be available for the other temporal adverbs as well. For example, we might introduce axioms like those in (44).

(44)
Val(x, always) iff x is always true
Val(x, never) iff x is never true

Now it might be argued that, even if it is plausible to treat 'yesterday' and 'always' as predicates, it is suspicious to try and treat "locating adverbials" in the same way, for they surely directly refer to specific dates. Following the exposition by Kamp and Reyle (1994), let us consider some of these cases—beginning with calendar names, as in (45).

(45)
The last class is July 4, 1995.

Is it really possible to avoid reference to times in this case? I fail to see why not. Following the assumptions set out above, this sentence must have an implicit when-clause; hence, it is natural to suppose that the date itself is merely a constituent of that clause:

(46)
The last class is when [... July 4, 1995].

The ellipsed part of the clause could indicate some form of conventional dating system, such as "standard calendar systems indicate ...."

Similar considerations apply to 'before' and 'after' with NP complements, as in (47).

(47)
The last class will be before July 5.

Examples such as (47) too are simply cases of partially ellipsed temporal conjunctions.

(48)
The last class will be before [. . . July 5].

Accordingly, it seems that temporal adverbs (even locating adverbials) need
not be regarded as referring expressions and hence need not pose conceptual difficulties for the A-theory.

We might wish to treat the standard B-theory predicates 'before' and 'after'
as composed out of more basic A-series relations. The idea here would be that
a sentence like (49) would have a logical form in which 'before' is treated as
composed of a past-tense morpheme and a simple when-clause as in (50).

(49)
TNS[S1] before TNS[S2]

(50)
[$_s$ TNS[PAST[S1] when [S2]]]

Notice that the original tense morphemes are now construed as a single morpheme that takes scope over the entire conjunction. (The second explicit morpheme might be construed as a kind of scope marker for tense.)

This is a little bit abstract, so consider the logical form that would be given
for the sentences 'I ate before I left the house', and 'I will eat before I leave the
house':

(51)
[$_s$ PAST[PAST[there is an eating by me] when [there is a leaving of the house
by me]]]

(52)
[$_s$ FUT[PAST[there is an eating by me] when [there is a leaving of the house
by me]]]

Notice that this story doesn't introduce nested tenses, since the outer tense applies to the conjunction and the inner one applies only to the first conjunct.

The analysis for 'after' would be analogous. A sentence having the surface
form (53) would have the logical form (54).

(53)
TNS[S1] after TNS[S2]

(54)
[$_s$ TNS[FUT[S1] when [S2]]]

One difficulty for this general strategy is going to be handling temporal adverbs like 'seldom' or 'often' in terms of 'past', 'present', and 'future'. Technical difficulties begin to emerge with predicates like 'since', which has the following two senses:

case 1

I've been in England since January 1 (been there continuously).

case 2

I've been in (to) England since January 1 (been there once or more).

If we attempt a reductive strategy, then 'since January 1' might be part of a restricted substitutional quantifier over when-clauses. (See section 4.3 for a discussion of substitutional quantification.)

   The gloss for case 1 might be as in (55), the gloss for case 2 as in (56).

(55)

(For all S, s.t. 'PAST['⌢S⌢'after January 1 . . .]]' is T) 'I've been in England when'⌢ S is T

(56)

(For some S, s.t. 'PAST['⌢S⌢'after January 1 . . .]]' is T) 'I've been in England when'⌢ S is T

So far so good, but when we move to adverbs of temporal quantification, we soon run into difficulties. Consider (57)–(58), for example.

(57)

We go to London often.

(58)

We've been to London six times.

One might suppose that these cases (certainly (58)) finally force us into the introduction of past and future times; we say "six times," after all. But if we were to look at translations of (58) into other languages, the quick acceptance of times would certainly seem premature—consider Italian, in which one would say "sei volte" (six turns).

   Still, second-order temporal adverbs do raise interesting issues. Note that in (57') and (58') it is not sufficient to quantify directly over when-clauses.

(57')

(For many S) 'we go to London when' ⌢ S is T

(58')

(For six S) 'we went to London when' ⌢ S is T

As was mentioned in note 14 to chapter 4, substitutional quantification breaks down in these cases: there can be many when-clauses that describe a single visit to London.

But we do need some way of talking about "times," even if we don't want to take them as being points of time in the sense of the B-series metaphysics. Once again, it turns out that we can solve the problem with off-the-shelf philosophical resources. Following a general strategy for substitutional quantification sketched in Ludlow 1985, we can go second order and build times out of when-clauses, as in (59).

(59)
In a given context c, for each clause S, tense morpheme tns, there is a unique "time" t, s.t. t = {S^i: tns⌢'['⌢S⌢'] when '⌢tns⌢'['⌢S^i⌢']' is T}

Intuitively, then, times are derivative of our primitive notion of when. We say that A and B happen at the same time because we know that A happens when B happens. Further, anything that happens when B happens also must, ipso facto, happen at the same "time" that A happens.

Further constraints are necessary, since the when-clause must uniquely specify when something happened. For example, it might be true that I went to London when I had a headache, but 'I had a headache' cannot be a relevant substitution instance. So apparently we end up with (59').

(59')
In a given context c, for each clause S, tense morpheme tns, there is a unique "time" t, s.t. t = {S^i: tns⌢'['⌢S⌢'] when '⌢tns⌢'['⌢S^i⌢']' is T, and tns⌢'['⌢S^i⌢'] only when '⌢tns⌢'['S⌢']' is true}

This allows the extension of t to include "anchoring" clauses like "when I celebrated my eighteenth birthday," but not "when I had one of my many headaches."

Notice the contextual variable here. This is crucial, since what counts as happening "at the same time" depends upon our interests. We might mean the same day, we might mean the same nanosecond, or we might mean during the brief history of the human species.

Given this revised notion of times as sets of when-clauses, we can now return to the non-first-order temporal adverbs and treat them as in (57") and (58").[9]

(57")
For many t, there is an S, S ∈ t, s.t. 'we go to London when' ⌢S is T

(58")
For six t, there is an S, S ∈ t, s.t. 'we went to London when' ⌢S is T

Thus, when we say that we have been to London six times we are not saying that our trips fell on six distinct time points (that wouldn't work in any case; a single trip could overlap six time points), nor are we talking about six events. We are talking about six non-overlapping event descriptions. Thus, I might characterize the six times I have been to London as being when I came to talk at Kings, when I came on my Nth birthday, and so on.

8.3   More on E-Type Temporal Anaphora

Although Partee (1984) observed a number of similarities between temporal and nominal anaphora, she failed to note one class of similarities: temporal constructions that mirror Evans's example 'John owns some sheep and Frank shears them.' The temporal analogues are as shown in (60).

(60)
Jack goes up the hill sometimes and then he comes tumbling down with Jill.

The traditional analyses of anaphora fail here. If temporal anaphora works as bound variable anaphora does, then we have something like (60').

(60')
(sometimes t)[Jack goes up the hill at t and he comes tumbling down with Jill at t]

But that doesn't get the truth conditions of (60) right, since it doesn't specify that each time he goes up he comes tumbling down. Likewise, it doesn't work to suppose that each of these clauses has an independent temporal quantifier. That merely gets us to (60").

(60")
(sometimes t)[Jack goes up the hill at t] and (sometimes t)[he comes tumbling down with Jill at t]

Of course, this doesn't get the truth conditions right either. What stands out in this instance is the fact that E-type temporal anaphora seems to work quite smoothly here[10]:

(60*)
(sometimes t)[Jack goes up the hill at t] and [he comes tumbling down with Jill (after he goes up the hill)]

Of course, it is also possible to adopt the treatment of temporal anaphora in Discourse Representation Theory (DRT), in particular as it is developed by

Hinrichs (1981, 1986) and by Kamp and Reyle (1993). This is not the place to open up a debate about the relative merits of E-type anaphora and DRT (some of this debate is taken up in Ludlow 1994), much less about the extension of those theories to temporal anaphora. This is not a book about anaphora; my interest in temporal anaphora here is philosophical, and it turns on precisely one concern: that the A-theory needs to avoid temporal reference. E-type anaphors present one possible (and workable) way of meeting that need. There may well be other solutions, and it may be that some of those solutions will employ DRT resources (or, perhaps, the dynamic semantics of Groenendijk and Stokhof (1991) and Chierchia (1995)). At present, however, the philosophical content of those theories is cloudy on this issue. If such approaches can help us to avoid temporal reference (in the technical sense of 'reference' I am using here), I have no objection to them.

8.4   Further Issues

In chapter 5, two of the more interesting extensions of the B-theory involved the incorporation of temporal "reference" in nominals and the phenomenon of sequence of tense. In this section I will show how these phenomena can be handled on the A-theory. I will then return to the philosophical objection raised by McTaggart and discussed in section 7.4 above.

Temporal Anaphora in Nominals
In section 5.2 I discussed an observation, due to Enç, that nominals often seem to have an implicit temporal reference of their own—possibly quite independently of the "temporal reference" of the sentence as a whole. The example from that discussion is repeated here as (61).

(61)
The hostages came to the White House.

There is an intuitive sense in which we wish the NP to pick out some time frame that is independent of the visit to the White House—intuitively, the hostages at a certain time and place (say, the hostages taken from the US Embassy during the Iranian revolution).

It is sometimes supposed that these sorts of cases present difficulties for A-theory semantics, presumably because they provide additional evidence of the need for temporal reference. As we have seen, however, armed with E-type temporal anaphora, one can account for a number of apparent cases of temporal reference cases without invoking reference at all. Can we do that here?

Just as the B-theory had to be augmented, we must say something more about the A-theory if we are to account for the temporal character of certain nominals. Clearly the when-clauses that we have introduced thus far will not do the job, since they are merely describing properties of the matrix event (in the case of (61), the visit to the White House). What can be said about temporal anaphora in NPs?

One attractive possibility would be to develop the idea, suggested by Bach and Cooper (1978), that there can be *implicit* relative clauses in NPs. For example, in the case of (61) there would be an implicit relative clause with the possible content indicated in (61').

(61')
[$_{NP}$ [$_{NP}$ The hostages] [$_S$ (who were captured in the US Embassy during the Iranian revolution)]] came to the White House.

The content of the relative clause would be extracted from previous discourse or from shared background information in a manner analogous to the treatment of E-type pronouns.[11] In sum, we can again avoid the move to temporal reference if we are prepared to accept a certain degree of abstract syntactic structure.[12]

Sequence of Tense

As was discussed in section 5.2, sequence of tense involves cases like (62), where Biff's illness may have occurred simultaneously with Mary's report or may have occurred at some time previous to the report.

(62)
Mary said that Biff was ill.

Higginbotham (1995) argued that the shifted reading was the core case, and that the unshifted reading involved the illusion of past tense in the complement clause. In Higginbotham's words, "the appearance of the past tense in a complement clause can be an appearance merely; cross-reference takes place as in the first case, but the tense of the complement is present, not past."

Clearly the same solution is available to the A-theorist, but just as clearly there is something unsatisfactory about it. If there is no past-tense morphology in these complement clauses, why does it *sound* as if there is? More urgently, what are the mechanisms by which we get illusory past tense in these cases?

If this approach is unattractive, there are other solutions available with the A-theory framework. For example, the "independent" theories of SOT discussed in chapter 5 have natural analogues within the A-theory. To see this, consider that the structure of a sentence like (62) is actually going to be something along the lines of (63).

(63)

[₍ₛ₎ Mary said that [₍ₛ'₎ Biff was ill (when) [. . .]] when [. . .]]

Focusing our attention on the internal complement clause, we know (following O2 above) that the principal constraint on when-clauses is that their lead tenses match those of the clauses with which they are conjoined. Hence, in the above example, we know that the when-clause paired with 'Biff was ill' must be past tense. But that is the only constraint. The clause might have a content like "as Mary was speaking" (giving us the unshifted reading), or it might have a content like "when she visited him last week" (giving us the shifted reading). In each case, the content of the when-clause is going to be extracted from previous discourse (or from some form of common knowledge) in fundamentally the same way that the content of E-type pronouns are reconstructed.

If this picture is right, then it is a mistake to think of tense being "shifted" or of there being a "sequence" of tense at all. Rather, what is happening is that, depending on how the implicit clause is reconstructed, the described situation may be cotemporaneous with any described past-tense situation. It might be cotemporaneous with the described event of the matrix clause (Mary's speaking), or it might be cotemporaneous with any other contextually salient past-tense event description (e.g., when Mary saw Biff last week, or when Biff missed his meeting with Napoleon, or whenever). Interestingly, this parallels the last (and in my view the most promising) of the B-theory solutions that we looked at: simply letting R pick up any past- or future-tense event.[13]

In sum, the extensions to the B-theory that we looked at in section 5.2 have analogous extensions in the A-theory. Importantly, the extensions are possible without the appeal to temporal reference, and hence there is no conceptual cost to the basic A-theory program. Other extensions will proceed in like manner. Whereas the B-theory appeals to temporal reference, the A-theory looks for implicit clausal structure to carry the E-type temporal anaphora. Whether this strategy can be carried out is an open empirical issue; perhaps the positing of this implicit clausal structure will collide with general principles of linguistic theory.[14] But notice how striking it is that every construction for which researchers are inclined to posit temporal reference happens also to be a construction for which an implicit-clause story seems plausible. Indeed, it is even more striking that the case for temporal reference routinely involves some sort of explanation that relies upon the requisite clausal structure to identify the supposed referent (e.g., "hostages who were captured in the US Embassy during the Iranian revolution"). Perhaps this is a clue that reference was never involved at all.

As was noted in chapter 4, reference does not come for free. The epistemological burden involved in positing reference in these cases is great, and I see no efforts in the literature to take responsibility for that burden. The positing of implicit clauses involves a burden of its own, and it will have to be shouldered. But at least we have a model for how implicit clauses can be incorporated into current linguistic theory.[15] Can the same be said for the liberal postulation of reference?

8.5 McTaggart Revisited

Having equipped ourselves with a better understanding of the revised A-theory, let us now return to McTaggart's original objection to the A-theory. Mellor (1981) has claimed that Prior's answer (discussed in section 7.4 above) fails to escape the vicious regress. But does it really fail? Generating the regress requires that we be able to move from (64) to saying that there is a time at which x is future and that there is a time at which x is past (thus delivering the contradiction: x is future and x is past).

(64)
x was future and will be past.

Prior's response was that we need not have made this step, but we are now in a position to make an even stronger response. We don't need to avoid the step. In a certain sense we could not make the step if we wanted to!

Here is the idea. (65) is shorthand for an LF representation of the form given in (65').

(65)
FUT[S]

(65')
FUT[S] when FUT[...]

But then the semantics delivers the following truth conditions for (65'):

(65*)
[]S[] will be true when [] [...] [] will be true

Similar considerations apply to (66), which will have the truth conditions shown in (66*).

(66)
PAST[S]

(66*)

[]S[] was true when [] [...] [] was true

We can never get to the point where we have a conjunction of two conflicting A-theory tensed claims. Clearly (65*) and (66*) are not incompatible, since the when-clauses will have different contents.

To illustrate, take a proposition like

[] [(∃e) e is the dying of Queen Anne] [].

That proposition was future and is now past, but we can't overlook the temporal anaphora. There is an implicit when-clause, so that what we actually have is that the proposition was future (say, <u>when Queen Anne was born</u>) and it is past (say, <u>as I write these words</u>). There is not even the illusion of a contradiction if we remember to include the temporal anaphora.

The reason for the failure of the McTaggart argument here is not one usually given, and I believe it is not one anticipated by Mellor. The claim is not merely that the B-theorist has attempted to strip away the tense from (63) and (64). The B-theorist must also strip away the temporal anaphora from these constructions. But, by hypothesis, all tensed sentences have implicit when-clauses which serve to do the work of temporal anaphora. But if (63) and (64) come complete with when-clauses, then they can't possibly contradict each other unless those when-clauses have the same content. But they don't.

Nor will it help to attempt to take this to a meta-level—for example, by suggesting that a given set of A-theory truth conditions like (66*) is future at some time, present at some time, and past at some time. If we try to formalize such claims, as in (67) and (68), we disguise the actual structure of such claims.

(67)

(66*) is PAST

(68)

(66*) is FUT

Spelled out properly according to the theory developed in this chapter, the truth conditions of (67) will be as in (67*).

(67*)

(66*) was true when [...] was true

The B-theorist can race along this path indefinitely looking for a contradiction, but no level of embedding is going to generate a contradiction.

This is the sense in which the theory developed here is stronger than Prior's with respect to the McTaggart argument. Prior had no recourse to temporal anaphora, and hence he had to allow that at every other step in the McTaggart argument there was an apparent contradiction. This gave the impression that Prior had to keep moving up a level to escape these contradictions, and hence that he was forced into an infinite regress. Though I am not convinced that this was a genuine regress, the entire question is now rendered moot. The contradiction is *never* generated. The McTaggart argument fails.

Chapter 9
Broadening the Investigation

As should be evident from the previous two chapters, I think the preponderance of evidence leans in favor of an A-theory semantics of tense. I hope it is also clear that I consider this semantical evidence to support the A-theory conception of time. In this chapter I want to broaden the investigation somewhat by taking up the question of whether evidence from psycholinguistics or even from phenomenology can change the verdict. However, there are a lot of arguments on the table, and perhaps it is time to try and put them together in a single package.

Let us review some of the reasons for favoring a A-theory conception of time and tense. First, we have good reasons to suppose that there is a close (if not isomorphic) relation between the semantics of tense and the metaphysics of time. As I rhetorically asked in previous chapters, what makes something the semantics of "tense" if not that it has some reflex in the temporal character of the external world? Moreover, appeals to the psychology of time consciousness only delay the inevitable connection between tense and time. After all, what makes something "time" consciousness if not some connection between those mental states and temporal reality?

What can we conclude about the semantics of tense? As we learned in chapter 6, the B-theorist is going to have profound difficulties in accounting for the indexical character of temporal discourse. Moreover, there are really only three options for the B-theorist in this matter:

• The B-theorist can follow a token-reflexive strategy in which the utterance event itself makes it into the content of a tensed utterance/thought. But, as we saw in chapter 6, that packs too much information into the biconditionals of the T-theory, and we soon collide with the problem of utterances like 'there is no spoken language'.

• The B-theorist can try to cut the link between indexical meaning and the semantics of natural language. But, as we saw in chapters 3 and 6, this strategy is a cheat.

• The B-theorist can disquotationally introduce the indexical predicates into the axioms of the T-theory. But this amounts to becoming an A-theorist.

It seems to me that all the extant objections to the A-theory semantics can be dealt with. Insofar as those objections turn on temporal anaphora, this does not force us to accept a theory of temporal reference; to the contrary, we can have a theory of E-type temporal anaphora. Not only does such a theory appear to cover the facts; it also allows us to skirt some otherwise embarrassing asymmetries between temporal reference and ordinary reference (for example, it allows us to avoid reference to times or events with which we have no causal connection).

Thus, the A-theory semantics has epistemological advantages as well as what I would argue to be an empirical advantage (namely, its ability to adequately handle the facts about temporal indexicals). But what if we throw out temporal indexicals? This is a funny bit of evidence to throw out, since by some lights these facts constitute the very core of the temporal phenomena that we want to account for. Furthermore, if I am right, the temporal morphemes PAST and FUT are themselves indexical predicates, so ignoring indexicality amounts to ignoring the phenomenon of tense *tout court*. For the sake of argument, however, let us say that these facts can be ignored. Also for the sake of argument, let us dismiss whatever purchase epistemological arguments may have. (Never mind the fact that epistemological concerns led to the invention of Russellian descriptions and E-type pronouns in the first place.)

If we throw out all the evidence adduced so far on behalf of the A-theory, do we get a stalemate? Or is there further evidence that weighs in favor of one position over the other? As it turns out, even if we decide to ignore temporal indexicals and epistemological considerations, there remains some very suggestive psycholinguistic research that supports the A-theory semantics developed in this book.

9.1   Psycholinguistic Considerations

In section 2.4 we considered a suggestion from Evans (1985b) that support for one of two competing semantic theories might be found by appealing to psychological evidence. In particular, we considered the possibility that evidence for a particular semantic theory might be found in facts about language acquisition and in facts about acquired language deficits. In this section, I will look at some suggestive psychological studies on temporal language, and I will show that these studies lend support to the A-theory semantics developed in chapters 7 and 8.

What psychological questions will be decisive in adjudicating between the alternative semantic theories for tense? Intuitively, we will be interested in questions that determine whether the language of the B-theory or the language of the A-theory is more fundamental. For example, according to the B-theory, the semantics given for the PAST, PRES, and FUT tense morphemes presuppose an understanding of the before/after (earlier-than/later-than) relation. Alternatively, the semantics for the A-theory might[1] give the semantics for 'before' and 'after' in terms of the predicates 'past', 'present', 'future', and the relational predicate 'when'. If it could be shown that knowledge of one set of these relations emerged significantly before the other, we would have strong evidence for the semantic theory that takes those relations as primitive.

Evidence also might be found in the study of acquired language deficits. As linguistic abilities erode, do we lose the ability to understand basic tense morphemes first, or do we lose the ability to understand terms like 'before' and 'after' first, or do these abilities always degrade together? If one ability degrades earlier, that may suggest that that ability was not the more fundamental—that it may have been a higher-level linguistic ability requiring the knowledge of other, more primitive linguistic abilities.

As it turns out, there has been extensive psycholinguistic research on the acquisition of temporal language, and a number of the studies are suggestive. However, for the most part, the psychological studies have not been designed to answer the kinds of questions that exercise us here, and hence not all of them can help us choose between our two semantic theories. This is not a criticism of the psychological research. The focus of research is inevitably tied to the interests of the field, and there is no reason that these interests should be in the ultimate outcome of linguistic or metaphysical debates.[2]

Still, some of the research has been very suggestive. For example, a great deal of research has gone into the investigation of our first question—whether knowledge of the meaning of 'before' and 'after' emerges simultaneous with or after our knowledge meaning of 'past', 'present', and 'future'. Here the evidence seems to suggest that the child's ability to comprehend 'before' and 'after' emerges significantly later. Indeed, the acquisition of simple tenses emerges quite early (by age 2), and, as Clark (1973) reports, as a *lower* limit children do not learn the relational temporal terms 'before' and 'after' until age of 5![3]

This order of progression is nicely illustrated by Weist (1986), who specifically tracks the development of temporal language using the event-based resources of Reichenbach's theory. According to Weist, children move through a series of "four temporal systems during the development of the capacity to express increasingly complex configurations of temporal concepts" (p. 357).

Utilizing Reichenbach's S (speech time), R (reference time), and E (event time), Weist proposes that children proceed through the following stages of temporal development.

stage 1: R and E are frozen at S; children can only talk about present events.
stage 2 (age 18–24 months): Children distinguish E from S (using simple tense forms like past and future), but R is frozen at S, so the children cannot talk about events occurring relative to other time points.
stage 3 (age 3 years): R may be distinguished from S, but when it is, E is restricted to R. (For example, a temporal adverb like 'yesterday' might modify R, yet E will still be fixed relative to S.)
stage 4 (age 4 years): R, S, and E can all be at separate times.

Contrary to Weist's analysis, however, it seems more natural to take these results as supporting the A-theory semantics of tense. On the face of it, there is no principled reason why, on B-theory semantics, the order of acquisition should proceed in this order; according to the B-theory, the PAST, PRES, and FUT tense morphemes are supposed to be high-level abilities relative to the before/after relation. On the other hand, this order of acquisition seems natural within the framework of the A-theory semantics. The order of acquisition would be (1) rule for PRES tense morpheme (if there is a present-tense morpheme), (2) rules for PAST and FUT tense morphemes, (3) rules for temporal adverbs, then (4) rules incorporating higher-level abilities involving temporal conjunctions and e-type temporal anaphora.

Some of the interpretations given to data of this sort in the psychological literature are interesting as well. For example, Cromer (1968) and McNeill (1979), working within a broadly Piagetian framework, argued that before age 4 children are unable to temporally "decenter" themselves—that they are temporally egocentric in a certain sense. This observation brings to mind the remarks in chapter 7 in which, following Dummett (1969), I characterized the distinction between the B-theory and the A-theory as a distinction between a perspective in which we are standing outside of time, surveying (as Dummett wrote) "all temporal positions in a single glance," and one where we are "immersed in temporality" and only able to describe the world "as it is now."[4]

Acquisition data is not the only suggestive evidence. It also appears that research on acquired linguistic deficits (for example, among Parkinson's patients) shows that comprehension of 'before' and 'after' degrades much more rapidly than other linguistic forms (see Goodglass et al. 1979). This might be taken as suggesting that 'before' and 'after' are not primitive predicates at all but are rather built out of simpler notions, such as the basic tenses and temporal conjunctions.

There are also narrower questions to be investigated. The A-theory of tense, as developed in chapter 8, necessarily incorporates a notion of *when* as a primitive, and this notion is supposed to be distinct from the notion of occurring *at the same time*. This is a very subtle distinction, and most psychological studies are not designed to tease apart the two notions. Nevertheless, some researchers have observed just such a distinction, and have noted that a particular sense of 'when' emerges before the child has a notion of temporal order and simultaneity.

For example, in a remarkable passage, Cromer (1968, p. 110) notes that first uses of 'when' (such as "When its got a flat tire, its needa go to the ... to the station") are more statements of co-occurring events than statements of genuine simultaneity. Cromer's fascinating conclusion is that "perhaps the ability to 'date' an event by a contemporaneous event is more 'primitive' than the notion of serial ordering." Interestingly, as Keller-Cohen (1974) noted, similar observations about early uses of 'when' (i.e., that it doesn't mean "at the same time") can be found in Chamberlain and Chamberlain 1904 and in Jesperson 1940.

Clearly this observation by Cromer and others does not by itself support the thesis that there is a nonsequential use of 'when' which is prior to the notion of two events occurring at the same time. The research necessary to come up with conclusive results in this area would be delicate indeed.[5] Yet Cromer's observation is promising, for it suggests that the question may have an empirical answer (and indeed that initial observations support one of the key suppositions of the A-theory semantics).

I hope that the kinds of questions raised here will help to focus future research on the acquisition of event structure, of tense, and of the general conception of temporal order. There is certainly much at stake in the answer to properly framed questions about relative order of acquisition. First, the semantics of tense for natural language may well be illuminated by the answer; second, if the general program followed in this book is correct, ultimately the metaphysics of time could be illuminated by the answers we get to these very low-level questions. It may seem surprising that answers to grand metaphysical questions should turn on answers to questions about the acquisition of language by children, but I hope the considerations outlined in this book will make such a conclusion seem more plausible, if nevertheless still surprising.

9.2   Saving the Phenomenology[6]

The A-theory is often supposed to be more faithful to our intuitions about time than the B-theory is, but in the theory I developed in chapters 7 and 8 this advantage may appear to be lost. After all, like the B-theorist, I have given up the

notion of genuine temporal change. Perhaps more significantly, I have rejected
the reality of future and past events. Surely, these moves also conflict with our
intuitions about the nature of time! Or do they?

A lot turns on what we mean by 'intuitions'. There are those intuitions which
we are trained to have in our philosophy classes, and then there are what we might
call "untutored intuitions." Obviously, I am unimpressed by philosopher-induced
intuitions in this domain. This leaves our untutored intuitions. It is fair to ask
whether there are such things, and, if there are, what they might be.

At a minimum, we might expect a theory that comports with our intuitions to
be consistent with the way we experience the world. That is, if we experience
some things as future and others as past, we would say that a theory which re-
verses that "direction" clashes with our intuitions. Likewise, if we experience the
world as having a genuine future "out there," then (barring some explanation) the
sort of theory advocated here might well count as conflicting with our intuitions
about time.

This talk of "experiencing the world," of course, lands us thick in phenomenology, Although the phenomenological method is controversial, it seems to me
that it can be instructive in cases like this, because it shows that even the notion
of how we experience the world has to be handled with delicacy—particularly
in the case of the phenomenology of time.

How *do* we experience time, then? One might suppose that the philosophically untutored way we experience time is as a dynamic system in which events
move from the future to the present and on into the past. That is certainly how
a number of philosophers have *written* about our experience of time. The
metaphors on this score are endless. Williams (1951, pp. 461–462) catalogued
them as follows:

Time flows or flies or marches, years roll, hours pass. More explicitly we may speak as
if the perceiving mind were stationary while time flows by like a river, with the flotsam
of events upon it; or as if presentness were a fixed pointer under which the tape of hap-
penings slides; or as if the time sequence were a moving picture film, unwinding from
the dark reel of the future, and rewound into the dark can of the past. Sometimes, again,
we speak as if the time sequence were a stationary plain or ocean on which we voyage,
or in a variegated river gorge down which we drift; or, in Broad's analogy, as if it were
a row of house fronts along which the spotlight of the present plays. "The essence of nowness," Santayana says, "runs like fire along the fuse of time."

However, these may all be examples of bad phenomenology. A number of phe-
nomenologists have argued that our experience of time is not like this at all, and,
more significantly, that our experience of time does not support an independent future and past. One case in point is the work of Merleau-Ponty (1962, p.

411), who categorically rejects the idea that we experience time as flowing or that we experience an independent future and past:

> We say that time passes or flows by. We speak of the course of time.... If time is similar to a river, it flows from the past towards the present and the future. The present is the consequence of the past, and the future of the present. But this often repeated metaphor is in a way extremely confused. For, *looking at the things themselves,* the melting of the snows and what results from this are not successive events....

The point is that if we think of time as a series of successive events, we have to think of an observer of the earlier and later events. For example, standing on the banks of a river today and watching the water pass by, I might say that there was an event of this water coming down from the mountains. But that supposes a witness up in the mountains, and our taking the perspective of that witness. Phenomenologically speaking, I really can't take that position. This blunder, in Merleau-Ponty's view, has "persisted from the time of Heraclitus to our own day," and the root of the blunder is "our surreptitiously putting into the river a witness of its course"(ibid., p. 411). That move is simply out of court if we are interested in how *we* experience the world.

If we concentrate on *our* experience of the world, we have to reject the idea that time is a process or that it involves reference to independent future and past events. Rather, we have to think of the future and past being, as it were, in the present. "Time," writes Merleau-Ponty (ibid., p. 412),

> is, therefore, not an actual process, not an actual succession that I am content to record. It arises from *my* relation to things. Within things themselves, the future and the past are in a kind of eternal state of pre-existence and survival; the water which will flow by tomorrow *is* at this moment at its source, what has just past *is* now a little further downstream in the valley. What is past or future for me is present in the world.

Note how smoothly this comports with the claim in chapter 7 that we evaluate past-tense and future-tense utterances by considering *current* evidence. Indeed, how could we *not* evaluate tensed propositions this way if the future and the past are "present in the world"?

Merleau-Ponty (ibid., p. 413) also cautions against appeals to memory to try and make sense of time as a sequence of events:

> ...it has passed unnoticed that our best reason for rejecting the physiological preservation of the past is equally a reason for rejecting its 'psychological preservation', and that reason is that no preservation, no physiological or psychic 'trace' of the past can make consciousness of the past understandable. This table bears traces of my past life, for I have carved my initials on it and spilt ink on it. But these traces in themselves do not refer to the past: they are present.... Nor can one, a fortiori, construct the future

out of contents of consciousness: no actual content can be taken, even equivocally, as evidence concerning the future. . . .

My appeal to Merleau-Ponty here is admittedly an appeal to authority, but the point is not to nail down one certain picture of how we experience time. Rather, the point is to illustrate that the picture of time as involving an independent future and past is by no means considered faithful to our experience by those who purport to be interested in the phenomenology of time. Accordingly, it cannot be said without sustained (and no doubt subtle) argumentation that the theory presented in chapters 7 and 8 clashes with the untutored way in which we experience the world. Very simply, the burden of proof rests with those who would advance the priority of one particular set of intuitions.

9.3   Conclusion

Let us take stock. In chapter 6 we saw that there were serious problems for any version of the B-theory that hoped to account for the phenomenon of temporal indexicals. As was shown in earlier chapters, this limitation of the B-theory cannot be dismissed out of hand. If the world is "tenseless," then one cannot appeal to semantics or psychology to deliver the missing tensed ingredient, for semantics and psychology are not disembodied enterprises—they cannot add tense to a tenseless world. Only a full A-theory semantics/metaphysics seems to be capable of making sense of our temporal discourse.

In chapter 7 we saw that the A-theory semantics and metaphysics could claim a number of strong epistemological advantages. For example, the A-theory frees us from the embarrassing B-theoretic claim that we can actually refer to times and events in the future and in the causally disconnected past. It further frees us from the claim that to evaluate past (future) tense sentences we must, as it were, travel into the past (future) and evaluate the sentence at that past (future) tense time. In short, the A-theory story seems much more plausible as an account of our semantical knowledge.

In this chapter we have seen that broadening our investigation leaves this conclusion intact. If we turn to cognitive psychology generally and to the theory of concept/language acquisition specifically, we find that the evidence weighs heavily in favor of the A-theory of tense. Moreover, by some accounts the A-theory does a better job of comporting with the phenomenology of time. I conclude that the A-theory (of both tense and time) is the more plausible general theory and that it should be adopted in future research on the nature of tense and time.

This is a strong conclusion in a number of respects. As regards metaphysics the A-theory is certainly a minority view, and as regards semantics the A-theory is virtually ignored. But the conclusion is also a strong one in that it entails a number of radical and far-reaching consequences for other domains of philosophy and linguistics. In the next chapter, I will outline some of these consequences and propose some directions for future research within this general framework.

Chapter 10
Consequences

So far, this investigation has been limited to some of the more immediate consequences of the A-theory. In particular, we have been interested in the consequences for semantical theory, and to a lesser extent for psychology. But, as was noted in the introduction, the doctrine of time is interwoven with virtually every branch of philosophy and indeed nearly every branch of human inquiry. For the most part these other forms of inquiry have been predicated on B-theory assumptions (either tacitly or explicitly). If those B-theory assumptions are abandoned and replaced by an A-theory metaphysics, it is natural to wonder what some of the consequences will be.

Because the consequences will be felt in areas ranging from the theory of causality and the philosophy of action to the philosophy of space to the philosophy of religion, it would be impossible to do justice to all of the potential areas affected.[1] Accordingly, I think it might be more useful for me to pick out one string of philosophical consequences, and one string of linguistic consequences, and follow them for a while in an effort to illustrate just how rich and complex they will be.

10.1 Philosophical Consequences

Logic and Truth-Value Links[2]
One of the most pressing issues for this particular defense of the A-theory is the apparent loss of truth-value links, and hence the loss of an apparently natural account of certain logical inferences. As an illustration of the problem, consider (1) below, already discussed in chapter 6.

(1)
Dinosaurs roamed the Earth.

On the presentist version of the A-theory adopted here, we do not evaluate this sentence by "traveling" to some time earlier than now and determining whether, at that time, 'Dinosaurs roam the Earth' is true. Rather, the truth of it is grounded by current facts—for example, existing fossils.

This general line of response is, of course, similar to one that has been pursued by Dummett (most notably in his 1969 paper) and other anti-realists, but there is arguably a difficulty for the position. It can be held that there are important truth-value links between statements about the past and statements about the present, and that anti-realists (and A-theorists) must provide some alternative account of these links. For example, we routinely make inferences like (2).

(2)
I am hungry.

Next Tuesday it will be true that I was hungry.

On a B-theory semantic theory like that sketched in chapter 5, it is clear how this sort of inference can be made. If I am hungry now, then there is a time t = now such that I am hungry at t. But then for any date t' later than t it will be true at t' that I was hungry. Since next Tuesday is later than t, next Tuesday it will be true that I was hungry.

The A-theorist, on the other hand, will need to articulate alternative (anti-realist) truth-value links that can be drawn on for these inferences. To illustrate, Wright (1993, chapter 5) formalizes the truth-value links grounding the B-theory inferences as follows:

for $t_1 < t_2$

A
$(\forall t_2)[Past{:}S$ is true at t_2 iff $(\exists t_1)(S$ was true at $t_1)]$

B
$(\forall t_1)[Fut{:}S$ is true at t_1 iff $(\exists t_2)(S$ will be true at $t_2)]$

C
$(\forall t_2)[S$ is true at t_2 iff $(\forall t_1)(Fut{:}S$ was true at $t_1)]$

D
$(\forall t_1)[S$ is true at t_1 iff $(\forall t_2)(Past{:}S$ will be true at $t_2)]$

and so on.[3]

Thus, if FUT[S] is true on May 1, 1998, there is a later date at which S will be true (by B), and so forth.

Here is the difficulty for the A-theorist: Since future- and past-tensed sentences are to be evaluated on the basis of the present, it is possible to envision a situation in which evidence that may have been present at t_1 is erased or eliminated and is hence not available at t_2. That is, suppose that today (t_1) I commit some crime (say, I kill Colonel Plum with a candlestick) and then erase all evidence and take amnesia pills so as to also forget the cover-up.[4] Now we appear to have a situation where 'I am (successfully) killing Col. Plum with a candlestick' is true. The problem is this: If my cover-up is good, at t_2 there will be absolutely no facts to support the truth of 'I killed Col. Plum with a candlestick'. Thus, if the t_2 statement is to be evaluated by facts holding at t_2, the statement will not be true at t_2. Then, by (D), it follows that 'I am (successfully) killing Col. Plum with a candlestick' is false, contradicting our initial assumption.

The move that looks fishy here is the one where we say that at t_2 there will be no facts to ground the truth of the statement in question. Doesn't this amount to traveling into the future and evaluating the situation—and isn't this precisely the sort of situation that is supposed to be blocked?

Indeed, all the A-theorist is compelled to admit is the following: We begin with the truth (now) of 'There will be no facts to ground the truth of 'I killed Col. Plum with a candlestick'. From this and our truth-value links, all that we can infer is that the following will be true at t_2: 'there are no facts to ground the truth of 'I killed Col. Plum with a candlestick'. But this isn't enough to move back to a contradiction.

Getting the contradiction requires the following additional postulate:

E
($\forall t$)['There are no facts to ground the truth of S' is/was/will be true at t iff S is/was/will not be true at t)]

Using this, we can infer that it will not be true that 'I killed Col. Plum with a candlestick' at t_2. Now (D) carries us to the falsity of 'I am (successfully) killing Col. Plum with a candlestick', and we have our contradiction.[5]

It appears that the A-theorist must find another way to escape contradiction here. One possible answer is that this worry about truth-value links has things upside down. Perhaps, as McDowell (1978) seems to suggest, the real issue is that the realist about the past *needs* truth-value links in order to support his or her realism. Accordingly, perhaps the burden is on the realist to justify the appeal to these links. McDowell (p. 132, note 10) thinks that no such justification can be forthcoming:

The truth-value link realist's view of what it is, say, for something to have occurred is unintelligible. He conceals that from himself with a confused thought of being with knowledge acquiring powers different from ours. Thus the realist's view of the reality of the past can be described, with only mild caricature, as the idea of another place, in which past events are still occurring, watched, perhaps, by God.

Like Wright (1993, chapter 3), I am inclined to think that this criticism is unfair. The realist about the future and the past is under no compulsion to claim special knowledge acquiring powers. We are talking logic here, not epistemology, and the realist is quite happy to cut the link between the two.

Of course, by parity of reasoning, an anti-realist is not compelled to accept truth-value links as grounding logical reasoning like that in (2). Still, one wonders what could ground such reasoning if not the usual truth-value links. Would it even be possible to dispense with such links? Wright (1993, p. 179) considers the prospects dim:

> The truth-value links are not to be compared to those features of, say, classical logic which undergo modification by the intuitionists. The intuitionistic modifications are deep-reaching; but they are relatively conservative with respect to our ordinary notion of valid inference. Wholesale rejection of the truth-value links, in contrast, would be bound to leave us, it seems, with no clear conception of how tensed language was supposed to work at all. What, for instance, is someone who asserts 'It will rain at noon tomorrow' to be taken as saying if the truth-conditions of his utterance are not held to coincide with that of any utterance of 'It is raining' at noon tomorrow? Maybe there could be a coherent revisionary programme for tensed discourse, pivoting around rejection of the truth-vaue links as the intuitionist revisions of classical logic pivot around rejection of Bivalence; and perhaps we should be left with a surprising amount to say. But it does not seem likely.

Let us suppose, then, that some form of truth-value links are indispensable. Is there a way out for the anti-realist here? Wright considers two possibilities.

The first way out—the one advocated by Wright—is to refigure truth-value links in a way that is more sympathetic to the anti-realist about the past and future. According to Wright, the anti-realist should reject (A)-(D) and opt instead for links like (A*)-(D*).

A*

$(\forall t_2)$[What *Past*:S expresses at t_2 is true iff $(\exists t_1)$(what S expressed at t_1 is true)]

B*

$(\forall t_1)$[What *Fut*:S expresses at t_1 is true iff $(\exists t_2)$(what S will express at t_2 is true)]

C*

$(\forall t_2)$[What S expresses at t_2 is true iff $(\forall t_1)$(what *Fut*:S expressed at t_1 is true)]

D*

$(\forall t_1)$[What S expresses at t_1 is true iff $(\forall t_2)$(what *Past*:S will express at t_2 is true)]

and so on.

The difference is that the proposed * links supplant the tense inflection in 'be true' with tense inflections in the verb 'to express'. Wright's idea is that by doing this we can retain the truth-value links by giving up the stability of the truth predicate—that is, by giving up on the timelessness of truth.

To illustrate with our example of Col. Plum: even if our evidence erasure program is successful, what 'I killed Col. Plum with a candlestick' will express at t_2 is (currently) true. It follows unproblematically that what 'I am (successfully) killing Col. Plum with a candlestick' now expresses is true. No contradiction need arise.

Wright's solution then is to allow that what we express by an utterance (tokening) of S will not be eternally true in the traditional sense (whatever that comes to once we have given up the reality of the future and the past), but rather that what is said might flip-flop between true and false over time.

This is a pretty strong conclusion. As Wright (1993, p. 201) puts the matter, "the prospect of rehabilitating something importantly akin to the classical notion of truth is, in effect, finally dashed." Though I have not been reluctant to embrace strong conclusions in this book, one naturally wonders if there isn't a less radical way out.

One alternative idea, which Wright attributes to Dummett (1969), is that what S expresses will shift over time. Truth could remain stable if we allowed that the content of an utterance (tokening) was temporally unstable. Put another way, perhaps an utterance at t_1 has a certain content C at t_1 but that very same t_1 utterance has another content at t_2.

Applied to the current problem of my killing Col. Plum, we might accept that what 'I killed Col. Plum with a candlestick' will express at t_2 is true but argue that it will express something rather different at t_2 than it does as uttered now (at t_1), and we are in no position now to know what the content of that utterance might be at t_2.

Wright (1993, p. 194) rejects this solution, not because of its paradoxical feel, but because of its alleged inability to cope with diachronic disagreements:

... if Dummett's anti-realist has indeed found a way to explain how he can avoid dismissing the views of his earlier and later self, the threatened cost is an unability to explain how there can be such a thing as conflicting views held by protagonists who are sufficiently separated in time.

Dummett's anti-realist is therefore open to a simple dilemma. Does his position permit the reconstruction of some sort of general notion of diachronic inconsistency, or does it not? If it does not, that merely furnishes the realist with a further powerful objection—what account are we now to give of the growth of human knowledge, the hard-won gradual defeat of superstition and error in which we are encouraged to believe, etc. etc.? But if some sort of notion of diachronic inconsistency can be saved, the task will still

remain of showing that the kind of clash which an indexical conception of truth *does* allow
to hold between statements widely separated in time does not obtain between his present and his later, and earlier opinions.

It seems to me that if one wants to break the dilemma and pursue the shifting-
content strategy, then one should hold that diachronic disagreements are possible but reject the idea that they can be thought of as conflicts between positions
held at t_1 and t_2. Rather, the idea would be that the relevant historical disagreements are all "in the present." Thus, if I now dispute Plato's doctrine of the
forms, it does not mean that the view I hold at t_2 conflicts with the content of
something that Plato said at t_1, but rather that the conflict between our views
must take place as they are couched at t_2. Although this subtle and complex gambit obviously must be played with care, I see no reason to suppose that it inevitably fails.

In my view, then, we are left with two solutions to the problem of truth-
value links, both of which need to be explored in more detail before they are fully
secured. Still, in the interim, it would be interesting to see what the consequences
of these gambits might be, since the A-theory will have to make good on at
least one of the two. In the next section we will begin exploring some of these
consequences.

Externalism, Self-Knowledge, and Memory
The two solutions that Wright discusses for the problem of truth-value links turn
out to have consequences that ripple into debates about the nature of memory,
particularly as it relates to the authority of our self-knowledge and the doctrine
of externalism about mental content. If (as Putnam (1975), Burge (1979), and
many others have argued) the contents of our mental states depend upon social
and environmental factors, then there are alleged to be consequences for our ability to know the content of our mental states without first investigating the environment. That is, if (as Putnam says) "meanings ain't in the head," it is not
clear how we can have authoritative self-knowledge. This would undermine basic
assumptions about the nature of self-knowledge that have been widely held at
least since Descartes.

But Davidson (1987), Burge (1988), and others have observed that there is
no tension in externalism and authoritative self-knowledge, since the second-order
knowledge of our mental states must be environmentally determined as well.
Thus, a second-order thought that might be expressed as "I am thinking that water
is wet" will be a second-order thought involving water or twater, depending upon
whether the agent is in a water environment or a twater environment.

This move has led to a further discussion about externalism and memory, driven in part by arguments made by Boghossian (1989) and Ludlow (1995). Memory comes in as follows. Boghossian argues for the incompatibility of externalism and self-knowledge based on the so-called slow-switching thought experiments of Burge (1988). We are asked to imagine an agent who unknowingly moves between Earth and Twin-Earth and is later informed that switches had been taking place. Would such an agent have authoritative knowledge of his mental states? According to Boghossian, the agent would not, since it appears possible for an agent S to know his thoughts at time t, forget nothing, yet at some time later than t (having been informed of the possibility or prevalence of slow-switching) be unable to say what the contents of his thoughts were at t. Boghossian argues:

> The only explanation, I venture to suggest, for why S will not know tomorrow what he is said to know today, is not that he has forgotten but that he never knew. Burge's self-verifying judgments do not constitute genuine knowledge. What other reason is there for why our slowly transported thinker will not know tomorrow what he is said to know directly and authoritatively today?

Ludlow (1995) reconstructs this argument as follows:

(1) If S forgets nothing, then what S knows at t_1, S knows at t_2.
(2) S forgot nothing.
(3) S does not know that P at t_2.
(4) Therefore, S did not know that P at t_1.

At which premise should the externalist take aim? According to Burge (1998), the weak link in Boghossian's argument is premise 3. According to Burge, memory provides something like "anaphoric links" to events in the past that allow us access to past contents. Thus we *do* have resources that allow us access to the content P at time t_2.

Of course, if we reject the reality of future and past events, then the Burge position is a non-starter. It cannot be the job of memory to "reach back" into the past for a content, for the simple reason that there is literally no past to reach back to. The picture of memory that we are left with is somewhat Humean in character—not in the sense that memories are simply vague sense impressions, but in the sense that the content of a memory is fixed entirely by present circumstances and not by its linking us to the past. Boghossian cannot be engaged on premise 3.

Alternatively, Ludlow (1995b) holds that the weak premise in the argument is the first one. The reasoning is that if the contents of our mental states are determined by our social environment, it is natural to suppose that the contents of our memories will depend upon our social environment. As we move from one environmental condition to another (perhaps without even noticing the environmental change), the contents of our memories will shift accordingly. Ludlow (ibid.) applies this line of reasoning to Boghossian's argument in the following manner:

> ...let's say that at time t_1 I know that I am thinking that arugula is bitter. Suppose that at time t_2 later than t_1, I recall that initial thought about arugula, but, due to undetected changes in my linguistic community, the content of my thoughts about arugula have shifted. Boghossian is arguably correct in asserting that I do not know at t_2 what I knew at t_1, but he is incorrect in supposing that "the only explanation" for this is that I "never knew" my thoughts in the first place. It is entirely consistent with the social externalist view of memory that I forgot nothing, but that the contents of my memories have nonetheless shifted.

Hofmann (1995) points out some apparent difficulties with this move. It appears that memory fails to reflect the content of memory targets, and further that it is not reliable regarding the truth of my earlier thoughts. Hofmann puts the first problem this way:

> ...if [the circumstances of recollection] determine memory content, then memory turns into an empty, absurd faculty. This is so, since memory no longer can do what it is supposed to do, namely, to recall the very same thoughts one earlier on had entertained. If Peter had come to believe at t_1 somehow that arugula only grows in Mediterranean climate, and now, at t_2, recalls this thought, then what he recollects will not be the same thought about arugula, but some other thought about, say, tarugula—according to the newly adopted individuating conditions.

Hofmann puts the second problem as follows:

> ...equally embarrassing, the truth values of the memories will have changed. So, for example, Peter's belief at t_1 that arugula only grows in Mediterranean climate will now, when recollected, turn into a falsehood.... For, at time t_2 it will be a thought about tarugula which is a vegetable (let's assume) that grows only in tropical climates. Even worse, if Peter recollects that he had had, at t_1, some arugula experience, then also this memory has turned by now into a falsehood, since it has become a memory-thought about tarugula which (let's assume) Peter never has had any direct encounter with. And, all of this has occurred without Peter being able to introspectively become aware of it. Memory, as social externalism will have it, has 'turned pseudo'. It is no longer a source of knowledge.

In response, Ludlow (1996) argues that, although memory is not faithful in certain respects, in most important respects it will be. For example, the veracity of most of my beliefs will survive the switching cases. If I believe at t_1 that water is wet, then at t_2 I will have a belief that twater is wet. If my earlier beliefs were on the whole reliable, then my later beliefs should be as well. As for the fact that my recollection of the initial thought is that it was a twater thought, we simply needed to rethink the point of having memories in the first place:

> ... is there any reason to suppose that it is the job of memory to "record the contents" of past mental episodes? On the face of it, this assumption begs the central question at issue. According to the externalist conception of memory that I have proposed, it is not the job of memory to record contents, but rather to provide information about past episodes relative to current environmental conditions. Even if there were a mechanism which could, as it were, freeze the contents of an initial mental episode and carry it in memory indefinitely, I'm not sure that it would have any utility. Indeed, it would be a way of preserving the content of a thought which we could no longer have. (ibid., p. 316)

However, the analysis of truth-value links proposed by Wright (the one that gives up the timelessness of truth) allows an even bolder response. If the switch is such as to make events on Earth in principle inaccessible to us, then it is simply no longer true that my original memory was a water memory. In a sense, then, a conception of memory that is sensitive to the current environment is crucial for *preventing* error, since otherwise it would be preserving contents that are no longer true. The second objection thus collapses.

Alternatively, suppose we adopt the alternative way out canvassed (and then dismissed) by Wright: suppose we hold that the timelessness of truth is preserved, but that the contents of our statements shift over time. This too gives us a way out.

In the latter case, the episode of my thought E that occurs at t_0 has water content when I am at t_0 but twater content when I am at t_2. Thus, the thought might not be identified with a single content, but rather with a series of contents at different times. What I was thinking at t_0 would depend upon when I happen to recollect my thought—or, more generally, where I happen to be at later points of time.

That is, a given episode of thought E occurring at t_0 might be assigned different contents at different times, as follows.

	t_0	t_1	t_2	t_3	t_4	t_5
E's content	H_2O	H_2O	XYZ	XYZ	XYZ	H_2O

Returning to the original Boghossian argument, we find that the Ludlow (1995b) reconstruction suppresses some important details. The full argument should have been as follows:

(0) If a first-order thought E has content P at t_1, then it has content P at t_2.
(1) If S forgets nothing, then what S knows at t_1 S knows at t_2.
(2) S forgot nothing.
(3) At t_2 S does not know the content of E to be P.
(4) Therefore, at t_1 S did not know the content of E to be P.

Obviously, the previously hidden premise (0) is seriously flawed, since E may well have the content P at time t_1 but something else altogether (say, Q), at t_2. Premise 1 is flawed too, of course, since what I know at t_1 is E's t_1 content, and what I know at t_2 is E's t_2 content. No longer knowing the t_1 content of E doesn't count as forgetting any more than the fact that I can no longer know that E is happening *now*. But the crucial thing to see is that, although my second-order knowledge of my thoughts shifts over time, that shift is crucial, since it allows me to track the shifting contents of my first-order thoughts. Memories that are sensitive to environmental conditions are crucial for us to keep track of what we were thinking.

This may seem a surprising conclusion. Episodes of belief are no longer stable objects; they are now highly dynamic and sensitive to the communities that we inhabit over time. On the other hand, if the conclusion is surprising it also has a certain elegance. Our revised theory of truth-value links was driven by our rejection of the reality of the future and the past. It is remarkable that the new way of thinking about truth-value links should also help to secure an approach to memory that is intimately interwoven with widely held views about mental content and self-knowledge. But, in view of the tight connections holding between time and memory, between memory and mental content, and between mental content and self-knowledge, the real surprise would have been if the move to the A-theory was philosophically inert. Clearly, it is anything but that.

10.2   Linguistic Consequences

The linguistic consequences for this proposal are, of course, vast. We have already seen that the proposal sketched here has wide-ranging consequences for the analysis of (implicit) temporal conjunctions, relative clauses, etc. Moreover, the consequences flowing from the analysis of temporal anaphora will not be insignificant.

Rather than dwell at length on some of these obvious consequences, in this section I want to pursue a much stronger and more provocative possible consequence: the possibility of eliminating the notion of tense as a grammatical category altogether.

In this book we have seen that there is no reference to future or past events—that (for example) the English tense system, such as it is, does not need reference times in the future or in the past in order to make sense of temporal adverbs, temporal anaphora, complex tenses, etc. What we have are basic temporal morphemes (PAST, PRES, FUT) that are predicates taking proposition-like objects as their arguments. Perhaps we can go one step further and exorcise the talk of temporality from what we sloppily call 'temporal adverbs', 'temporal anaphora', 'tense morphemes', and so on.

This might sound crazy, but in a sense it is entirely natural, since that many natural languages don't have tense morphemes anyway. We need not look to unfamiliar languages such as Hopi. English doesn't have a genuine future-tense morpheme; rather, it relies on modals to do (or so we think) the work of a future-tense morpheme. As we move from English to other languages, we find that future-tense morphemes—in those rare languages where they are purported to exist—are always suspicious looking. In Romance languages, they appear to have modal elements packed within them. Purported past-tense morphemes are no less suspicious, usually being nothing more than aspectual markers.

The standard view supposes that we are using modals and aspectual markers to express future tense and past tense (hence, to express things about the future and the past),[6] but why should we suppose that? Why not suppose we are just using modals to express modality (potentiality or probability, for example) and aspectual markers to express aspect (perfect aspect, for example)? Perhaps somewhere (maybe it was Aristotle's fault) bad philosophy infected linguistic theorizing. We moved from the assumption that there must be a future and a past to the conclusion that there must be linguistic elements that allow us to speak about such things. Perhaps this philosophical assumption has become a procrustean bed in which we categorize things as temporal elements, when to a Martian linguist with no knowledge of western philosophy of time, these elements would look like ordinary modals and aspectual markers.

No Future

To make this discussion a little less abstract, let us take up the question of the future tense in Romance languages.[7] What we are taught when we learn Spanish, for example, is that there are future-tense morphemes that in the regular form conjugate as in (3) for a verb like 'hablar' (to speak).

(3)
hablaré
hablarás
hablará
hablarémos
hablaréis
hablarán

And we are taught that the future-tense morphemes are as shown in (4).

(4)
-aré
-arás
-ará
-arémos
-aréis
-arán

Or perhaps we are taught that the future ending is attached to an infinitive stem, so that the actual morphemes are as shown in (5).

(5)
-é
-ás
-á
-émos
-éis
-án

Either way, one cannot help but notice the striking similarity between these morphemes and the Spanish axillary 'haber' ('have'), which conjugates as shown in (6).

(6)
he
has
ha
hemos
habéis[8]
han

In the case of (5) there is near identity with (6). In the case of (4) the picture that emerges is that rather than a single unbroken future-tense morpheme we have a modal element and an irrealis marker 'ar', so that the actual structure is something like (7).

(7)
habl - ar - é
habl - ar - ás
habl - ar - á
habl - ar - émos
habl - ar - éis
habl - ar - án

Some version of this paradigm holds in each of the Romance languages that has an apparent future tense. (It is worth noting that many Romance "dialects" do not have a future tense at all.[9])

Now it might be objected that, although this story tells us something about the origin of the future tense, it doesn't say much about how tense is actually represented in I-language. That is, it may be that the structure proposed in (7) has long since vanished, and we now represent the future as a single unstructured morpheme. As it turns out, however, there is good reason to suppose that this sort of multiple-morpheme approach persists to this day.

One piece of evidence on this score comes from European Portuguese, in which clitic pronouns can be inserted between what I have characterized as the modal element and the irrealis element. That suggests that these two elements are in fact distinct representations and are not merely part of a single unbroken future-tense representation. Furthermore, in other Romance dialects the very same elements (e.g. the auxiliary 'have') do not appear attached to the verb stem at all—as in certain southern Italian and Sardinian dialects in which, e.g., 'I will speak' can be expressed as 'Ho a parlare', utilizing the auxiliary 'avere' (have) followed by a preposition and an infinitive. Here we lose even the illusion of a genuine unbroken future-tense morpheme.

Following this general strategy, we can proceed apace with all the Indo-European languages. All the future-tense forms appear to be modal in origin. I would merely suggest that perhaps they *remain* modals (or something very much like modals). This is certainly consistent with the interpretations commonly given to these elements in spoken language. Indeed, in spoken standard Italian present tense is generally *not* what one uses to express the future. For example, if one wants to say "I am going to the theater tomorrow," one says (8) and not (9).

(8)
Vado   al teatro   domani
(go-1SG-PRES to the theater tomorrow)

(9)
Andrò   al teatro   domani
(go-1SG-FUT   to the theater tomorrow)

When the future *is* used, it is most likely being used to express possibility or uncertainty, as when one says (10) (which has the sense of "It must be around 8 o'clock").

(10)
Saranno   le otto
(be-3PL-Fut eight)

In short, what gets called future tense not only *looks* like modality; in many cases it *acts* like modality.

But, one might ask, what exactly are these modals referring to, if not to the future?

One idea that can be found in the linguistics literature is that modals such as 'will' do not refer to the future but rather specify an epistemic notion similar to predictability.[10] This idea can be only partially satisfactory for our purposes, however, since one is tempted to take the talk of prediction or predictability as involving prediction *of the future,* in which case we land back where we started.

Alternatively, we might consider modals as referring to *dispositions,* construed as real properties of the world. So if I say that 'I will leave' I am talking not about some distinct future out there but about a disposition of the present world—a certain potentiality, as it were.

It might be useful to think for a moment about simple, relatively primitive clocks. When the Wicked Witch of the West turns over the hourglass, the amount of sand left on top reflects how much time Dorothy has remaining. But rather than think about the remaining time being spooled up out there in Dorothy's future, perhaps it would be better to think of the hourglass as having a certain dispositional property which reflects something about the temporal disposition of Dorothy. When the top of the hourglass is full of sand, Dorothy's position is only somewhat precarious. As the sand drains into the bottom, as the system loses its potential energy, Dorothy's position is rather more precarious. It is not precarious because of some event waiting for her out there in the future. Rather, it is precarious because of the present disposition of events in the world. The hourglass merely shares certain dispositional properties with Dorothy.

Caution is necessary in this treatment of dispositions, of course. We can't turn around and say that a disposition of this sort is something that will come about under certain circumstances (as Aristotle seemed to say in places). The notion of disposition has to be grounded without appeal to temporal notions. But there is no apparent reason to doubt that dispositions can be so grounded.

No Past

The situation only *seems* more complex when we move to the past tense. Again, in most non-Indo-European languages the so-called past is generally just some form of aspectual marker. Is the same true for Indo-European languages? The case is certainly good for English, in which our so-called past-tense morphemes are dead ringers for perfect aspectual markers. (A prime example is the '-ed' morpheme, which is taken to show that the event in question has culminated.)

Indeed, just as there are numerous reasons to be suspicious of the future tense, there are plenty of reasons to be equally suspicious of the past. For example, it is a notorious fact that past tense does not behave like past tense in counterfactuals. Consider (11).

(11)
If I had a million dollars....

This led Isard (1974) to speculate that the PAST morpheme does not refer to the past but has a more general sense of "remote." (In the case of (11), the sense would be "remote from reality.") A somewhat similar idea is pursued by Iatridou (1996), who develops a general notion of "exclusion" that covers both possible worlds and temporal intervals. In both cases there is a sense that some deeper third element underlies both tense and counterfactual modality—that tense can't simply be a primitive element that refers to the past.[11]

Although these approaches help to show that there is something more fundamental than the notion of tense, they probably don't go far enough for present purposes. Obviously, even if an event is remote, it is either remote in time or possibility, and what we really want to do is avoid the notion of temporal order (and temporal remoteness) altogether. Ideally, what we would like to say about so-called past-tense morphology is that it is really telling us something about the kind of evidence that we currently have for our claims.

On this score, we might benefit from the study of languages with *evidentials*.[12] In these languages (which range from Native American languages to Bulgarian), there are morphemes which have the function of indicating something about the source of the information that we have for our claim. For example, a particular morpheme might indicate that we have first-hand evidence for our claim. Another might indicate that our evidence is based on second-hand testimony. It is interesting to note that in some cases these morphemes are found in complementary distribution with whatever resources these languages have for expressing the past, perhaps suggesting that what we are taking to be tense morphemes or aspectual markers might actually be evidentials.

Here is the idea. In the case of modals we have so-called "root modals," or modals of obligation, which are often taken to be the core cases of modality; then there are also more sophisticated forms of modality (epistemic, metaphysical, etc.). Perhaps an analogous story holds for evidentials. That is, perhaps evidentials indicating whether the source of information is experience or testimony are the root evidentials, and then there are more abstract forms that include aspectual markers. A language like Bulgarian, then, which is often taken to have past-tense morphemes, perfect aspect, and evidential morphemes, would simply have three kinds of evidentials.

This idea is certainly consistent with current work on tense and on evidentiality. Izvorski (1997) has argued that the present perfect in many languages (ranging from Turkish to Norwegian to Bulgarian) in fact expresses what she calls the "perfect of evidentiality." For example, the examples in (12) all express a meaning akin to "I apparently/evidently arrived."

(12)
Turkish
gel   -miş   -im
come PERF   1SG
Bulgarian
Az sâm   došâl
I   be-1sg,PRES   come-P.PART
Norwegian
Jeg har   kommet
I   have-1SG,PRES come-P.PART

As Izvorski notes (ibid., p. 1), because "the perfect of evidentiality is observed in languages that are not all genetically related or geographically proximate, it is quite unlikely that the present perfect-evidential connection is simply a case of accidental syncretism."

What I am suggesting is consistent with these claims, but it is much more general. Why not suppose that *all* past-tense morphology is simply a kind of evidential? We have already seen that, philosophically speaking, past-tense claims really amount to claims about evidence that is currently available in the world. Why not make the obvious next step and take so-called past-tense morphology to, in fact, be a kind of evidential marker?

All of this is extremely sketchy, of course. My point is not that any of this is an inevitable consequence of the A-theory, but rather that this is a possible avenue of investigation that has been opened up. Whether this particular avenue will prove successful is far from clear, and I for one would be hesitant to speculate.

If this general strategy for the elimination of tense does pan out, however, it appears to leave us in a paradoxical situation. Throughout this book I have argued from the semantics of tense to the nature of time, and now I am suggesting that the grammatical category of tense can be dispensed with altogether. But this is not a genuine paradox; I am not kicking away the ladder that got us this far. There is a real grammatical phenomenon (or class of phenomena) that we sloppily call tense and which we suppose to be connected to temporal reference.

What we really have on our hands is most likely not a single phenomenon but a mixture of modality and evidentiality. Likewise, what I have been calling temporal anaphora can perhaps more accurately be considered a combination of propositional anaphora and implicit modal and evidential conjunctions (e.g., when-clause conjunctions). But whatever we choose to call these grammatical phenomena, we have seen how they allow us to exorcise the future and the past from semantical theory and consequently from metaphysics.

If we sweep away the grammatical category of tense in this fashion, we do not thereby end up with a "detensed" world—at least not in the sense advocated by Mellor and other B-theorists. To the contrary, by reducing talk of tense to evidentiality and aspect we are finally able to locate the indexical character of so-called temporal discourse in the world: it resides in the nature of evidentiality, as well as in the dispositions and aspectual properties that furnish the world.[13]

Just as metaphysics has no room for the future and the past, linguistics may have no call for a grammatical category of tense. Still, if the grammatical category of tense is dissolved into more basic and fruitful concepts, those concepts will have to preserve the basic features of the A-theory (including the indexical nature of so-called temporal discourse). Whatever the outcome, however, tense and time will remain intimately linked. And if they are ultimately dissolved, it stands to reason that they will be dissolved simultaneously, and that the resulting semantical concepts will in large measure mirror the resulting metaphysical concepts.

10.3   Conclusion

I hope that the illustrations I have given in this chapter have shown just how rich and far-reaching the consequences of adopting the A-theory will be. I realize that a number of philosophers and linguists may look at the emerging questions, loose ends, and philosophical puzzles as grounds for retreat. On the other hand, I see a new and largely unexplored intellectual territory opening up before us—one without nicely paved roads, and with dangers and logical conundrums at nearly every turn, but also one with new ways of thinking about old (often stalled) philosophical projects, and certainly one in which formerly disconnected philosophical puzzles begin to dovetail in marvelous ways.

Whether philosophers and linguists choose to pursue this course may depend in large measure on intellectual temperament. Do we stay on the well-charted B-theory approach in which we ignore the obvious big problems (like failure to account for indexicality) and are rewarded with a stable class of tractable mini-problems? Or do we leave that path for the wild and woolly world that the A-theory offers us? At this point I can speak only subjectively: I would prefer to leave the beaten path to explore the rich and complex consequences of the A-theory.

This is not an indictment of the idea of a community of scholars. To the contrary, I am hoping that others will join in this investigation of the A-theory—in part because one can see how vast and intricate this new world is. This book is a partial testimony to that. We have had to move through linguistics, the philosophy of mind, logic, and epistemology, and on into investigations of self-knowledge and memory. In view of the breadth and complexity of this undertaking, it is really impossible for any one person to work through the details or even anticipate what the final outcome will be.

More important, this need for a community effort is evidence of the progress that has been made in philosophy, and of how philosophy has outgrown the stage where an individual or a small group can synthesize the field and work out the details. No longer is it possible for an individual with the stature of Descartes or Leibniz to singlehandedly argue through a philosophical position. The problems have become so subtle, and their interrelationships so complex, that the lone genius must yield to collaborative interdisciplinary research teams. Among other things, this tells us that the age of giants has passed in philosophy; and while that is sad, perhaps it is also for the best.

Appendix P1

Is I-Language the Language
of Thought?

In section 1.3, I briefly entertained the possibility that I-language might be the language of thought (LOT). Here I return to that theme and examine in more detail some arguments against the thesis that have been offered by Ray Jackendoff and by Steven Pinker. Once again I will be unable to draw strong conclusions, but perhaps it is enough to see that the thesis is not out of the question, and indeed that the extant arguments against the thesis are very weak indeed. I will begin with Jackendoff's arguments and then move on to some of Pinker's.

Jackendoff (1993, p. 185) argues that if natural language were the language of thought it would be a mystery why it is possible to translate from one language to another—say from Japanese to English:

> The basic reason for keeping language and meaning separate is that pretty much anything we can say in one language can be translated into any other, preserving the thought that the original language conveys. This means that thoughts can't be embalmed in the form of any single language—they must be neutral as to what language they are to be expressed in.

Jackendoff concludes (ibid., p. 186) that a single independent thought "must be distinct from the linguistic garb in which it is clothed."

Let us set aside for the moment the question whether such meaning-preserving translations are possible. If they are possible, it is arguably because the LF representations of different languages (say, English and Chinese) do not vary markedly. Indeed, there is some speculation that the LFs for the two language might be identical, so it is hard to see what ice this argument is going to cut.[1]

Even less compelling, in my view, is Jackendoff's argument (ibid., p. 187) to the effect that some thinking is not present to consciousness but is intuitive. It is no part of an I-language/thought identity thesis that all I-language thoughts be conscious. Why should they be?

One of Jackendoff's arguments appears to speak directly to the possible identification of I-language with what he calls I-concepts. According to that argument
(ibid., p. 186), "the syntactic structure of language is built out of things like nouns
and verbs, prepositional phrases and tenses," but "thought isn't built out of such
units—thought concerns things like objects, actions, properties, and times." That
is, there is supposed to be a mismatch between language (even I-language) and
thought. I have to confess that I find the argument unpersuasive.

Suppose, as Jackendoff says, that language is built out of things like tenses,
and that thought concerns things like times. Wouldn't our natural supposition
be that the tenses of language concern things like times? So what prevents I-
language (with its tenses) from being the language of thought?

Of course, we have long known that there are apparent mismatches between
syntactic and semantic categories. For example, Williams (1983) has argued that
in certain environments indefinite NPs like 'a lawyer' are not quantified expressions but predicates, as, for example, in 'Mary is a lawyer'. Suppose this
story is right.[2] All that follows is that the interpretation of an NP will depend
upon the syntactic position in which it appears. This is no offense to the LOT
thesis, for the LOT thesis is not committed to the view that something of a certain syntactic category must always have the same interpretation; it is merely
committed to the view that we can state the principles of interpretation for the
language in question. It is a trivial matter to have the semantics reflect a difference in syntactic position.

But perhaps Jackendoff has something more in mind. Observing that some
nouns denote objects and others denote events, he argues that "object nouns like
'chair' and event nouns like 'earthquake,' which are not distinguished in syntax, must be radically distinguished in thoughts." Suppose that the thoughts involving the noun 'chair' are radically different from thoughts involving
'earthquake'. Exactly why are these not radically distinguished in the syntax?
Jackendoff, after all, proposes radically different lexical concepts for these sorts
of nouns. But what is the difference between a lexical concept and the sort of
lexical entry commonly assumed to occur in syntax?

It has been supposed since the earliest days of generative grammar that the
lexicon and structured lexical entries are parts of syntactic theory. In current
theory, it is even more urgent that the lexicon (robustly construed) be part of the
syntax. Why? Because in current theory (e.g., Chomsky 1995b) syntactic forms
are projected from richly structured lexical entries by virtue of several very
simple syntactic principles (greed, last resort, etc.). Without the lexicon, there

simply are no syntactic forms. Nor is there much point in saying that the conceptual representation of a noun or a verb is more richly structured than the corresponding representation that we get in the linguistic lexicon. It is not clear that there are any features of "conceptual representation" that are not relevant to the derivation of structure in the syntax. But in the second place, suppose that there was some property *foo* that a given conceptual representation C had but which the corresponding lexical entry L did not require for the derivation of linguistic forms in the syntax. Is there any reason to say that L *couldn't* or *shouldn't* contain the additional information? That is, is there any reason why L and C must be distinct?

Jackendoff (1992) appears to think that the richly structured "conceptual representations" that he gives are not part of "straight syntax." For example (p. 30), we "should be clear…that [conceptual structure] is as different from "straight" syntax (the grammar of NPs, VPs, etc.) as straight syntax is from phonology." But what *is* "straight syntax"? In current linguistic theory we have two levels of representation: PF and LF. Accordingly, if "straight syntax" means anything, it must refer to these two level of representation. If PF is part of straight syntax, then why is straight syntax distinct from phonology? Likewise, is there any non-question-begging way to argue that LF (which already encodes scope distinctions and at least as much lexical structure as is necessary to project phrase structure) cannot encode the information that Jackendoff attributes to conceptual structure? I can't imagine what such an argument would look like.

So much for Jackendoff's arguments. The arguments catalogued by Pinker (1994, p. 78ff.) fare no better. Let me consider those arguments in turn before offering criticism.

First, Pinker notes that thoughts are ambiguous, and argues that linguistic forms supposedly are not. He gives several amusing newspaper headlines (e.g., 'Stud Tires Out') as examples of this phenomenon, but other sorts of examples from written text are certainly legion.

Second, Pinker suggests that natural language representations lack "logical explicitness," meaning that certain inferences that intuitively make sense to us do not follow on the basis of natural language form: "English sentences do not embody the information that a processor needs to carry out common sense."

Third, Pinker argues that natural language is unable to account for coreference. We might introduce a subject in our discourse as "the tall blond man with one black shoe" but subsequently refer to the individual as "him." How do we know that we are talking about the same individual? Allegedly, nothing in the English language tells us.

Fourth, Pinker argues that natural language is unable to handle conversation specific words such as 'I', 'you', 'here', and 'now', since their meanings vary from context to context. Supposedly these cases do not pose a problem for a distinct language of thought.

Fifth and finally, Pinker argues that natural languages, unlike the language of thought, fail to account for synonymy. Thus, they allegedly cannot account for why 'John sprayed the wall with paint' and 'John sprayed paint onto the wall' mean the same thing.

Pinker's conclusion is that "people do not think in English or Chinese or Apache; they think in a language of thought." If English and Chinese and Apache are construed as E-languages, I do not dispute the conclusion (though I doubt these arguments support that conclusion[3]). On the other hand, if we take talk of these languages to be standing in for talk of various possible I-language states, the arguments fail miserably.

We have already seen that I-language representations are richly structured. The structure of LF representations seems particularly relevant when we consider Pinker's line of reasoning. Consider the argument from ambiguity. The inscription 'Every man loves some woman' has two distinct LF representations, which intuitively encode the relevant scope ambiguity. But of course other kinds of ambiguities are structurally encoded too—a famous example being Chomsky's 'Visiting relatives can be boring'. Is the expression 'visiting relatives' gerundive or a noun phrase? Clearly that makes all the difference.

There is no barrier to our saying that LF representations also reflect lexical ambiguity. If I say 'John went to the bank', there may be several possible interpretations of what I say, depending upon which lexical entry for 'bank' is inserted. I assume that in the I-language representation there is a fact about which lexical entry has been inserted.

Likewise, Pinker's example 'Stud Tires Out' reflects a combination of lexical and structural ambiguity. Is the LF representation structured as (1), or as (2)?

(1)

[$_{NP}$ Stud tires][(are) out]

(2)

[$_{NP}$ Stud][tires out]

Again, I assume that these two meanings correspond to two distinct LF representations.

Similar considerations apply to the logical explicitness of LF representations. Typical LF representations are no less explicit than anything offered in an AI inference engine, and there is certainly no barrier to defining logical inference rules directly for LF representations.[4]

Would LF representations fail to account for pronominal coreference? Again it is hard to see why. Indeed, much of the most interesting work in discourse-representation theory has assumed some form of the LF hypothesis and has defined the relevant anaphoric relations for LF representations. Likewise for the context dependency of indexicals and like expressions.

Finally, it is far from clear why two structurally diverse syntactic forms can't have the same meaning. Hence it is unclear why synonymy presents an argument against the identification of I-language (or even E-language) with the language of thought. It is entirely possible that there should be two distinct LOT representations with the same interpretation, so why shouldn't there be distinct I-language representations with the same interpretation? Now, it may well be that Pinker does not intend these arguments to cut against the candidacy of I-languages for the language of thought. One thing is clear, however. If so intended, the arguments fail miserably.[5]

Appendix P2
Language/World Isomorphism?[1]

In chapter 4 I argued for a strong connection between semantics and metaphysics, but I also hinted that there might be the possibility of an even stronger relation— one that takes the structure of language and the structure of the world to be isomorphic to each other. Let's call this thesis the language/world isomorphism (LWI) hypothesis.

The LWI label is a little bit crude, since the key idea is that there is an isomorphism holding between logical forms and the world. The basic idea is not restricted to the analytic tradition in philosophy. It has been at the root of the "semantic tradition" (in the sense of Coffa 1991) from Kant, through Bolzano and the early Wittgenstein, up to the present. As early as Kant we find some suggestion that there is an isomorphism between a representation and the thing represented:

[Representation] is that determination of the spirit (*Bestimmung der Seele*) that refers to other things. What I call referring (*Beziehen*) is when its features conform to those of the external things.[2]

[The representation] is composed out of its component concepts in the same way in which the entire represented thing is composed out of its parts. Just as, for example, one can say that the notes of a musical piece are a representation of the harmonic connection of the notes, not because each note is similar to each tone but because the notes are connected to each other just as the tones themselves.[3]

The most celebrated version of this general idea is surely the picture theory of meaning advanced by Wittgenstein in the *Tractatus*. On the view articulated there, just as "what a picture must have in common with reality, in order to be able to depict it—correctly or incorrectly—in the way it does, is its pictoral form" (1961b, 2.17), a proposition must be isomorphic in structure to a state of affairs in order to represent or be about that state of affairs.

Of course, we are not talking about the "surface form" of a proposition (whatever that might be). We are talking about the proposition "under analysis"—in other words, we are talking about its logical form. For Wittgenstein, only if one were to get down to the complete analysis of proposition would it reflect the structure of the world.[4]

Chomsky's Arguments against LWI

In Chomsky's recent writings contain a number of arguments designed to show that if we were to adopt a referential semantics the kind of ontology we would predict does not appear to track our intuitions about the kinds of things we are really talking about. Such theories allegedly commit us to things that we would never acknowledge as existing. They also allegedly commit us to types of things which are different from the types of things that we ordinarily suppose we are talking about. And the things we talk about are allegedly too unruly for such theories to handle. To have labels for all these possibilities, let us call them the "argument from implausible commitments," the "type-mismatch argument," and the "misbehaving-object argument." I will review all three of Chomsky's arguments before offering what I take to be the most natural reply to them.

The Argument from Implausible Commitments

Chomsky (1981, p. 324) draws attention to the fact that a referential semantics (apparently in conjunction with the LWI hypothesis) commits us to some apparently implausible entities (flaws for example) and suggests that we really can't take seriously a theory that commits us to such entities:

> If I say "the flaw in the argument is obvious, but it escaped John's attention," I am not committed to the absurd view that among things in the world are flaws, one of them in the argument in question. Nevertheless, the NP the flaw in the argument behaves in all relevant respects in the manner of the truly referential expression the coat in the closet. . . .

Pursuing a similar line of attack, Hornstein (1984, p. 58) has drawn attention to constructions like (1).

(1)
The average man is concerned about his weight.

Hornstein contends that "no one wishes to argue that there are objects that are average men in any meaningful sense."

The general concern introduced by examples like 'flaw in the argument' and 'the average man' is that the doctrine that there must be a tight connection between semantics and ontology is suspect, for it commits us to apparently absurd views.

This argument needs to be fixed up a bit before it is fully functional. As it stands, the argument makes the assumption that the logical form of these constructions is transparent—e.g., that the expression 'the flaw' really is nothing more than a simple NP containing a determiner and a noun. This is not such an innocent assumption. After all, the LWI hypothesis does not hold that there is an isomorphism between surface linguistic form and the world, but rather that there is an isomorphism between some ultimate logical form and the world. As Higginbotham (1985) has argued, before admitting a commitment to objects like flaws and average men we would have to look more closely at the underlying logical form of these constructions.

Higginbotham suggests that 'flaw in the argument' is parallel to 'bad singer'. The semantics of 'bad singer' is not such that we say someone is a bad singer iff he is bad and is a singer. Rather, we understand that someone is a singer and that his singing is bad. Likewise, we should not say that 'that is a flaw in the argument' is true iff that is a flaw and that is in the argument. Rather, we should say that the phrase is true iff something is an argument and it is flawed. Despite appearances, 'flaw' may not be a nominal; it may be a modifier like 'bad'.

Higginbotham offers a similar analysis for the case of 'the average man'. First, he notes that the expression is actually ambiguous between the case of an individual who has typical properties and the sense in which we say that the average family has 2.3 children. It is presumably the latter sense that is problematic here. In this latter case, Higginbotham suggests that 'average', despite appearing to be an adjective, is functioning as a kind of adverbial. The construction is parallel to examples like (2), discussed by Haïk (1983).

(2)
Let's have a quick cup of coffee.

Clearly, in (2) we are not suggesting that there are cups of coffee that are in some sense quick. Rather, 'quick' is behaving as an adverbial, modifying the activity. Higginbotham proposes that in a construction like (3) the analysis will be something along the lines of (3').

(3)
The average family has 2.3 children.

(3')
On average, a family has 2.3 children.

Chomsky might reply in a number of ways here.[5] Consider the somewhat more complex sentence (4).

(4)
Your report on the average family fails to make it clear that it has 2.3 children.[6]

Even if suitable glosses can be worked out, they will technical spellouts, of course, and these spellouts may introduce difficulties of their own. But the glosses themselves are not necessarily innocent. As Chomsky (personal communication) asks, are we to continue with the strategy for examples like (5)?

(5)
That his income is falling bothers John Doe.

That is, are we to take John Doe to be standing proxy for 'an average man', which in (5) is to be further unpacked with 'average' operating as a kind of adverbial? This begins to constitute a very strong and possibly counterintuitive thesis about the logical form of these constructions.

In the case of 'flaw in the argument', there are likewise responses to Higginbotham available. For example, Chomsky (personal communication) asks, how could one treat 'flaw' as a kind of predicate in an example like (6)?

(6)
We fixed three of the flaws you found but the rest of them resisted our efforts.

One possible answer is to say that (6) can be glossed as in (6'), where it is the steps in the argument that are intuitively flawed.

(6')
We fixed three of the flawed steps you found but the rest of them resisted our efforts.

Again glosses of this nature have to be justified at some point, and there is a heavy burden to show that the introduction of this proposed hidden structure comports well with the rest of what we know about the syntactic form of these constructions. Still more, it has to be shown that general rules are available, not only case-by-case fixes. Any attempt to pursue the Higginbotham course here will not be a trivial exercise.

The Type-Mismatch Argument
Even if we are comfortable with potentially counterintuitive entities such as flaws, Chomsky (1995a) notes that there is an apparent mismatch between the type individuation that objects and substances intuitively have and the type

individuation that a referential semantics will provide. To get clear on the issue, a terminological distinction will be helpful. Suppose we distinguish an I-substance from a P-substance, where a P-substance (if there is such a thing) is the sort of stuff that would play a role in physical theory (H_2O, for example) and an I-substance (if there is such) is the stuff that we are intuitively talking about when we use language (the intuitive referent of 'water'). To put the point in a more theory-neutral way, the I-substance is what it appears we are talking about based upon our use of language. The alleged problem is that P-substances and I-substances just don't match up right.

If, following Putnam (1975), 'water' refers to H_2O, then a referential semantics will assign a P-substance (H_2O) as the semantic value of 'water'. But the problem is that the stuff we are actually talking about when we use the term 'water'—the I-substance—is something else altogether. To see this, consider the fact that what we find in the Hudson River is called 'water' though it could hardly be considered H_2O. Also problematic is the fact that there are substances (e.g., iced tea) that chemically approximate H_2O much more closely than Hudson River water does, yet we don't call them 'water'. According to Chomsky, the situation is even more problematic than this. If someone at the water company were to pour tea leaves into the system, so that what came out of the tap was chemically identical to Lipton Iced Tea, we would still call it 'water'—although we might complain about its impurity.

Thus, what we are talking about when we use the term 'water'—the I-substance—depends upon the social setting in which we find that substance. But according to referential semantics, the meaning of the term is supposed to depend upon the chemical composition of the substance referred to—it is supposed to be a P-substance. Conclusion: Referential semantics (if respecting the LWI hypothesis) will not track the intuitive notion of meaning.

One might think it possible to get off the hook by appealing to social theories of external (referential) content (in the sense of Burge 1979). Rather than P-substances, we might posit S-substances: substances that are individuated according to community norms. Thus, while my concept of water might not accord with H_2O, it might still accord with a certain socially determined object that has the property of being water when it comes from the faucet but not when it is served at a restaurant. The problem here is that there are plenty of examples where such S-substances (if there could be such things) would not track our intuitions about the extension of terms—Burge's own examples about tharthritis and brisket are cases in point. That is, there is a mismatch between I-substances and S-substances. We will come back to this point a bit later.

The Misbehaving-Object Argument

There are a number of interesting features to the water/tea story, one of which can be broken out as a separate objection to referential semantics.

We have already seen in the type-mismatch argument that I-substances don't track P-substances, but there is another problem. The water/tea story also seems to show that the I-substance we are talking about when we use the term 'water' is a most ill-behaved sort of substance. Something may cease to be water even if no internal physical changes have taken place. For example, the same chemical compound is water when it comes from the tap but ceases to be water when it is served at a restaurant. If that is the intuitive character of I-substances, then there is really little hope that referential semantics can "give the reference" of what we talk about when we talk about 'water' and 'tea', since referential semantics is supposedly going to say that the content of these terms is H_2O in the first case and H_2O plus certain other elements in the latter. That is, I-substances are so unruly that it is wildly implausible to suppose that they could have any counterparts in the physical world. Hence, they have no counterparts that a referential semantics could utilize as their referents.

Chomsky (1975, p. 203) makes a related if somewhat more general point when notes that the very notion of whether we are talking about a single object or a collection of objects turns on any number of social and institutional factors:

We do not regard a herd of cattle as a physical object, but rather as a collection, though there would be no logical incoherence in the notion of a scattered object, as Quine, Goodman, and others have made clear. But even spatiotemporal contiguity does not suffice as a general condition. One wing of an airplane is an object, but its left half, though equally continuous, is not. . . . Furthermore, scattered entities can be taken to be single physical objects under some conditions: consider a picket fence with breaks, or a Calder mobile. The latter is a "thing," whereas a collection of leaves on a tree is not. The reason, apparently, is that the mobile is created by an act of human will. If this is correct, then beliefs about human will and action and intention play a crucial role in determining even the most simple and elementary of concepts.

Moving that discussion into the current debate, we might say that it is implausible for even such simple semantic concepts as object and collection to correspond in any interesting sense with P-substances.

Analysis of the Arguments: Some Replies

The conclusion that we can draw from examples like the above is that any referential semantics purporting to respect the LWI hypothesis is going to misfire badly since it is bound to utilize as referents P-substances, which just don't track the intuitive meanings of natural language expressions.

One reply for the semanticist is to simply reject the LWI hypothesis. That is, one could say: Yes, a semantic theory is concerned about the connection between language and the world (as part of a four-place relation also involving speaker and context), but this says nothing about there being an isomorphic mapping between primitive linguistic expressions (under analysis) and things (or kinds of things) in the world. If there is a single lexical entry corresponding to 'water', it does not map onto any single substance; rather, it maps onto various things, depending on circumstances, discourse participants, etc. Such theories are no less referential than those that respect LWI. After all, they are still in the business of articulating language/world relations, albeit through a very complicated story, and despite the fact that these relations are often dynamic one-to-many relations. Is there another way out?

Why not give up the P- and S-substances? That is, why not bite the metaphysical bullet and acknowledge that there really are I-substances—that is, things like flaws. They are clearly not logically absurd entities, and it need not be conceded that they are particularly odd entities. In the case of flaws, at least, one might say that they are altogether common in the arguments one runs across, and one might wonder why they should be considered any less real than, say, tables and chairs. Likewise, coats hanging in the closet need not have any particular ontological priority over average families and flaws.

But is this a metaphysical bullet that we can bite? Can our ontology admit such things? Here (finally) we come to the issue of "aspects of the world" and the kinds of things that we can be realists about.

Aspects of the World

Operating throughout all three of Chomsky's arguments cited above is the assumption (shared with Putnam and others) that P-substances are the kinds of substances that a referential semantics is going to favor. For example, Chomsky (1993) remarks:

To be an Intentional Realist, it would seem, is about as plausible as being a Desk- or Sound-of-Language- or Cat- or Matter-Realist; not that there are no such things as desks, etc., but that in the domain where questions of realism arise in a serious way, in the context of the search for laws of nature, objects are not conceived from the peculiar perspectives provided by the concepts of common sense.

But why should we make the assumption that "the domain where questions of realism arise in a serious way" is "in the context of the search for laws of nature"? One possible answer would be that physical theory gets to say what is real, and that hence if we are to have a genuine referential semantics in which the referents are "real" existing entities then we are stuck with the kinds of entities and substances posited by physical theory. But this answer makes a strong assumption about scientific realism—an assumption that is controversial to say the least, and most likely false in my view.

A great deal of literature in the philosophy of science (e.g., van Fraassen 1980) holds that the entities posited by science do not exist in the same sense as midsize earthbound objects like tables and chairs. Pursuing this line of thinking, we might say that scientific theories, despite their great interest and utility, are not the arbiters of what is real.

If we set aside the exclusive claim of the physical sciences on our ontology (i.e., if we dismiss P-substances as our semantic values), then we may well find that I-substances are entirely plausible candidates for the referents of a semantic theory. For example, it may be that the semantic value of 'water' just is water—the complicated I-substance that moves through pipes into our homes. If we take that route, then it is far from clear that the LWI hypothesis must be surrendered.[7]

But perhaps the appeal to I-substances is a cheat,[8] or perhaps it is entirely parasitic on the notion of I-language representations. What is an I-substance if not simply "whatever corresponds to a particular I-language representation"? Seen in this light, isn't the talk of I-substance vacuous? At best, isn't it a misleading way of talking about I-language?

Here we need to head off a confusion. Even if it should turn out that I-language representations are in some sense prior to I-substances (perhaps logically prior or metaphysically prior), it does not follow that our path as empirical investigators will begin with the linguistic representations. The idea is that the linguistic representations will indeed underwrite our metaphysical intuitions, but that because of this we can expect our metaphysical intuitions to shed some light on the nature of I-language. A concrete example: The lexical entry for 'water', when fully fleshed out, is bound to be a very complicated representation (at least, if it is to interact in complex ways with other I-language representations). Our knowledge of this fact does not come from direct investigation of the lexicon; rather, it is guided by metaphysical intuitions about water like those that Chomsky evinces in his articles—intuitions that take into account rich contextual information about whether the material in question is coming from a faucet or whether it is being served in a restaurant.

It will not do to argue that Chomsky's water intuitions are not metaphysical—that they are only about his "I-concept" of water, or about the phenomenology of water. If there is no world beyond these concepts or beyond the phenomenology, then once we have made the step from talking about linguistic representations to talk of concepts, or phenomena, or sense data, we have basically stepped into the world—or as far into it as we are ever going to get.[9]

Of course, this picture is as Kantian as it can be. We have metaphysical intuitions, and we want to know what underwrites those intuitions. The first departure from Kant lies in the answer given—not "the categories of reason" but rather the structure of I-language. The second departure lies in the fact that our approach need not be entirely transcendental. We do have substantial independent knowledge of the language faculty, and we can use that knowledge to gain insight into the nature of reality.

Appendix T1
A Basic Quantificational Fragment

Following Chomsky (1995b), suppose that a "sentence" is in fact an ordered pair of representations ⟨PF, LF⟩, where PF representations interface with the "perceptual-articulatory" component and LF representations interface with the "conceptual-intensional" system (or, as I would prefer to put it, LF is the level of representation that is visible to the semantic theory).

Since our principal interest will be with LF representations, a few words are in order about their nature (for present purposes we can skip over their derivation). I will assume, following work dating back four decades now, that the form of a linguistic representation can be characterized as a branching tree structure like the following.[1]

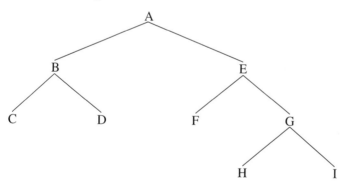

In this particular case we have a binary branching structure, but there is an empirical question as to whether other forms are possible in natural language.[2] The terminal nodes of such a structure will be the lexical items, and the branching nodes will be labels for grammatical categories S (clause), NP (noun phrase), VP (verb phrase), PP (prepositional phrase), and so on. Of particular interest to us are the geometric relations that hold between the nodes of such structures, and the role that those relations play in allowing us to formally characterize the notion of scope in natural language.[3]

Recall, first, that in formal logics such as the propositional calculus we can utilize parentheses as scope markers. For example, in '~(A∨B)&(C∨D)' we understand that the negation is to have scope over the first conjunct ('A∨B') but not the second. Many philosophers have despaired (and some have rejoiced) that matters are apparently not so tidy in natural language. In fact, however, very tight definitions of scope are possible for the kinds of representations utilized in linguistic theory.

Let us say that a node A *dominates* B iff there is a path moving uniformly down the tree from A to B. So, for example, in the diagram above, A dominates all other nodes, and B dominates only C and D. Following Reinhart (1976), we can also define a relation of *c-command* as follows: X c-commands Y iff neither of X and Y dominates the other and every branching node dominating X also dominates Y. For example, according to this definition, B will c-command I (because the first branching node dominating B, that is A, also dominates I), but C will not c-command I. C-command is a relatively simple geometrical relation on phrase-structure representations, but it is also a very good candidate for specifying scope relations in natural language. That is, we can assume for purposes of this book that c-command just is scope.[4]

We can further assume, following work dating back to Chomsky (1976) and May (1977), that LF representations are generated (in part) by movement of quantified expressions. For example, a sentence with the "surface form" shown in (1) will have the (LF) representation shown in (2), where 'e' is a co-indexed trace of movement (later we will see how these traces can be treated as bound variables).[5]

(1)
John loves everyone

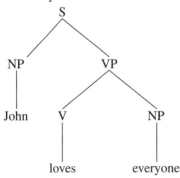

(2)

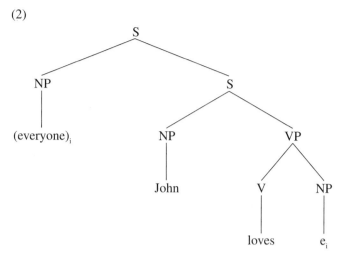

We can also "linearize" representations like (2) as in (3).

(3)

[$_S$ [$_{NP}$ everyone]$_i$ [$_S$ [$_{NP}$ John][$_{VP}$ [$_V$ loves][$_{NP}$ e$_i$]]]]

It is often supposed that certain ambiguities in natural language reflect multiple LF representations for a given utterance. Thus, an utterance of (4) will have two different possible LF representations, reflecting two possible scope relations that might hold between the noun phrases.

(4)

Every man loves some woman

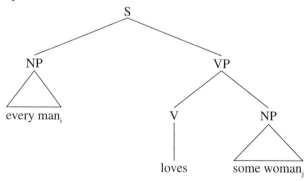

(4')

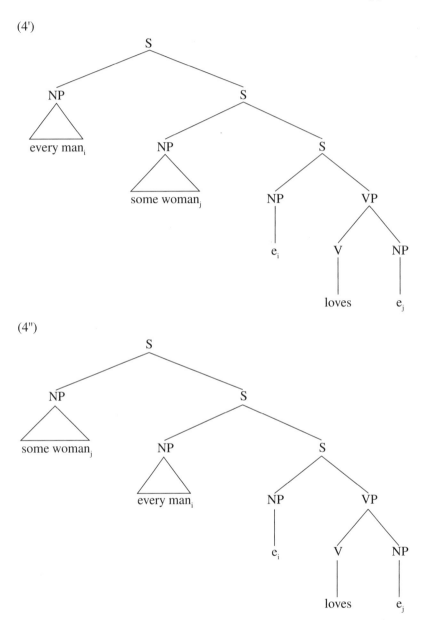

(4")

The fragment introduced in section 2.2 incorporated the distinction between predicates and referring expressions. Here, following Larson and Ludlow (1993) and Larson and Segal (1995), we expand that fragment by adding basic first-order quantification, as well as some basic resources for more complex noun phrases.

Syntax of L1

S → S1 and/or S2
S → it is not the case that S
S → NP VP
VP → V2 NP
VP → V1
V1 → <u>barks</u>, <u>walks</u>
V2 → <u>sees</u>, <u>likes</u>
NP → <u>every</u> N
NP → <u>some</u> N
NP → <u>Smith</u>, <u>Jones</u>
N → <u>man</u>, <u>woman</u>, <u>cat</u>, <u>dog</u>

In addition to these simple phrase-structure rules, we can assume (following our discussion above) that there is a rule that maps the product of these rules onto other phrase markers (which will be called LF representations). This rule—which, following Chomsky (1976) and May (1977, 1985), we can call "QR", for quantifier raising—states that a quantified noun phrase can be Chomsky-adjoined to S, leaving behind a co-indexed trace. The resulting LF representation is analogous to a restricted quantifier form of first-order logic. As was noted above, QR will also provide a way of representing certain scope ambiguities. (Recall the LF representations given for 'Every man loves some woman' in (4') and (4").)

But how do these two representations give rise to two distinct interpretations, and precisely what is the relation between the quantified noun phrases and their co-indexed traces? For that matter, precisely how can c-command function as scope?

The short answer to these questions is that the valuation predicate Val is defined in such a way that the co-indexed traces are treated as bound variables in the sense familiar from first-order logic, and the compositional axioms of the T-theory ensure that c-command relations will reflect scope relations. The basic idea is to incorporate Tarski's idea of sequences into the axioms of our T-theory. Specifically, we can introduce the predicate Val(A, B, σ) to be read as "A is the value of B with respect to assignment σ," where σ is an assignment of values to all the variables of the language.

If we think of the variables as being of the form x_i, where i is a numerical subscript, then a sequence σ will assign an object to each variable x_i. This idea will be reflected in our basic axiom for the interpretation of trace as in (5), where $\sigma(i)$ is the ith position of the sequence.

(5)
Val(x, t_i, σ) iff x = $\sigma(i)$ for i ≥ 1.

The crucial axioms for the interpretation of the quantifiers are as shown in (6), where $\sigma' \approx_i \sigma$ indicates that the sequence σ' differs from σ at most in the ith position.

(6)

a.

Val(T, $[_S \ [_{NPi} \ \underline{\text{every}} \ N \ ], \ S1 \ ], \ \sigma$) iff for every $\sigma' \approx_i \sigma$ such that Val($\sigma'(i), N, \sigma$), Val(T, S1, σ')

b.

Val(T, $[_S \ [_{NPi} \ \underline{\text{some}} \ N \ ], \ S1 \ ], \ s$) iff for some $\sigma' \approx_i \sigma$ such that Val($\sigma'(i), N, \sigma$), Val(T, S1, σ')

c.

Val(T, $[_S \ NP_i \ S1 \ ], \ \sigma$) iff for $\sigma' \approx_i \sigma$ such that Val($\sigma'(i), NP, \sigma$), Val(t, S1, σ')

With the axioms and rules introduced thus far, the theorem derived for 'Every dog barks' would be as shown in (7).

(7)

Val(T, $[_S \ [_{NP} \ \underline{\text{every}} \ [_N \ \underline{\text{dog}}]]_i \ [_S \ [_{NP} \ e_i] \ [_{VP} \ [_{V1} \ \underline{\text{barks}}]]]]$) iff for every $\sigma' \approx_i \sigma$ such that $\sigma'(i)$ is a dog, $\sigma'(i)$ barks

It is also possible to incorporate generalized quantifier theory into this framework (see chapter 8 of Larson and Segal 1995); however, for current purposes we can make do with the two standard first-order quantifiers 'every' and 'some'.

We are now ready to see how the c-command relation cashes out the notion of scope. No stipulation is necessary; as Larson and Segal (ibid., p. 252 ff.) note, the situation is exactly parallel to the way scope and quantifier/variable binding are related in the standard predicate calculus.

As an illustration, consider the sort of structure that would arise in the multiply quantified sentence 'every man loves some woman'. Abstracting from detail, the structure will be as follows:

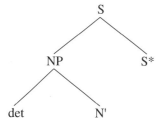

Given the way the axioms are defined for this structure, the interpretation of S* will be relativized to the sequence introduced in the resolution of the S node.

Thus, Larson and Segal offer the following contrasting theorems, reflecting the different interpretations of the two LFs:

(8)
Val(T, [$_S$ [$_{NP}$ every [$_N$ man]]$_i$ [$_{S^*}$ [$_{NP}$ some [$_N$ woman]] [$_{S'}$ [$_{NP}$ e$_i$] [$_{VP}$ [$_{V2}$ loves] [$_{NP}$ e$_j$]]]]) iff for every $\sigma' \approx_i \sigma$ such that $\sigma'(i)$ is a man, for some $\sigma'' \approx_j \sigma'$ such that $\sigma''(j)$ is a woman, $\sigma''(i)$ loves $\sigma''(j)$

(9)
Val(T, [$_S$ [$_{NP}$ some [$_N$ woman]]$_i$ [$_{S^*}$ [$_{NP}$ every [$_N$ man]] [$_{S'}$ [$_{NP}$ e$_i$] [$_{VP}$ [$_{V2}$ loves] [$_{NP}$ e$_j$]]]]) iff for some $\sigma' \approx_i \sigma$ such that $\sigma'(i)$ is a woman, for every $\sigma'' \approx_j \sigma'$ such that $\sigma''(j)$ is a man, $\sigma''(i)$ loves $\sigma''(j)$

In the words of Larson and Segal (ibid., p. 253): "The correlation [between scope and c-command] is a simple outcome of the way in which the semantics uses the object-language syntax to construct the T sentence, compositionally building parts of the latter using the 'skeleton' provided by the former."

Semantics of L1

I now introduce a three-place Val predicate Val(A, B, C), to be read as "A is the value of B with respect to assignment C."

Terminal Nodes

(1)
a.
Val(x, Smith, σ) iff x = Smith
Val(x, Jones, σ) iff x = Jones
Val(x, t$_i$, σ) iff x = $\sigma(i)$ for i $\geq$ 1
b.
Val(x, dog, σ) iff x is a dog
Val(x, cat, σ) iff x is a cat
Val(x, man, σ) iff x is a man
Val(x, woman, σ) iff x is a woman
c.
Val(x, barks, σ) iff x barks
Val(x, walks, σ) iff x walks
d.
Val($\langle x,y \rangle$, sees, σ) iff x sees y
Val($\langle x,y \rangle$, likes, σ) iff x likes y

Nonterminal Nodes

(2)

a.

Val(T, [$_S$ NP VP], σ) iff for some x, Val(x, NP, σ) and Val(x, VP, σ)

b.

Val(x, [$_{VP}$ V NP], σ) iff for some y, Val(⟨x,y⟩, V, σ) and Val(y, NP, σ)

c.

Val(x, [$_α$ β], σ) iff Val(x, β, σ) (where α ranges over categories, and β ranges over categories and lexical items)

(3)

a.

Val(T, [$_S$ S1 <u>and</u> S2], σ) iff it is both the case that Val(T, S1, σ) and Val(T, S2, σ)

b.

Val(T, [$_S$ S1 <u>or</u> S2], σ) iff either Val(T, S1, σ) or Val(T, S2, σ)

c.

Val(T, [$_S$ <u>it is not the case that</u> S1], σ) iff it is not the case that Val(T, S1, σ)

(4)

a.

Val(T, [$_S$ [$_{NPi}$ <u>every</u> N], S1], σ) iff for every σ' ≈$_i$ σ such that Val(σ'(i), N, σ), Val(T, S1, σ')

b.

Val(T, [$_S$ [$_{NPi}$ <u>some</u> N], S1], s) iff
for some σ' ≈$_i$ σ such that Val(σ'(i), N, σ), Val(T, S1, σ')

c.

Val(T, [$_S$ NP$_i$ S1], σ) iff for σ' ≈$_i$ σ such that Val(σ'(i), NP, σ), Val(T, S1, σ')

Definitions

i.

For any sequence σ, σ(i) is the ith element of σ.

ii.

For any sequences σ and σ', σ' ≈$_i$ σ iff σ' differs from σ at most on σ'(i).

iii.

Val(T, S) iff Val(T, S, σ) for all sequences σ.

Finally, let us again make use of two derivation rules that were introduced with the language L.

Derivation Rules
(SoE)

$$\ldots \alpha \ldots$$
$$\alpha \text{ iff } \beta$$
———

therefore $\ldots \beta \ldots$

(SoI)

$$\phi \text{ iff for some } x, x = \alpha \text{ and } \ldots x \ldots$$
————————————

therefore ϕ iff $\ldots \alpha \ldots$

Recall that these are not logical rules, and that the steps in each derivation are much more tightly constrained than they would be if the full resources of logic were at our disposal. These are simply rules for deriving T-theorems.

This fragment is significantly more involved than the language L introduced earlier, and it might be useful to work through a derivation in order to more fully grasp the mechanisms at play. Consider a derivation for the sentence 'Every dog barks'. Recall that the truth definition will apply to a structural description of a sentence, and in this case will apply to the LF of the sentence: $[_S [_{NP} \text{every} [_N \text{dog}]]_i$ $[_S [_{NP} e_i] [_{VP} [_{V1} \text{barks}]]]]$. The derivation will proceed as follows:

$[_S [_{NP} \text{every} [_N \text{dog}]]_i [_S [_{NP} e_i] [_{VP} [_{V1} \text{barks}]]]]$ is true iff

(1)
for every $\sigma' \approx_i \sigma$ such that $\text{Val}(\sigma'(i), [_N \text{dog}], \sigma)$, $\text{Val}(T, [_S [_{NP} e_i] [_{VP} [_{V1} \text{barks}]]]], \sigma')$
[instance of (4a)]

(2)
for every $\sigma' \approx_i \sigma$ such that $\text{Val}(\sigma'(i), [_N \text{dog}], \sigma)$, for some x, $\text{Val}(x, [_{NP} e_i], \sigma')$
and $\text{Val}(x, [_{VP} [_{V1} \text{barks}]], \sigma')$
[from (1), by (2a), SoE]

(3)
for every $\sigma' \approx_i \sigma$ such that $\text{Val}(\sigma'(i), \text{dog}, \sigma)$, for some x, $\text{Val}(x, e_i, \sigma')$ and
$\text{Val}(x, \text{barks}, \sigma')$
[from (2), by (2c), SoE]

(4)
for every $\sigma' \approx_i \sigma$ such that $\sigma'(i)$ is a dog, for some x, $x = \sigma'(i)$ and x barks
[from (3), by (1a), (1b), (1c), SoE]

(5)
for every $\sigma' \approx_i \sigma$ such that $\sigma'(i)$ is a dog, $\sigma'(i)$ barks
[from (4) by SoI]

Appendix T2

A Quantificational Fragment with Events

(from Larson and Segal 1995)

Following a proposal due to Davidson (1967b), we can hold that there is an implicit quantification over events in English action sentences like 'John buttered the toast slowly'. Subsequent writing in this vein has suggested that the logical form is even more complex than this, perhaps that it is along the lines of 'There is an event e, such that e is a buttering, John is the agent of e, the toast is the patient of e, e is past, and e is slow'.[2]

The standard assumption is that the Davidsonian event analysis will require us to introduce an explicit reference event quantification into the syntax itself. We can probably do this, but, as Larson and Segal (1995) have shown, it is unnecessary.

Suppose that we have a simple extension to the language discussed in appendix T1, so that we have adverbs and prepositions introduced as follows.

VP → V ADV
VP → V PP
P → P NP
ADV → slowly, quickly
P → in, with
V → swims, kicks
NP → the lake

Then the task is to show how the resulting structures can be interpreted as involving a kind of quantification over events. As with the simpler fragment in appendix T1, the axioms for the adverbs and prepositions will essentially be disquotational. The axioms for the verbs will likewise be disquotational with the twist that they are taken to be predicates of events, rather than individuals. Axioms for NPs will be as in the quantificational fragment introduced in appendix T1.

The crucial step for introducing the event structure will come in the rule for the interpretation of S and the rule for the interpretation of the VP. The first rule introduces the agency thematic role, the second introduces the theme (or some other relevant thematic role, depending upon a number of factors).[3] The rules for the ADV and PP categories will be straightforward.

Syntax of L2

Add the following to the syntax of L1:

VP → V ADV
VP → V PP
P → P NP
ADV → slowly, quickly
P → in, with
V → swims, kicks
NP → the lake

Semantics for L2[4]

Terminal Symbols

(1)
a.
Val(e, <u>slowly</u>, σ) iff e is slow (for something of e's kind)
Val(e, <u>quickly</u>, σ) iff e is quick (for something of e's kind)
b.
Val(⟨e,x⟩, <u>in</u>, σ) iff e is in x
c.
Val(e, <u>swims</u>, σ) iff e is a (event of) swimming
Val(e, <u>kicks</u>, σ) iff e is a kicking
Val(e, <u>barks</u>, σ) iff e is a barking
Val(e, <u>walks</u>, σ) iff e is a walking
Val(e, <u>sees</u>, σ) iff e is a seeing
Val(e, <u>likes</u>, σ) iff e is a liking
d.
Val(x, <u>Smith</u>, σ) iff x = Smith
Val(x, <u>Jones</u>, σ) iff x = Jones
Val(x, <u>the lake</u>, σ) iff x = the lake
Val(x, t_i, σ) iff x = σ(i) for i ≥ 1

e.

Val(x, <u>dog</u>, σ) iff x is a dog

Val(x, <u>man</u>, σ) iff x is a man

Val(x, <u>woman</u>, σ) iff x is a woman

Nonterminal Nodes

(2)

a.

Val(T, [$_S$ NP VP], σ) iff, for some e, Val(e, VP, σ) and, for some x, x is the agent of e and Val(x, NP, σ)

b.

Val(e, [$_{VP}$ V NP], σ) iff Val(e, V, σ) and, for some y, y is the theme of e and Val(y, NP, σ)

c.

Val(e, [$_{VP}$ V ADV], σ) iff Val(e, V, σ) and Val(e, ADV, σ)

d.

Val(e, [$_{VP}$ V PP], σ) iff Val(e, V, σ) and Val(e, PP, σ)

e.

Val(e, [$_{PP}$ P NP], σ) iff, for some z, Val(⟨e,z⟩, P, σ) and Val(z, NP, σ)

f.

Val(x, [$_α$ β], σ) iff Val(x, β, σ) (where α ranges over categories, and β ranges over categories and lexical items)

(3)

a.

Val(T, [$_S$ S1 <u>and</u> S2], σ) iff it is both the case that Val(T, S1, σ) and Val(T, S2, σ)

b.

Val(T, [$_S$ S1 <u>or</u> S2], σ) iff either Val(T, S1, σ) or Val(T, S2, σ)

c.

Val(T, [$_S$ <u>it is not the case that</u> S1], σ) iff it is not the case that Val(T, S1, σ)

(4)

a.

Val(T, [$_S$ [$_{NPi}$ <u>every</u> N], S1], σ) iff for every σ' ≈$_i$ σ such that Val(σ'(i), N, σ), Val(T, S1, σ')

b.

Val(T, [$_S$ [$_{NPi}$ <u>some</u> N], S1], σ) iff, for some σ' ≈$_i$ σ such that Val(σ'(i), N, σ), Val(T, S1, σ')

c.

Val(T, [$_S$ NP$_i$ S1], σ) iff, for σ' ≈$_i$ σ such that Val(σ'(i), NP, σ), Val(T, S1, σ')

(5)

derivation rules (repeated from L1)

(SoE)

$$\ldots α \ldots$$
$$α \text{ iff } β$$
_____

therefore   . . . β . . .

(SoI)

φ iff for some x, x = α and . . . x . . .
_____

therefore φ iff . . . α . . .

definitions

i.

For any sequence σ, σ(i) is the ith element of σ.

ii.

For any sequences σ, σ', σ' ≈$_i$ σ iff σ' differs from σ at most on σ'(i).

iii.

Val(T, S) iff Val(T, S, σ) for all sequences σ.

To better understand how these axioms may be deployed, consider a couple of sample derivations. First, consider the derivation of the truth conditions for the sentence 'Smith swims slowly'.

Val(T, [$_S$ [$_{NP}$ Smith][$_{VP}$ [$_V$ swims][$_{ADV}$ slowly]]]) iff . . .

(1)

there is an e, Val (e, [$_{VP}$ [$_V$ swims][$_{ADV}$ slowly]]], σ), and for some x, x is the agent of e, and Val(x, [$_{NP}$ Smith], σ)
[instance of (2a)]

(2)

there is an e, Val (e, [$_V$ swims], σ) and Val (e, [$_{ADV}$ slowly], σ), and, for some x, x is the agent of e, and Val(x, [$_{NP}$ Smith], σ)
[from (1) by (2c), SoE]

(3)

there is an e, e is a swimming and Val(e, [$_{ADV}$ slowly], σ), and, for some x, x is the agent of e, and Val(x, [$_{NP}$ Smith], σ)
[from (2) by (1c), SoE]

(4)

there is an e, e is a swimming and e is slow, and, for some x, x is the agent of e, and Val(x, [$_{NP}$ Smith], σ)
[from (3) by (1a), SoE]

(5)

there is an e, e is a swimming and e is slow, and, for some x, x is the agent of e, and x = Smith
[from (4) by (1d), SoE]

(6)

there is an e, e is a swimming and e is slow, and Smith is the agent of e
[from (5) by SoI]

In this fragment, prepositional phrases function basically like adverbs, although the derivations for sentences containing PPs are slightly more complex. To see this, consider the derivation of the truth conditions for the sentence 'Smith swims in the lake'.

Val(T, [$_S$ [$_{NP}$ Smith][$_{VP}$ [$_V$ swims][$_{PP}$ [$_P$ in] [$_{NP}$ the lake]]]]), iff . . .

(1)

there is an e, Val(e, [$_{VP}$ [$_V$ swims][$_{PP}$ [$_P$ in][$_{NP}$ the lake]]], σ), and, for some x, x is the agent of e, and Val(x, [$_{NP}$ Smith], σ)
[instance of (2a)]

(2)

there is an e, Val(e, [$_V$ swims], σ) and Val(e, [$_{PP}$ [$_P$ in] [$_{NP}$ the lake]], σ) and for some x, x is the agent of e, and Val(x, [$_{NP}$ Smith], σ)
[from (1) by (2d), SoE]

(3)

there is an e, Val(e, [$_V$ swims], σ) and, for some z, Val(⟨e,z⟩, [$_P$ in], σ) and Val(z, [$_{NP}$ the lake]], σ), and for some x, x is the agent of e, and Val(x, [$_{NP}$ Smith], σ)
[from (2) by (2e), SoE]

(4)

there is an e, Val(e, [$_V$ swims], σ) and, for some z, e is in z and Val(z, [$_{NP}$ the lake]], σ), and for some x, x is the agent of e, and Val(x, [$_{NP}$ Smith], σ)
[from (3) by (1b), SoE]

(5)

there is an e, e is a swimming and for some z, e is in z and Val(z, [$_{NP}$ the lake]], σ), and for some x, x is the agent of e, and Val(x, [$_{NP}$ Smith], σ)
[from (4) by (1c), SoE]

(6)

there is an e, e is a swimming and for some z, e is in z and z = the lake, and
for some x, x is the agent of e, and x = Smith
[from (5) by (1d), SoE]

(7)

there is an e, e is a swimming and e is in the lake, and Smith is the agent of e
[from (6) by SoI]

Appendix T3

A Fragment with ILFs for Propositional Attitudes

(from Larson and Ludlow 1993)

Syntax of L3

Same as L1, with addition of the following:

$VP \rightarrow V_{int}S$
$V_{int} \rightarrow$ believes, claims, thinks

Semantics of L3

Terminal Nodes

(1)
a.
Val(x, <u>Smith,</u> σ) iff x = Smith
Val(x, <u>Jones,</u> σ) iff x = Jones
Val(x, t_i, σ) iff x = σ(i) for i ≥ 1
b.
Val(x, <u>dog</u>, σ) iff x is a dog
Val(x, <u>cat,</u> σ) iff x is a cat
Val(x, <u>man</u>, σ) iff x is a man
Val(x, <u>woman</u>, σ) iff x is a woman
c.
Val(x, <u>barks</u>, σ) iff x barks
Val(x, <u>walks</u>, σ) iff x walks
d.
Val(⟨x,y⟩, <u>sees</u>, σ) iff x sees y
Val(⟨x,y⟩, <u>likes</u>, σ) iff x likes y
Val(⟨x,y⟩, <u>believes</u>, σ) iff x believes y
Val(⟨x,y⟩, <u>thinks</u>, σ) iff x thinks y

Val($\langle x,y \rangle$, <u>claims</u>, σ) iff x claims y

Nonterminal Nodes

(2)

a.

Val(T, [$_S$ NP VP], σ) iff, for some x, Val(x, NP, σ) and Val(x, VP, σ)

b.

Val(x, [$_{VP}$ V NP], σ) iff, for some y, Val($\langle x,y \rangle$, V, σ) and Val(y, NP, σ)

c.

Val(x, [$_\alpha$ β], σ) iff Val(x, β, σ) (where α ranges over categories, and β ranges over categories and lexical items)

d.

Val(x, [$_{VP}$ V$_{int}$S], σ) iff, for some y, Val($\langle x,y \rangle$, V$_{int}$, σ) and y = []S[] w.r.t. σ

(3)

a.

Val(T, [$_S$ S1 <u>and</u> S2], σ) iff it is both the case that Val(T, S1, σ) and Val(T, S2, σ)

b.

Val(T, [$_S$ S1 <u>or</u> S2], σ) iff either Val(T, S1, σ) or Val(T, S2, σ)

c.

Val(T, [$_S$ <u>it is not the case that</u> S1], σ) iff it is not the case that Val(T, S1, σ)

(4)

a.

Val(T, [$_S$ [$_{NPi}$ <u>every</u> N], S1], σ) iff, for every $\sigma' \approx_i \sigma$ such that Val(σ'(i), N, σ), Val(T, S1, σ')

b.

Val(T, [$_S$ [$_{NPi}$ <u>some</u> N], S1], σ) iff, for some $\sigma' \approx_i \sigma$ such that Val(σ'(i), N, σ), Val(T, S1, σ')

c.

Val(T, [$_S$ NP$_i$ S1], σ) iff, for $\sigma' \approx_i \sigma$ such that Val(σ'(i), NP, σ), Val(T, S1, σ')

Definitions (repeated from L1)

i.

For any sequence σ, σ(i) is the ith element of σ.

ii.

For any sequences σ, σ', $\sigma' \approx_i \sigma$ iff σ' differs from σ at most on σ'(i).

iii.

Val(T, S) iff Val(T, S, σ) for all sequences σ.

Definition: Let α be a phrase marker with root S, let σ be a sequence, and for each node β of α, let x be the semantic value assigned to β, assuming Val(T, α, σ). Then:

1.
If β is a terminal node and Val(x, β, σ), then $[]\beta[] = \langle \beta, x \rangle$

2.
If β is $[_\gamma \delta_1 \delta_2 \ldots \delta_n]$ for $n \geq 1$ and Val(x, $[_\gamma \delta_1 \delta_2 \ldots \delta_n]$, σ), then
$[]\beta[] = [_{\langle \gamma, x \rangle} []\delta_1[] \ []\delta_2[] \ldots []\delta_n[]]$

3.
If the semantic value assigned to β, assuming Val(T, α, σ), is not defined, and
(a) β is a terminal node, then $[]\beta[] = \langle \beta \rangle$
(b) β is $[_\gamma \delta_1 \delta_2 \ldots \delta_n]$ for $n \geq 1$, then $[]\beta[] = [_{\langle \gamma \rangle} []\delta_1[] \ []\delta_2[] \ldots []\delta_n[]]$

Finally, we shall use two derivation rules we used in L1 and L2.

(5)
Derivation Rules

(SoE)
$$\frac{\ldots \alpha \ldots \quad \alpha \text{ iff } \beta}{}$$
derive $\ldots \beta \ldots$

(SoI)
$$\frac{\text{for some x, } x = \alpha \text{ and} \ldots x \ldots}{}$$
derive $\ldots \alpha \ldots$

Consider a sample derivation for 'Smith believes Jones walks'.

Val(T, $[_S [_{NP} \underline{\text{Smith}}][_{VP} [_V \underline{\text{believes}}][_S [_{NP} \underline{\text{Jones}}][_{VP} [_{Vint} \underline{\text{Sings}}]]]]$, σ) iff

(1)
for some x, Val(x, $[_{NP} \underline{\text{Smith}}]$, σ) and Val(x, $[_{VP} [_{Vint} \underline{\text{believes}}][_S [_{NP} \underline{\text{Jones}}][_{VP} [_V \underline{\text{walks}}]]]]$, σ)
[instance of (2a)]

(2)
for some x, Val(x, $[_{NP} \underline{\text{Smith}}]$, σ) and for some y, Val($\langle x, y \rangle$, $[_V \underline{\text{believes}}]$, σ) and y = $[][_S [_{NP} \underline{\text{Jones}}][_{VP} [_{Vint} \underline{\text{walks}}]]][]$ w.r.t. σ
[from (1) by (2d), SoE]

(3)

for some x, x = Smith and for some y, Val($\langle$x,y$\rangle$, [$_{Vint}$ <u>believes</u>], σ) and y = [][$_S$
[$_{NP}$<u>Jones</u>][$_{VP}$[$_V$<u>Walks</u>]]][] w.r.t. σ
[from (2) by (1a), SoE]

(4)

for some x, x = Smith and for some y, x believes y, and y = [][$_S$[$_{NP}$<u>Jones</u>][$_{VP}$[$_V$
<u>walks</u>]]][] w.r.t. σ
[from (3) by (1d), SoE]

(5)

Smith believes [][$_S$[$_{NP}$<u>Jones</u>][$_{VP}$[$_V$<u>walks</u>]]][] w.r.t. σ
[from (4) by SoI]

Construction of the ILF proceeds as follows: First, the truth definition must be
applied to the embedded clause to determine the semantic values of each node
of the embedded p-marker. Recall that the embedded p-marker in this case is just
the following.

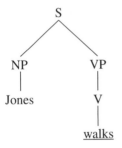

We can get the semantic value of each node from the following (partial)
derivation.

Val(T, [$_S$ [NP <u>Jones</u>][$_{VP}$ [$_V$ <u>walks</u>]]], σ) iff . . .

(1)

for some x, Val(x, [NP <u>Jones</u>], σ) and Val(x, [$_{VP}$ [$_V$ <u>walks</u>]], σ)
[instance of (2a)]

(2)

for some x, Val(x, <u>Jones</u>, σ) and Val(x, <u>walks</u>, σ)
[from (1) by (2c), SoE]

(3)

for some x, x = Jones and x walks
[from (2), by (1a), (1c), SoE]

Given the calculation of these semantic values, we can construct the ILF following the definition introduced above.

$[][_S[_{NP}$ Jones$] [_{VP}[_V$ <u>walks</u>$]]][]$

   $= [_{\langle S, True\rangle}[][_{NP}$ <u>Jones</u>$][] [][_{VP}[_V$ <u>walks</u>$]]][]]$
   [by (3ii)]

   $= [_{\langle S, True\rangle}[_{\langle NP, Jones\rangle} []$ <u>Jones</u>$][]][_{\langle VP, Jones\rangle}[_{\langle V, Jones\rangle} []$ <u>walks</u> $[]]]]$
   [by (3ii)]

   $= [_{\langle S, True\rangle}[_{\langle NP, Jones\rangle} \langle$ <u>Jones</u>, Jones$\rangle]] [_{\langle VP, Jones\rangle}[_{\langle V, Jones\rangle} \langle$ <u>walks</u>, Jones$\rangle]]]$
   [by (3i)]

In a more familiar tree representation, we have the following.

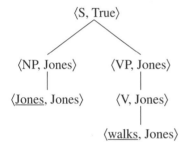

Finally, then, we have derived the following theorem:

<u>Smith believes Jones walks</u> is true iff Smith believes

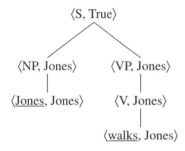

Appendix T4

A B-Theory Technical Fragment

This appendix, which builds on the "EC" fragment of Larson and Segal 1995, shows the basic B-theory axioms in a fragment without quantification and without complement clauses.

Syntax for LB

Terminal Symbols

(1)
ADV → yesterday, today, tomorrow
P → in, with
V → swims, walks
NP → Smith, Jones, The Lake
TNS → PAST, PRES, FUT, PRES PERF, etc.
ASP → PROG, CUL
CON → before, after, when

Nonterminal Symbols

(2)
IP → NP I'
I' → I VP
VP → V (PP) (ADV)
PP → P NP
I → TNS ASP
IP → IP CON IP

Semantics for LB

Terminal Symbols

(1)

a.

Val(e, <u>yesterday</u>, S, R, E) iff R is the day before S

Val(e, <u>today</u>, S, R, E) iff R is the same day as S

Val(e, <u>tomorrow</u>, S, R, E) iff R is the day after S

b.

Val(⟨e,x⟩, <u>in</u>, S, R, E) iff e is in x

c.

Val(e, <u>swims</u>, S, R, E) iff e is a swimming

Val(e, <u>walks,</u> S, R, E) iff e is a walking

d.

Val(x, <u>Smith</u>, S, R, E) iff x = Smith

Val(x, <u>Jones</u>, S, R, E) iff x = Jones

Val(x, <u>The Lake</u>, S, R, E) iff x = The Lake

e.

Val(e, PAST, S, R, E) iff S is later than R/E

Val(e, PRES, S, R, E) iff S, R, and E temporally overlap

Val(e, FUT, S, R, E) iff S is earlier than R/E

Val(e, PRES PERFECT, S, R, E) iff E is earlier than S/R

Val(e, PAST PERFECT, S, R, E) iff E is earlier than R and R is earlier than S

Val(e, FUT PERFECT, S, R, E) iff S is earlier than E, E is earlier than R

Val(e, FUT PERFECT, S, R, E) iff E is earlier than S, S is earlier than R

Val(e, FUT PERFECT, S, R, E) iff E and S temporally overlap, S is earlier than R

Val(e, FUT IN PAST, S, R, E) iff R is earlier than S, R is earlier than E

f.

Val(e, <u>PROG</u>, S, R, E) iff in-progress-at(e, E)

Val(e, <u>CUL</u>, S, R, E) iff culminates-at(e, E)

g.

Val(⟨x,y⟩, <u>before</u>, S, R, E) iff x is earlier than y

Val(⟨x,y⟩, <u>after</u>, S, R, E) iff x is later than y

Val(⟨x,y⟩, <u>when</u>, S, R, E) iff x temporally overlaps with y

Axioms for Nonterminal Symbols

(2)

a.

Val(T, [$_{IP}$ NP I'], S, R, E) iff, for some x, e, Val(e, I', S, R, E) and at(e, E) and, for some x, x is the agent of e and Val(x, NP, S, R, E)

b.

Val(e, [$_{I'}$ I VP], S, R, E) iff Val(e, I, S, R, E) and Val(e, VP, S, R, E)

c.

Val(e, [$_{VP}$ V], S, R, E) iff Val(e, V, S, R, E)

Val(e, [$_{VP}$ V PP], S, R, E) iff Val(e, V, S, R, E) and Val(y, PP, S, R, E)

Val(e, [$_{VP}$ V ADV], S, R, E) iff Val(e, V, S, R, E) and Val(e, ADV, S, R, E)

Val(e, [$_{VP}$ V PP ADV], S, R, E) iff Val(e, V, S, R, E) and Val(e, PP, S, R, E) and Val(e, ADV, S, R, E)

d.

Val(e, [$_{PP}$ P NP], S, R, E) iff, for some z, Val(⟨e,z⟩, P, S, R, E) and Val(z, NP, S, R, E)

e.

Val(e, [$_{I}$ TNS ASP], S, R, E) iff Val(e, TNS, S, R, E) and Val(e, ASP, S, R, E)

f.

Val(T, [$_{IP}$ IP1 CON IP2], S, R, E) iff Val(T, IP1, S, R1, E1) and Val(T, IP2, S, R2, E2) and Val(⟨E1,E2⟩, CON, S, R, E)

g.

Val(x, [$_{\alpha}$ β], S, R, E) iff Val(x, β) where α ranges over categories and β ranges over categories and lexical items.

Production Rules

(SoE)

$$\begin{array}{c} \ldots \alpha \ldots \\ \alpha \text{ iff } \beta \\ \hline \end{array}$$

therefore ... β ...

(SoI)

$$\frac{\phi \text{ iff for some x, x} = \alpha \text{ and } \ldots x \ldots}{}$$

therefore φ iff ... α ...

To illustrate, the derivation for 'Smith swam yesterday' in this fragment would proceed as shown in (1).

Val(T, [$_{IP}$ [$_{NP}$ Smith] [$_{I'}$[$_I$[$_{TNS}$ PAST][$_{ASP}$ CUL]][$_{VP}$[$_V$ swims][$_{ADV}$ yesterday]]]], S, R, E) iff . . .

(1)

for some x,e, Val(e, [$_{I'}$[$_I$[$_{TNS}$ PAST][$_{ASP}$ CUL]][$_{VP}$[$_V$ swims][$_{ADV}$ yesterday]]], S, R, E) and At(e,E) and x is the agent of e and Val(x, [$_{NP}$ Smith], S, R, E)
[instance of (2a)]

iff

(2)

for some x,e, Val(e, [$_I$[$_{TNS}$ PAST][$_{ASP}$ CUL]], S, R, E) and Val(e, [$_{VP}$[$_V$ swims][$_{ADV}$ yesterday]], S, R, E) and At(e,E) and x is the agent of e and Val(x, [$_{NP}$ Smith], S, R, E)
[from (1), by (2b), SoE]

iff

(3)

for some x,e, Val(e, [$_{TNS}$ PAST], S, R, E) and Val(e, [$_{ASP}$ CUL], S, R, E) and Val(e, [$_{VP}$[$_V$ swims][$_{ADV}$ yesterday]], S, R, E) and At(e,E) and x is the agent of e and Val(x, [$_{NP}$ Smith], S, R, E)
[from (2), by (2e), SoE]

iff

(4)

for some x,e, Val(e, [$_{TNS}$ PAST], S, R, E) and Val(e, [$_{ASP}$ CUL], S, R, E) and Val(e, [$_V$ swims], S, R, E) and Val(e, [$_{ADV}$ yesterday], S, R, E) and At(e,E) and x is the agent of e and Val(x, [$_{NP}$ Smith], S, R, E)
[from (3), by (2c), SoE]

iff

(5)

for some x,e, Val(e, PAST, S, R, E) and Val(e, CUL, S, R, E) and Val(e, swims, S, R, E) and Val(e, yesterday, S, R, E) and At(e,E) and x is the agent of e and Val(x, Smith, S, R, E)
[from (4), by (2g), SoE]

iff

(6)

for some x, e, Val(e, PAST, S, R, E) and Val(e, CUL, S, R, E) and Val(e, swims, S, R, E) and R is the day before S, and At(e,E) and x is the agent of e and Val(x, Smith, S, R, E)
[from (5), by (1a), SoE]

iff

(7)

for some x,e, Val(e, PAST, S, R, E) and Val(e, CUL, S, R, E) and e is a swimming, and R is the day before S, and At(e,E) and x is the agent of e and Val(x, Smith, S, R, E)
[from (6), by (1c), SoE]

iff

(8)

for some x,e, Val(e, PAST, S, R, E) and Val(e, CUL, S, R, E) and e is a swimming, and R is the day before S, and At(e,E) and x is the agent of e and x = Smith
[from (7), by (1d), SoE]

iff

(9)

for some x,e, S is later than R/E, and Val(e, CUL, S, R, E) and e is a swimming, and R is the day before S, and At(e,E) and x is the agent of e and x = Smith
[from (8), by (1e), SoE]

iff

(10)

for some x,e, S is later than R/E, and culminates-at(e, E) and e is a swimming, and R is the day before S, and At(e,E) and x is the agent of e and x = Smith
[from (9), by (1f), SoE]

iff

(11)

for some e, S is later than R/E, and culminates-at(e, E) and e is a swimming by Smith, and R is the day before S, and At(e,E) and Smith is the agent of e
[from (10), by SoI]

Appendix T5

A Basic A-Theory Fragment

This appendix, which borrows from the ILF fragment of Larson and Ludlow 1993, combines an ILF theory with an event-based analysis of aspect. To keep matters simple and to keep the crucial axioms at center stage, basic quantifiers are not introduced here (although they could be introduced along the lines of appendix T1 without difficulty). Propositional attitude verbs are also omitted here.

Syntax of LA

Terminal Symbols

As in LB (appendix T4).

Nonterminal Symbols

S → IP when/before/after IP
IP → TNS IP (ADV)
IP → NP I'
I' → I VP
VP → V (PP)
PP → P NP
I → ASP

Semantics of LA

Terminal Nodes

(1)
a.
Val($\langle$x,y$\rangle$, <u>sees</u>) iff x sees y
Val($\langle$x,y$\rangle$, <u>hits</u>) iff x hit y

b.
Val($\langle$e,x$\rangle$, <u>in</u>) iff e is in x
c.
Val(e, <u>swims</u>) iff e is a swimming
Val(e, <u>walks</u>) iff e is a walking
d.
Val(x, <u>Smith</u>) iff x = Smith
Val(x, <u>Jones</u>) iff x = Jones
Val(x, <u>the lake</u>) iff x = the lake
e.
Val(x, PAST) iff x was true
Val(x, FUT) iff x will be true
Val(x, PRES) iff x is true
f.
Val(e, CUL) iff e culminates
Val(e, PROG) iff e is in progress
g.
Val(x, <u>yesterday</u>) iff x was true yesterday
Val(x, <u>tomorrow</u>) iff x will be true tomorrow
Val(x, <u>today</u>) iff x is true today
Val(x, <u>now</u>) iff x is true now

Nonterminal Nodes

(2)
a.
Val(T, [$_S$ IP1 <u>when</u> IP2]) iff Val(T, IP1) when Val(T, IP2)
Val(T, [$_S$ IP1 <u>before</u> IP2]) iff Val(T, IP1) before Val(T, IP2)
Val(T, [$_S$ IP1 <u>after</u> IP2]) iff Val(T, IP1) after Val(T, IP2)
b.
Val(T, [$_{IP}$ TNS IP1]) iff, for some x, Val(x, TNS), and x = []IP1[]
c.
Val(T, [$_{IP}$ TNS IP1 ADV]) iff, for some x, Val(x, TNS), Val(x, ADV), and x = []IP1[]
d.
Val(T, [$_{IP}$ NP I']) iff for some e, Val(e, I') and for some x, x is the agent of e and Val(x, NP)

e.

Val(e, [$_{I'}$ I VP]) iff Val(e, I) and Val(e, VP)

f.

Val(e, [$_{VP}$ V PP]) iff Val(e, V) and Val(e, PP)

g.

Val(e, [$_{PP}$ P NP]) iff for some z, Val($\langle$e,z$\rangle$, P) and Val(z, NP)

i.

Val(x, [$_{\alpha}$ β]) iff Val(x, β) where α ranges over categories and β ranges over lexical items.

Definition

Let α be a phrase marker with root S and for each node β of α, let x be the semantic value assigned to β, assuming Val(T, α). Then:

1.

If β is a terminal node and Val(x, β), then []β[] = $\langle$β,x$\rangle$

2.

If β is [$_{\gamma}$ δ$_1$ δ$_2$ . . . δ$_n$] for n≥1 and Val(x, [$_{\gamma}$δ$_1$ δ$_2$ . . . δ$_n$]), then []β[] = [$_{\langle\gamma,x\rangle}$ []δ$_1$[] []δ$_2$[] . . . []δ$_n$[]]

3.

If the semantic value assigned to β, assuming Val(T, α), is not defined, and

(a) β is a terminal node, then []β[] = $\langle$β$\rangle$

(b) β is [$_{\gamma}$ δ$_1$ δ$_2$ . . . δ$_n$] for n ≥ 1,

then []β[] = [$_{\langle\gamma\rangle}$ []δ$_1$[] []δ$_2$[] . . . []δ$_n$[]]

Derivation Rules

(SoE)

. . . α . . .

α iff β

———

. . . β . . .

(SoI)

φ iff for some x, x = α and . . . x . . .

——————————————————

φ iff . . . α . . .

(RR)

Redundancy Reduction

ϕ iff x is/was/will be true, and x is/was/will be true . . .

ϕ iff x is/was/will be true . . .

This can be illustrated with a sample derivation for 'Smith swam yesterday'. Here we assume a syntax in which there is an implicit temporal conjunction. We assume, further, that the adverb modifies this conjunct (analogous to the way in which adverbs modify the R event on the Reichenbach proposal).

Val(T, [$_{IP}$ [$_{IP1}$ [$_{TNS}$ PAST][$_{IP2}$ [$_{NP}$ Smith][$_{I'}$[$_{I}$[$_{ASP}$ CUL]][$_{VP}$[$_{V}$ swims]]]]] when [$_{IP3}$ [$_{TNS}$ PAST][$_{IP4}$ . . .][$_{ADV}$ yesterday]]]) iff

(1)

Val(T, [$_{IP1}$ [$_{TNS}$ PAST][$_{IP2}$ [$_{NP}$ Smith][$_{I'}$[$_{I}$[$_{ASP}$ CUL]][$_{VP}$[$_{V}$ swims]]]]]) when Val(T, [$_{IP3}$[$_{TNS}$ PAST][$_{IP4}$ . . .][$_{ADV}$ yesterday]])

[instance of (2a)]

iff

(2)

for some x, y Val(x, [$_{TNS}$ PAST]) and x = [] [$_{IP2}$ [$_{NP}$ Smith][$_{I'}$[$_{I}$[$_{ASP}$ CUL]][$_{VP}$[$_{V}$ swims]]]] [] when Val(y, [$_{TNS}$ PAST]), Val(y, [$_{ADV}$ yesterday]) and y = [] [$_{IP4}$ . . .] []

[from (1), by (2b), (2c), SoE]

iff

(3)

for some x, y Val(x, PAST]) and x = [] [$_{IP2}$ [$_{NP}$ Smith][$_{I'}$[$_{I}$[$_{ASP}$ CUL]][$_{VP}$[$_{V}$ swims]]]] [] when Val(y, PAST), Val(y, yesterday) and y = [] [$_{IP4}$ . . .] []

[from (2), by (2i), SoE]

iff

(4)

for some x, y, x was true and x = [] [$_{IP2}$ [$_{NP}$ Smith][$_{I'}$[$_{I}$[$_{ASP}$ CUL]][$_{VP}$[$_{V}$ swims]]]] [] when y was true, y was true yesterday and y = [] [$_{IP4}$ . . .] []

[from (3), by (1a), (1e), (1g), SoE]

iff

(5)

for some x, y, x was true and x = [] [$_{IP2}$ [$_{NP}$ <u>Smith</u>][$_{I'}$[$_I$[$_{ASP}$ CUL]][$_{VP}$[$_V$ <u>swims</u>]]]] []
when y was true yesterday and y = [] [$_{IP4}$ . . .] []

[from (4), by RR]

iff

(6)

[] [$_{IP2}$ [$_{NP}$ <u>Smith</u>][$_{I'}$[$_I$[$_{ASP}$ CUL]][$_{VP}$[$_V$ <u>swims</u>]]]] [] was true when [] [$_{IP4}$ . . . [] was
true yesterday

[from (5), by SoI]

The treatment of the ILFs proceeds as in appendix T3.

Notes

Introduction

1. See chapter 3 of Sorabji 1983 for discussion. Kretzman (1976) argues that the issue is also taken up by Aristotle, although this claim is somewhat more controversial.

2. In any case, that is the received view of Einstein's position. But see p. 287 of Shimony 1993 for dissension on this point. It is worth noting that direct evidence of Einstein's position on the matter is hard to come by; one of the best pieces of evidence for his B-theory sympathies is a letter of condolence written to the family of a friend (Einstein 1955).

3. This page reference is to the version in Yourgrau 1990.

4. This in fact echoes a point made several decades earlier by Reichenbach (1956, p. xiii): "If the speculatively oriented philosophy of our time denies to contemporary science its philosophical character, if it calls contributions such as the theory of relativity or the theory of sets unphilosophical and belonging in the special sciences, this judgement expresses only the inability to perceive the philosophical content of modern scientific thought."

5. See, e.g., Smith 1993 and Craig 1990. The following passage from Craig (p.339) illustrates this point of view nicely: "I find it surprising that anyone reading Einstein's 1905 paper can think that Einstein demonstrated that absolute simultaneity does not exist and that time is therefore relative to a reference frame. For the entire theory depends upon acceptance of Einstein's arbitrary (and, indeed, highly counterintuitive) definition of simultaneity, coupled with a philosophical positivism of Machian provenance according to which absolute simultaneity is meaningless if it is empirically undetectable. . . . One who is not a positivist and who therefore rejects Einstein's definitions would regard these relatively moving observers as deceived due to the nature of their measurements, which fail to detect true time. In a real sense, he would not regard Einstein's theory as a theory about time and space at all, but, as Frank put it, 'as a system of hypotheses about the behavior of light rays, rigid bodies, and mechanisms, from which new results about this behavior can be derived.'" But see Shimony 1993 for further discussion (and criticism) of this view of relativity theory.

6. This view also appears to have been held by Gödel. See Yourgrau 1991.

7. I don't mean that physicists can't do philosophy. The point is that the questions can't be answered in isolation of philosophical inquiry—whether carried out by persons in philosophy departments or in physics departments.

8. Strawson 1959 is a classic example of this general approach.

9. A caveat is necessary here. Some so-called Priorean tense logics are not genuine Priorean theories, because their semantics import B-series resources. As van Benthem (1982) notes, on many "Priorean" theories the semantics for 'past', 'present', and 'future' are often given in terms of the relations before and after. For example, it is typically asserted that x satisfies 'past' iff x is earlier than y, where y is the utterance time. It seems to me that this way of giving the semantics for a Priorean tense logic is quite out of the spirit of Prior's general program, which happens to eschew future and past events as well as the B-series time line.

10. Of course neither Kaplan nor Perry advocates truth-conditional semantics, but the key point here is independent of the semantical framework we choose to work with. This way of thinking about the Kaplan-Perry view of indexicals within the truth-conditional framework is due to Larson and Segal (1995).

11. Although the objection turns on a theory in which the operators apply to events rather than to propositions, the objection is readily adapted to propositions. The idea would be that a given proposition is future, then present, and then past.

Chapter 1

1. Portions of this section are drawn from Ludlow (forthcoming).

2. Chomsky would add that I-language is "individualistic," meaning that the properties of the system depend on the individual in isolation rather than on relations between the individual and the external environment. I don't need to make that assumption here, and I'll reject the thesis for psychology in general a bit later.

3. The hedge about "co-opting" (more accurately, exaptation) is to cover Chomsky's view that the language faculty may not have been the product of gradual evolution. For more on this, see section 1.2.

4. See Lewis 1975a for an articulation of this view of language. See Lewis 1969 for a discussion of the nature of convention.

5. Strictly speaking, the difference between I-language and E-language may not even count as an actual distinction, since on Chomsky's view there is I-language and then there is a collection of poorly defined if not incoherent views which might be lumped together as "E-language theories."

6. Davidson (1986) reaches a similar conclusion, though by a much different route. In a funny sense, although neither would admit it, Davidson and Chomsky are in accord on one point: that there is no such thing as a language (construed as an E-language).

7. An alternative would be to regard languages as abstract objects in the sense of Katz 1981. For reasons outlined by Higginbotham (1983), I will set aside that possibility here.

8. For a general discussion of this issue, see Beakley 1991.

9. See Gould and Lewontin 1979. For some of Gould's popular writings on this theme, see Gould 1980.

10. For a description of the phenomena, see Hayes 1995.

11. The influence of Fodor (1975) and Carruthers (1996) will be evident in portions of this section.

12. In one amusing episode, Russell, while taking an intelligence test that required him to manipulate certain geometric shapes, asked if he could terminate the exam on the ground that he no longer had names for shapes.

13. This concession is controversial. For a sample of the literature on whether mental images are fundamentally pictorial or discursive, see Beakley and Ludlow 1992.

Chapter 2

1. For an example of someone whose alarm has gone off, see Devitt 1993.

2. An interesting puzzle arises if one wants to hold to this externalist conception of knowledge and to the idea that one has a priori knowledge of the meanings of the expressions. Some have argued that a priori self-knowledge and externalism of this character are incompatible. However, it is fair to say that the issues are very subtle. This is not the place to take up these questions. For a survey of the current literature on the topic, see Ludlow and Martin 1998.

3. See, e.g., Chomsky 1986.

4. For discussions of this possibility, see p. 209 of Montague 1974.

5. Dummett (1991) has stressed that model-theoretic semantics cannot provide such connections, but that it nonetheless is useful for characterizing entailment relations between expressions. Whether model-theoretic semantics can even account for entailment relations also turns out to be controversial. For skepticism about model-theoretic treatments of logical entailment, see Etchemendy 1990 and Field 1991.

6. Having an interpretive T-theory without knowing that it is interpretive, or without knowing to what use it may be put, is like having a map without knowing whether it is to scale, or without knowing what it is a map of. For a discussion of this concern, see Foster 1976.

7. There would be no harm in writing a fragment that utilized the semantical notions of satisfaction and reference instead. In that case, 'x = Sally' might give way to 'Sally refers to x', and 'x walks' might give way to 'x satisfies 'walks''.

8. Reification of "the True" can be avoided if we wish. I use the notion here merely for convenience and not out of Fregean intuitions that there is such a thing as The True.

9. Were this constraint to be relaxed, we would end up proving theorems like "'Snow is white' is true iff snow is white and the number 7 is prime." For a discussion of this issue, see Davies 1981a.

10. For some criticism of this line of investigation, see Fodor and Lepore 1997 and Fodor and Lepore 1998. This criticism appears to be driven by the assumption that lexical decomposition and the like drive us into holism. I fail to see why this must happen.

11. For further discussion of Evans's argument, see Wright 1986; Davies 1981b, 1987; Peacocke 1986.

12. See, e.g., McDowell 1980; Evans 1982; Bilgrami 1987; Lepore and Loewer 1987. These authors are influenced by remarks in Dummett 1973 and Dummett 1975.

13. I'm not sure if Lepore and Loewer saw this.

14. See Ludlow 1993.

15. One might suppose that, within a broadly Davidsonian program, T-theories are treated in a "deflationary" way, so that they do not refer to objects, states of affairs, etc. Lepore and Loewer (1987, p. 103) argue as follows: "If one thinks . . . that a truth theory assigns possible states of affairs or facts to indicative sentences then we can see why [certain] truth theories assign the same truth conditions to the two sentences 'Cicero is bald' and 'Tully is bald'. But it is not necessary to think of truth theories in this way. Davidson rejects the reification of truth conditions. . . ." Contrary to this line of thinking, I fail to see how we can stipulate T-theories to be deflationary. The fundamental problem is that, because one is using (e.g.) English on the right-hand side of a T-sentence, what is stated on the right-hand side cannot be more or less than what is stated by that English expression. One way to get a handle on this issue is to think of the axioms and theorems in a T-theory as akin to the laws in any other science. One may not want to reify talk about planets and quasars, but it is hard to see how, short of general scientific anti-realism, one can escape commitment to them. The problem is not unique to certain kinds of T-theories in which it is stipulated that the right-hand side of the T-sentences refers to a state of affairs. Rather, the problem stems from the fact that natural language is used to state the truth conditions, and thus that the T-theory can "state" no more or less than what is said by the natural language expression used to give the truth conditions.

16. This reference was first brought to my attention by Richard Larson.

Chapter 3

1. See, e.g., Cresswell 1985, 1990; Hintikka 1962, 1969a, 1975; Lewis 1972; Stalnaker 1984.

2. See, e.g., Richard 1990; Salmon 1986; Soames 1987.

3. See appendix T3 for technical details.

4. The philosophers include Buridan (1966), Montague (1960), and Quine (1960); the linguists include McCawley (1974), Karttunen (1976), and Ross (1976).

5. For attempts, see den Dikken, Larson, and Ludlow 1996 and Larson, den Dikken, and Ludlow 1997.

6. Here apparently I depart from Higginbotham (1986a).

7. The following few paragraphs are drawn from Larson and Ludlow 1993.

8. Reiber (1997, p. 289) objects to ILF theories at precisely this point, arguing that such theories—particularly the version advanced by Larson and Ludlow—still face the "content problem": "The point I wish to make is that no matter how successful [Larson and Ludlow] may be in this project, it will leave the central objection unanswered. Explaining (i) how two belief reports can differ in content but report the same attitude

may be a first step in explaining (ii) why ordinary thinkers mistakenly think they have the same content, but explaining (i) does not suffice for explaining (ii). A 'pragmatic' explanation of (ii) would have to go beyond Larson and Ludlow's; it would need to be an 'error theory' that tells us why our judgements abut content are mistaken." This objection fails because it assumes that we *have* intuitions about contents (apart from those intuitions we are taught to have in philosophy graduate seminars). Clearly we have intuitions about when two sentences say the same thing, but it is quite another matter to suppose that we have natural intuitions about contents. The situation is somewhat related to that in syntax, where Chomsky has argued that we have intuitions about the acceptability of a sentence but not about its grammaticality. The latter notion is a theoretical construct (just like, I submit, the notion of content). Accordingly, no error theory is necessary; we have no natural content intuitions about which to be in error.

9. For what it's worth, I find this a plausible reconstruction of what Frege was trying to say. It is certainly a reasonable way of taking remarks like the following (quoted earlier in this chapter): "Although the thought is the same, the verbal expression must be different so that the sense, which would otherwise be affected by the differing times of utterance, is readjusted." In other words, the verbal expression must change with circumstances in order to express the same sense.

10. Does it follow that there must be an independently existing sense, or is talk of sense just a handy way of talking about our ability to keep track of when two indexical expressions or attitude attributions say the same thing? I am inclined to suppose that the latter is the case, although of course it would be possible to say that such abilities underwrite any epistemic relation we might have to senses construed as abstract objects. Such a possibility will be discussed in more detail (if obliquely) in chapter 4.

11. In recent years there has been a great deal of work on these sorts of simulation theories. For surveys of this literature, see Carruthers and Smith 1986; Davies and Stone 1995a,b.

12. For a proposal in this vein, see Nolan 1970.

13. Divide yes, but not wall off. Thus we have a proliferation of disciplines in the natural sciences (molecular biology, primate ecology, etc.) which ignore traditional disciplinary boundaries and which suppose that the various sciences are connected at some level and that postulating theories which rely on these connections is entirely appropriate.

Chapter 4

1. Consider, for example, the following fragment from Parmenides (1984): "It must be that what is there for speaking of and thinking of is; for it is there to be." The idea is also clearly articulated in Plato's *Sophist* (237 D-E), where a stranger points out to Theatetus that if we fail to refer when we use the expression 'something' we have failed to express a determinate proposition:

Str: Surely we can see that this expression 'something' is always used of a thing that exists. We cannot use it just by itself in naked isolation from everything that exists, can we?
Theatetus: No.
Str: Is your assent due to the reflection that to speak of 'something' is to speak of 'some one thing'?

Theatetus: Yes.

Str: Because you will admit that 'something' stands for one thing, as 'some things' stands for two or more.

Theatetus: Certainly.

Str: So it seems to follow necessarily that to speak of what is not 'something' is to speak of no thing at all.

Theatetus: Necessarily.

Str: Must we not even refuse to allow that in such a case a person is saying something, though he may be speaking of nothing? Must we not assert that he is not even saying anything when he sets about uttering the sounds 'a thing that is not'?

Aristotle broke with Plato on a number of metaphysical issues, but not on the connection between language and metaphysics. In chapter 1 of Book Z of the Metaphysics, for example, Aristotle addresses the question of whether predicates must refer to independent forms: "And so one might even raise the question whether the words 'to walk,' 'to be healthy,' 'to sit,' imply that each of these things is existent, and similarly in other cases of this sort; for none of them is either self-subsistent or capable of being separated from substance, but rather, if anything, it is that which walks or sits or is healthy that is an existent thing. Now these are seen to be more real because there is something definite which underlies them (i.e., the substance of individual) which is implied in such a predicate; for we never use the word 'good' of 'sitting' without implying this." Here Aristotle disagrees with Plato on the question of whether there must be independent forms, but crucially bases his argument on the linguistic fact that predicates cannot stand alone. (See p. 2 of Alston 1964 for a brief discussion of this passage.)

2. The idea that the domain should be stipulated in advance may be grounded in certain assumptions about the desirability of formal rigor in semantic theory (and the sciences generally); however, as is argued in Ludlow 1992, such a desideratum reflects a misunderstanding about the role of formal rigor in science generally.

3. It may well be that either (2) or (3) is inadequate for certain psycholinguistic reasons, but this would be a question for investigation.

4. For a discussion of a fragment of this kind, see subsection 4.3.2 of Larson and Segal 1995.

5. A similar argument has been raised against using singular event anaphora as an argument for the existence of events.

6. For a less pessimistic view, see Bealer 1982, Chierchia and Turner 1988, and many of the essays in Chierchia and Turner 1989.

7. Some philosophers have suggested that we can escape the apparent commitment to objects like Pegasus if we make a couple of basic assumptions. The first assumption, standard in free logics, is that we need not assume existential generalization holds, so that from (i), for example, we need not infer (ii).

(i)
Pegasus = Pegasus

(ii)
for some x, x = Pegasus.

We can grant this point, since our concern is whether referring expressions themselves raise ontological commitments (quite independently of the involvement of quantification). The question is whether an axiom like (17) by itself must commit us to an object like Pegasus. The issue is complicated by the fact that (i) appears to be contentful in a way that (iii) does not.

(iii)
Val(x, Egref) iff x refers to Egref.

One way of distinguishing axioms like (17) from axioms like (iii) is by supposing that they invoke concepts. So, for example, (17) is contentful because we have a concept of Pegasus, but (iii) is not because we have no concept corresponding to Egref. The prima facie problem with this solution is that axioms like (17) do not appear to be about concepts, but rather about objects. So, for example, a philosopher who believed in the existence of Pegasus might well distinguish his beliefs about Pegasus from his beliefs about the concept of Pegasus, and in turn may distinguish the two in his speech. In such a case, (17) may play a role in giving the semantics for this philosopher's utterances about Pegasus, but not his utterances about the concept of Pegasus. That would require a second axiom referring specifically to the concept. In any case, following considerations raised in section 1.3, I am highly skeptical of any analysis of concepts as being distinct from their I-language manifestations.

8. See, e.g., Kripke 1980.

9. There is probably also room to wonder about the relevance of rigidity intuitions here. Though it may be conceded to Kripke that names rigidly designate in a way that descriptions do not, Stanley (1997a) has argued that Kripke merely assumes that rigidity is relevant to the theory of meaning. Pointing to Kripke's (1980, p. 14) remarks that "we have a direct intuition of the rigidity of names, exhibited in our understanding of the truth conditions of particular sentences," Stanley holds that Kripke begs the question. The intuitions about rigidity, if there are such things, may have no bearing on our understanding of truth conditions.

10. Note the parallel between this and my discussion of indexicals in section 3.2.

11. I am indebted to Ernie Lepore for discussion of this point.

12. For a statement of the concerns, see Wallace 1972. For criticism, see Kripke 1976.

13. See Dreyfus 1982 for just a sample.

14. In this section I have focused exclusively on the question of whether substitutional quantification in fact frees us from ontological commitment. There are also numerous technical difficulties that arise for substitutional quantification as a thesis about natural language, some of which bear mentioning—for example, the question of whether substitutional quantification can be extended to quantifiers like 'most' and 'few' (Davies 1981a; Ludlow 1985, section 4.B; Lewis 1985). For example, if the truth conditions of 'Most spies are bored' are given as in the following example, the truth conditions come out wrong, since spies will go by many names, and it is possible that one spy in particular (say, Jones) may be the only bored spy, but by virtue of his having thousands of names, the following will be true:

For most terms t, such that t⌢'is a spy' is true and t⌢'is bored' is true.

Although these technical difficulties are interesting, I have set them aside because it must first be demonstrated that substitutional quantification frees us from all ontological commitments. I will return to this problem (under another guise) in chapter 8.

Chapter 5

1. This is basically the approach to tense in very early efforts within Montague Grammar—in particular, in the PTQ fragment of Montague 1974. It has also been adopted in truth-conditional semantics; see Lepore and Ludwig 1998.

2. Variations on this theme are possible. See Vickner 1985 for an example.

3. A more comprehensive T-theory can be found in appendix T4.

4. See Vickner 1985 and chapters 2 and 3 of Hornstein 1990 for proposals on deriving complex tenses from simpler ones in the Reichenbachian framework.

5. Others have observed that a quantificational treatment of these connectives is in order. See Bonomi 1997 for one such proposal and for a survey of some of the relevant literature.

6. This treatment of temporal connectives relies upon a syncategormatic treatment of the connectives. That is, they are assigned no specific category and are immediate daughters of S. If we make the natural assumption that they should be assigned a category CONJ, then a set of axioms along the lines of (7') could be employed.

(7')
a.
Val(T, $[_{\text{CONJP}}$ S1 CONJ'], S, R, E, σ) iff Val(T, S1, S, R, E, σ) and Val(T, CONJP, S, R, E, σ)
b.
Val(x, $[_{\text{CONJ'}}$ CONJ S2], S, R, E, s) iff there is a y, s.t. Val($\langle x,y \rangle$, CONJ, S, R, E, s) and Val(y, S, S, R, E, s)
c.
Val($\langle x,y \rangle$, [CONJ α], S, R, E, σ) iff Val($\langle x,y \rangle$, α, S, R, E, σ) (where α is 'before', 'after', or 'when')
d.
Val($\langle x,y \rangle$, 'before', S, R, E, σ) iff x is earlier than y
e.
Val($\langle x,y \rangle$, 'after', S, R, E, σ) iff x is later than y
f.
Val($\langle x,y \rangle$, 'when', S, R, E, σ) iff x temporally overlaps with y.

7. See appendix T4 for details of the derivation.

8. Here 'Infl' stands for verbal inflection.

9. See Higginbotham 1989 for further motivation for the introduction of event positions into nouns.

10. The label is from Abusch 1997.

11. Abusch (1997; see especially p. 4) argues that it does not work, but I don't find her judgements on the crucial data persuasive.

12. See Giorgi and Pianesi 1998 for discussion.

13. Proposals for the reduction of times to sets of events or propositions are common in the philosophical literature on time. See, e.g., Quine 1960.

Chapter 6

1. The discussion that follows owes much to Smith (1993).

2. It also appears to be the course taken by Mellor (1981). However, as we will see in a bit, Mellor proposes another way out.

3. Smith (1993) suggests that there is a difference between Reichenbach's and Smart's strategies in that, whereas Reichenbach ultimately makes use of the notion of the time or event of this very utterance, Smart dispenses with talk of times or events.

4. Here I am ignoring another serious difficulty for the B-theorist: Precisely what does it mean to give detensed truth conditions? If the truth conditions are to be expressed in the metalanguage, and the metalanguage is English, and all expressions of English are tensed, by virtue of what power are we supposed to strip the metalanguage of its tensed vocabulary? And if we can strip the metalanguage of such vocabulary, is the remaining language one that we actually understand? In addition, quite apart from our interest in giving a truth-conditional semantics, there is the very real question whether a tenseless language is even possible. (See Teichmann 1998 for a discussion.)

5. Smith (1993) puts this as an epistemological point rather than a logical one; he claims we can see a priori that (9) is false, but not so with (8).

6. See Davidson 1967b, Evans 1985a, and Butterfield 1985 for various versions of this idea.

7. I am grateful to Richard Larson and Ernie Lepore here. An alternative story (Ludlow 1997b) suggests that we think of (8) as containing a strict biconditional—or, if one prefers, as being in the scope of a modal operator, as in (i).

(i)

□(An utterance at time t of 'There is no spoken language' is true iff there is no spoken language at t)

(Even if we suppose that the theorems themselves are extensional, as in Davidson 1967a and in Larson and Segal 1995, we might want to allow such operators, since we take the theorems to be derived from what we know to be a true T-theory for the language. In that case, the hidden operator is something like "we know it is a theorem of true T-theory for English that . . .". Accordingly, we need to be on alert for scope ambiguities. Intuitively, what is amiss here is that we want the actual tokening to simply fix the reference time, but we don't want to be committed to the absurd view that necessarily there is an utterance of the token in question at the time that there is no spoken language. If we want to capture this intuition we need to make sure that the event quantification has scope over the modal operator in (i). Paying attention to the relative scope of the utterance-event quantification and the modal operator, we get the following truth conditions for (8):

(ii)

An utterance u at time t of 'There is no spoken language' is such that □(u is true iff there is no spoken language at t)

As above, this fixes the evaluation to the time of utterance of the token, but it keeps the quantification outside the scope of the modal operator. The rest of the reasoning proceeds as above.

8. It does, however, entail some consequences for how we think about the T-theory introduced in chapter 5. Now it is no longer sentences that are to be evaluable but utterances,

and the structural description of the sentence in question will not be on the LHS of the biconditional but will be outside the biconditional altogether! Consider axiom (i):

(i)

Val(T, [$_{IP}$ NP I'], S, R, E, σ) iff for some x, e, Val(e, I', S, R, E, σ) and x is the agent of e and Val(x, NP, S, R, E, σ)

We will have to rewrite this as the conditionalized axiom in (ii) if we are to incorporate the lessons learned from our discussion of token-reflexives.

(ii)

If u is utterance at S, of [$_{IP}$ NP I'], then Val(T, u, S, R, E, σ) iff for some x,e, Val(e, I', S, R, E, σ) and x is the agent of e and Val(x, NP, S, R, E, σ).

9. The proposal in Higginbotham 1995, after all, is for tensed thoughts and not merely tensed utterances.

10. See also Higginbotham 1986b.

11. I realize that appeals to psychology are common enough among B-theorists (and have been since Russell 1915), but such proposals seldom get beyond hand waving. Constructive proposals are few and far between, but when they are made it becomes clear that they face conceptual difficulties in their own right. Atkins (1986, p. 98), for example, suggests that our time consciousness is simply our experience of entropy: "We have looked through the window on to the world provided by the Second Law, and have seen the naked purposelessness of nature. The deep structure of change is decay; the spring of change in all its forms is the corruption of the quality of energy as it spreads chaotically, irreversibly, and purposelessly in time. All change, and time's arrow, point in the direction of corruption. The experience of time is the gearing of the electrochemical processes in our brains to this purposeless drift into chaos as we sink into equilibrium and the grave." Obviously the core of Atkins's position needs to be spelled out in rather more detail. Just how is it that we are conscious of entropy? How does entropy leave an electrochemical imprint on our brains? How does any of this give rise to consciousness of time, and in particular to the experience of time as being fundamentally tensed? Needless to say, these questions are profoundly difficult, and Atkins has not provided any suggestion as to how they may be answered. Nor, frankly, has anyone else.

Chapter 7

1. I am indebted to Ed Keenan for discussion on this matter.

2. Nor would this simply imply that I am glad that a certain proposition was no longer true. My state of relief is not about the character of a certain abstract proposition. A better way of glossing this is as "I am in a state of relief, and the content of the state is that [][(∃e)(e is the event of my having a root canal)][] is past."

3. Here I treat the temporal connectives syncategormatically. Ultimately one would want a categormatic treatment. I am taking the former approach for expository purposes only.

4. Of course this strategy runs afoul of assumptions that syntactic structure must be binary branching, but the same general idea can be cashed out in binary branching structures. One way of doing this (perhaps not the best way) is to suppose that there are both adverb phrases (AdvPs) and tense phrases (TPs) and to hypothesize structures like [$_{TP}$ Tense [$_{AdvP}$ Adv S]], and to write axioms like the following:

Val(T, [$_{TP}$ Tense AdvP]) iff there is an x, such that Val(x, Tense) and Val(x, AdvP)

Val(x, [$_{AdvP}$ Adv S]]) iff there is an x, such that Val(x, Adv) and x=[]S[]

5. For a clear statement of this objection, see Comrie 1985.

6. Obviously, if φ is an eternal (e.g. mathematical) proposition then it may well be both future and past. Here we are concerned with bounded events.

7. Although the objection turns on a theory in which the operators apply to events rather than to propositions, the objection is readily adapted to propositions. The idea would be that a given proposition is future, then present, and then past.

8. That is, from the rejection of the idea that there are only two possible truth values. Truth-value gaps are also possible.

Chapter 8

1. For discussion see Prior 1971; Evans 1982; Neale 1990; Ludlow and Neale 1991.

2. For example, by Strawson (1950) and Donellan (1966). For criticism of the view, see Kripke 1976 and Neale 1990.

3. Of course Russell (1905) was the first to introduce the possibility of names as descriptions in disguise. Numerous others have advocated such a view. See Kripke 1980 for criticism.

4. Of course, though they often are infelicitous, examples like (15b), (16b), (17b), and (18b) can on occasion be perfectly natural. In fact, in the computer science community the task is often not to explain the infelicity of such examples but rather to find techniques by which the subsequent pronoun's "intended specification" can be determined. For a discussion of this point see p. 317 of Sidner 1983.

5. The proposal of Evans (1977) differs from the others in that, while such pronouns do not stand proxy for descriptions, they have their referents fixed (rigidly) by description.

6. Among the various theories of descriptive pronouns, there are a number of proposals as to how descriptive content is to be recovered. In some cases it is to be recovered pragmatically; in others it is to be recovered by a general syntactic algorithm.

7. Axioms can also be written for binary branching structures like the following:

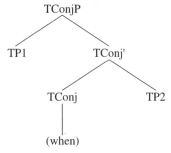

8. One idea would be to introduce numerical subscripts into these operators (e.g., to indicate "N days ago") and to develop the semantics accordingly.

9. I am grateful to Greg Ray and Murali Ramachandran for discussion of the material in this section.

10. Are there also cases of temporal donkey anaphora? Partee (1984) suggests that (i) below would be an example of E-temporal donkey anaphora.

(i)
Whenever Mary telephoned on a Friday, Sam was asleep.

It seems to me that this is mistaken. The problem is that the tense variable in '[Sam was asleep]' seems to be straightforwardly bound by 'whenever Mary telephoned on a Friday', not by some embedded temporal quantifier (i.e., not by 'a Friday'). The difference is that donkey anaphora has the pattern shown in (ii) below, where braces indicate the donkey anaphor.

(ii)
[All x: R(x, [some y: Py])]R'(x, {y})

But Partee's example follows the pattern of (iii).

(iii)
[All t: R(x, y, [some t': Pt'])]R'(y, {t})

The problem of course is that the temporal anaphor in (iii) is anaphoric on t rather than t'. It is simply a case of bound variable anaphora. I have yet to discover a convincing case of temporal donkey anaphora.

11. Notice that in (61), as with stand-alone sentences, there is a when-clause ("during the Iranian revolution") in the relative clause.

12. I am probably conceding too much here by calling the needed structure abstract, since I doubt that it is any more abstract than the sort of structure we posit every day—beginning with sentence and word boundaries. Strictly speaking, those boundaries are not pronounced either. It remains a mystery to me why the positing of such structures should meet resistance in certain quarters while the liberal positing of reference to abstracta is allowed to pass without complaint—as though reference came for free!

13. These were the solutions initially explored by Smith (1975), Ladusaw (1977), and Dowty (1982).

14. This is a challenge which I take seriously and which will have to be met at some point. Furthermore, arguing for the plausibility of these structures within current linguistic theory is not a trivial enterprise. As an illustration of the kind of effort that is necessary, see the treatment of implicit complement clauses in Larson et al. 1997. The arguments for implicit when-clauses and implicit relative clauses will be no less subtle and no less intertwined with the principles of current linguistic theory.

15. Here I am thinking of the argument for implicit complement clauses found in den Dikken et al. 1996 and in Larson et al. 1997.

Chapter 9

1. Not necessarily, since, as we saw in chapter 7, it is possible to treat 'before' and 'after' disquotationally. The critical thing for the A-theories is simply that 'before' and 'after' not be cashed out in terms of a precedence relation holding between events on a B-series time line.

2. For example, a great deal of psychological research has been devoted to the question of whether 'before' or 'after' is acquired first. This research may initially appear unlikely to shed a great deal of light on whether the B-theory or the A-theory is correct; however, this appearance may be deceptive. For example, it is possible to argue that if 'before' and 'after' essentially express the same relation (as, for example, they do according to the B-theory), then the acquisition of these two terms should occur at the same time. If so, then the question of whether one might be more easily learned than the other might become significant. It might suggest that the before/after relation is not a primitive after all, and that the meanings of 'before' and 'after' have rather different fine structure. Unfortunately, the results here are inconclusive. Early studies by Eve Clark (1970, 1971) suggested that children learned 'before' prior to learning the meaning of 'after'. Clarke further hypothesized that this could be accounted for if one supposed that these predicates were decomposible into more primitive semantic features (including, on her theory, +/– simultaneous and +/– prior). Though Clarke's findings have been confirmed by some studies (e.g. Weil and Stenning 1978; Munro and Wales 1982), a great deal of subsequent research (Amidon and Carey 1972; Keller-Cohen 1974, 1987; French and Brown 1977; Coker 1978; Goodz 1982; Trosborg 1982) has shown no consistent order of acquisition. These studies showed that other factors may be involved in the order of acquisition—for example, whether the clauses are arbitrarily or logically ordered, or the order of mention of the events described, or some combination of these factors.

3. Subsequent research (see e.g. French 1986) has reported other results, although caution is necessary in interpreting the results. Crucially, in the experiments reported by French, children showed facility with such terms when reporting causal or logical connections between events. But this is not the same as suggesting that children have facility with the temporal uses of 'before' and 'after' (which is of course what is at issue here).

4. Presumably the psychologists regarded the ability to decenter as a certain form of achievement, though one can imagine philosophical critiques suggesting that it really amounts to our adopting a certain alien perspective on the world.

5. Among other matters, there is the thorny problem of separating out causal uses of 'when' (as in "when I touch the stove I burn myself"). As Keller-Cohen (1974) found, the causal and temporal uses are not well differentiated in early child language.

6. I owe this section heading to Brian Beakley. The material on Merleau-Ponty was drawn to my attention by at least half a dozen colleagues and students at Stony Brook.

Chapter 10

1. Each of these questions would require a book-length treatment. On the philosophy of space, for example, it should be apparent that the argument from indexicality employed in chapter 6 applies just as well to spatial indexicals like 'here' and 'there'. Accordingly, one might anticipate the collapse of space into a point, or perhaps one might find support for a Leibnizian picture of space. The issues are very subtle, however, and demand very careful study. Parenthetically, Mellor (1981) has argued that the fact that no one has advocated spatial indexical predicates tells against their application in the case of time. Calling this the B-theorist's *tu quoque* argument, Craig (1996b) has argued that space and time are fundamentally different in this respect. That is certainly a plausible response, but it seems to me that it would at least be an interesting exercise to treat

space in an A-theory-like manner (that is, building spatial co-ordinates out of indexical predicates like 'here', 'there', etc.). The obvious problem is that where we all share the same temporal perspective (modulo relativistic effects it is currently now for all of us), we do not share the same spatial position, so 'here', 'there' etc. allegedly can't be real features of physical space. The challenge for an A-theory of space is therefore to carry out the project without collapsing into a kind of extreme solipsism.

2. I am indebted to Michael Potter for discussion of this matter.

3. It appears that the A-theorist cannot appeal to the same truth-value links without changes, since all these links employ what appears to be quantification over times. This problem is only superficial, however, since the A-theorist could reinterpret the quantifiers here as substitutional quantifiers over calendar dates. The result might be something like the following (where the substituends of t are dates):

A'
$(\forall t2)[\text{Past:S is true when } [\ldots t2] \text{ iff } (\exists t1)(\text{S was true when } [\ldots t1])]$

B'
$(\forall t1)[\text{Fut:S is true when } [\ldots t1] \text{ iff } (\exists t2)(\text{S will be true when } [\ldots t2])]$

C'
$(\forall t2)[\text{S is true when } [\ldots t2] \text{ iff } (\forall t1)(\text{Fut:S was true when } [\ldots t1])]$

D'
$(\forall t1)[\text{S is true when } [\ldots t1] \text{ iff } (\forall t2)(\text{Past:S will be true when } [\ldots t2])]$

and so on.

4. Can *all* records of an event be erased? Couldn't one argue that it is physically impossible to erase all records of a crime? Imagine, for example, an explosion in deep space. What would it take to erase all records of such an event? The criminals could certainly eliminate all witnesses near ground zero, and the criminals could take memory-erasing pills to strike their memories of the witness-elimination program as well as the original explosion. But of course the problem is that information about the explosion is departing the scene at the speed of light. The criminals can't catch up to that signal, so in principle the information is out there.

Now it might be objected that while the criminals can't catch up to the information, barring help from someone who reflects the information back to us neither can we, so the evidence is in principle out of our grasp. That might be a problem for the thoroughgoing idealist, but we might try to argue that we are only committed to anti-realism about the future and the past. The present is another matter. Unless we move to some sort of verificationist semantics it should be enough to say that the information is there in the present (here I am overlooking relativistic troubles involving the notion of simultaneity, as well as the epistemological burdens this might place on our semantic theory).

What holds for events in deep space could then be argued to hold for events that take place in zippered-up rooms as well. The criminals might soundproof the room and find a way of blocking electromagnetic emissions, but there is a genuine question of physics about whether they can thereby "erase" the information of what took place in that room. It is arguable that the walls of the room cannot annihilate the information present in the room. At best they can absorb it as a state change or bury it in noise. Reconstructing the information would no doubt be a tall order, but it appears to be possible in principle.

And if the room is later destroyed, well then the information is still not annihilated, but now released into the environment albeit with yet more noise.

I am not sure about how plausible this line of argument is with respect to physical theory. At some point the whole universe may collapse into a giant black hole. Do we really want to say that the evidence of the crime is preserved even then? If we extend the question to quantum physics then the preservation of all information seems even less likely, since measurements taken between the time of the crime and the time of our attempt to reconstruct the crime will introduce an element of indeterminacy.

Moreover, even if it could be shown that all information is preserved until the end of the physical universe, it certainly seems conceivable that there should be possible worlds where this is not the case. But then our concept of logical inference seems far too brittle. It should survive in worlds with different physical properties, should it not? Of course we are talking about extremely general physical properties so the matter is far from clear. As I have no idea how to tackle these questions I pass over them here. However, they are no doubt well worth pursuing. (I am indebted to Emiliano Trizio and Emiliano Boccardi for discussion of these matters.)

5. There is a question, however, as to whether the A-theorist is compelled to accept (E). One supposes that the answer is yes, since giving it up appears to entail giving up the general thesis that current facts determine truth. The issue is subtle, however, and perhaps there are ways for the A-theorist to block (E). Until we have some justification for blocking (E), however, we need to proceed on the assumption that the truth-value links (A)-(D) will drive the A-theorist to contradiction in situations where all evidence of an action can be erased.

6. For defenses of the standard view, see Wekker 1976 and Davidsen-Nielsen 1988.

7. For a very interesting discussion of the origin of future tense in Romance languages, see Fleischman 1982.

8. This is the only case where the identity breaks down, although not by much. Notice that one difference here is that the intervocalic "b" has dropped out—a familiar process in the history of Romance languages.

9. Examples include Sicilian and Southern Italian dialects and spoken Portuguese.

10. For discussions, see Jenkins 1972 (p. 73ff.); Huddleston 1976 (p. 69ff.); Coates 1983 (p. 177ff.). There is also a brief review of this literature in Palmer 1990 (p. 163ff.).

11. For the record, in Romance languages the conditional morphemes and the perfect (preterite) morphemes come from the same Latin forms, and in many cases the common origin is obvious. Consider the following paradigm from Italian:

passato remoto	condizionale
cred -ei	cred -er -ei
-esti	-er -esti
-è (-ette)	-er -ebbe
-emmo	-er -emmo
-este	-er -este
-erono	-er -ebbero

12. See Chafe and Nichols 1986; Palmer 1986; Willett 1988.

13. The indexical character of evidentials should be obvious. In the root case, something that is first-hand evidence for you might be second-hand evidence for me. Likewise, I might have perceptual evidence for something in the beginning, but archival evidence at another time. A similar story can be told for modal dispositions in the world. Each time we return to the Wicked Witch's hourglass, it has a different dispositional property. Obviously these remarks are loose, since I am using sequential visits and times to illustrate the indexical character of evidentials and dispositions. Strictly speaking, evidentiality and modal dispositions will be the fundamental notions that underwrite our talk of times and temporal sequence.

Appendix P1

1. Still, there are differences in the parametric settings of different I-languages, and, although we should not exaggerate these differences, I think it is flatly false to suppose that everything is in principle translatable—at least, if preservation of sense and shade of meaning are important to us. On this score Jackendoff's claims are completely at odds with what professional translators know. For a historical discussion of translation theory, see Venuti 1995.

2. In point of fact, as is argued in Ludlow 1985, I think the story is false. For the sake of argument, however, let us suppose otherwise.

3. In fact, these arguments are at best arguments against a thesis that would deny any structure to a sentence apart from that visible in the written form of the sentence.

4. Indeed, doing just that is a pet project of mine. See Ludlow 1998.

5. I have already hinted that I doubt they tell against the thesis that E-language could be the language of thought. The idea is that one can quite readily hold that E-language sentences have LF representations with all the structure that I-language representations are supposed to have. Indeed, a number of individuals hold precisely this thesis.

Appendix P2

1. The material in this section is drawn from Ludlow (forthcoming).

2. Kant 1910–1983, volume 15, pp. 76–77; translation from Coffa 1991 (p. 31).

3. Kant 1910–1983, volume 15, p. 78; translation from Coffa 1991 (p. 31).

4. Wittgenstein explains the matter as follows in his 1915 notebooks (1961a, p. 46): "It is clear that the constituents of our statements can and should be analyzed by means of definitions, and must be, if we want to approximate to the real structure of the statement.... The analyzed proposition mentions more than the unanalyzed. The analysis makes the proposition more complicated than it was, but it cannot and must not make it more complicated that its reference was from the first. When the proposition is just as complex as its reference, the it is *completely* analyzed."

5. In the following discussion I am indebted to personal communication with Chomsky.

6. One possible response for Higginbotham here is to render (4) along the lines of (4').

(4')
Your report fails to make it clear that on average a family has 2.3 children.

There are, however, potential pitfalls in the (4') gambit. For starters, the report described in (4') need not be *about* the average family at all; it could very well be a report on milk consumption in urban areas. Is (4") a possibility?

(4")
Your report on the average family fails to make it clear that on average a family has 2.3 children.

Obviously not, since this brings us back to the apparent quantification over the average family. But perhaps the upstairs NP can be analyzed away in another fashion, along the lines of (4''').

(4''')
Your report on what, on average, the state of families is, fails to make it clear that on average a family has 2.3 children.

But this might not do either, since (4) does not say that the report is on the general *state* of families.

7. Some might claim to see a paradox emerging here. I am claiming that science has no special claim on ontology, yet I-language does. The apparent paradox is that the nature of I-language is supposed to be the product of scientific investigation. I am not sure there is anything more to the tension here than one expects to find in naturalization projects—whether it is epistemology that we are naturalizing or the philosophy of language and metaphysics. (For surveys of some issues in naturalizing philosophy, see Quine 1969; Kornblith 1994; Shimony and Nails 1987; Papineau 1993.)

8. Both Paul Horwich and Noam Chomsky have suggested as much to me.

9. Nor does it help to argue that the concepts mediate between language and the world. In that case, the same considerations apply to the concept/world relation. If conceptual structure underwrites our metaphysical intuitions about I-substances, then our intuitions about I-substances will provide insights into our conceptual structure, and our conceptual structure will provide insights into the structure of I-language. For the record, I consider conceptual structure to be a dispensable "middleman" here.

Appendix T1

1. Here I ignore issues about the proper formalism for representing linguistic phrase markers. Among efforts to address this issue, see Lasnik and Kupin 1977.

2. See Kayne 1984 for a defense of the thesis that only binary branching structures are possible in natural language. See Kayne 1994 for a defense of the view that they must be rightward branching.

3. See Neale and Ludlow (forthcoming) for further discussion of this point.

4. There is an empirical question as to whether it is the optimal way of characterizing c-command in natural language. Other candidate theories are offered by Aoun, Hornstein, and Sportiche (1981) and by May (1985). The differences between these proposals will not be consequential to any claims made in this book.

5. These representations are a bit retro from the perspective of the "minimalist program" (Chomsky 1995b). For a good discussion of LF in the minimalist program, see Hornstein 1995.

Appendix T2

1. The notation and the specific execution of the event analysis here are from the (EC) fragment of Larson and Segal 1995.

2. See, e.g., Higginbotham 1989, Parsons 1985, and Parsons 1991.

3. Clearly this is an oversimplification. In particular, an NP in subject position is not always the agent (at least not in English). Our goal, however, is not to give a full account of English, but merely to introduce the basic mechanisms of the event calculus, ultimately to see if they may be useful in the semantics of tense.

4. Following the (EC) fragment of Larson and Segal 1995.

Bibliography

Abusch, D. 1997. The Sequence of Tense and Temporal De Re. *Linguistics and Philosophy* 20: 1–50.

Alston, W. 1964. *Philosophy of Language*. Prentice-Hall.

Amidon, A., and Carey, P. 1972. Why Five-Year Olds Cannot Understand Before and After. *Journal of Verbal Learning and Verbal Behavior* 11: 417–423.

Aoun, J., N. Hornstein, and D. Sportiche. 1981. Some Aspects of Wide Scope Quantification. *Journal of Linguistic Research* 1: 69–95.

Åqvist, L. 1976. Formal Semantics of Verb Tenses as Analyzed by Reichenbach. In *Pragmatics of Language and Literature*, ed. T. van Dijk. North-Holland.

Atkins, P. W. 1986. Time and Dispersal: The Second Law. In *The Nature of Time*, ed. R. Flood and M. Lockwood. Blackwell.

Bach, E. 1981. On Time, Tense, and Aspect: An Essay in English Metaphysics. In *Radical Pragmatics*, ed. P. Cole. Academic Press.

Bach, E. 1986. Natural Language Metaphysics. In *Logic, Methodology and Philosophy of Science VII*, ed. R. Marcus et al. North-Holland.

Bach, E., and R. Cooper. 1978. The NP-S Analysis of Relative Clauses and Compositional Semantics. *Linguistics and Philosophy* 2: 145–150.

Beakley, B. 1991. The Structure of Scientific Explanation in Cognitive Science. Ph.D. thesis, SUNY Stony Brook.

Beakley, B., and P. Ludlow, eds. 1992. *The Philosophy of Mind: Classical Problems/Contemporary Issues*. MIT Press.

Bealer, G. 1982. *Quality and Concept*. Oxford University Press.

Bilgrami, A. 1987. An Externalist Account of Psychological Content. *Philosophical Topics* 15:191–226.

Boghossian, P. 1989. Content and Self-Knowledge. *Philosophical Topics* 17: 5–26.

Boguraev, B., and T. Briscoe, ed. 1989. *Computational Lexicography for Natural Language Processing*. Longman.

Bonomi, A. 1997. Aspect, Quantification and When-Clauses in Italian. *Linguistics and Philosophy* 20: 469–514.

Brennan, S., and H. Clark. 1992. Lexical Choice and Local Convention. Manuscript, SUNY Stony Brook and Stanford University.

Broad, C. D. 1938. *An Examination of McTaggart's Philosophy*. Cambridge University Press.

Burge, T. 1979. Individualism and the Mental. In *Studies in Epistemology*, volume 4, ed. P. French et al. University of Minnesota Press.

Burge, T. 1986. Individualism and Psychology. *Philosophical Review* 95: 3–45.

Burge, T. 1988. Individualism and Self-Knowledge. *Journal of Philosophy* 85: 649–663.

Burge, T. 1998. Self-Knowledge and Memory. In *Externalism and Self-Knowledge*, ed. P. Ludlow and N. Martin. CSLI Publications (Cambridge University Press).

Buridan, J. 1966. *Sophisms on Meaning and Truth*. Appleton-Century-Crofts.

Butterfield, J. 1985. Indexicals and Tense. In *Exercises in Analysis*, ed. I. Hacking. Cambridge University Press.

Carruthers, P. 1989. *Tractarian Semantics: Finding Sense in Wittgenstein's Tractatus*. Blackwell.

Carruthers, P. 1996. *Language, Thought, and Consciousness: An Essay in Philosophical Psychology*. Cambridge University Press.

Carruthers, P., and P. Smith, eds. 1996. *Theories of Theories of Mind*. Cambridge University Press.

Casteñada, H.-N. 1967. Indicators and Quasi-Indicators. *American Philosophical Quarterly* 4: 85–100.

Chafe, W., and J. Nichols, eds. 1986. *Evidentiality: The Linguistic Coding of Epistemology*. Ablex.

Chamberlain, A., and Chamberlain, I. 1904. Studies of a Child. *Pedagogical Seminary* 11: 264–291.

Chierchia, G. 1984. Topics in the Syntax and Semantics of Infinitives and Gerunds. Ph.D. thesis, Department of Linguistics, University of Massachusetts, Amherst.

Chierchia, G. 1995. *Dynamics of Meaning : Anaphora, Presupposition, and the Theory of Grammar*. University of Chicago Press.

Chierchia, G., and McConnell-Ginet, S. 1990. *Meaning and Grammar: an Introduction to Semantics*. MIT Press.

Chierchia, G and R. Turner. 1988. Semantics and Property Theory. *Linguistics and Philosophy* 11: 261–302.

Chierchia, G., and R. Turner, eds. 1989. *Properties, Types, and Meaning*, volume 1: *Foundational Issues*. Kluwer.

Chomsky, N. 1975. *Reflections on Language*. Pantheon.

Chomsky, N. 1976. Conditions on Rules of Grammar. *Linguistic Analysis* 2: 303–351. Reprinted in *Essays on Form and Interpretation* (North-Holland, 1977).

Chomsky, N. 1981. *Lectures on Government and Binding*. Foris.

Chomsky, N. 1986. *Knowledge of Language*. Praeger.

Chomsky, N. 1993. Explaining Language Use. *Philosophical Topics* 20: 205–231.

Chomsky, N. 1995a. Language and Nature. *Mind* 104: 1–61.

Chomsky, N. 1995b. *The Minimalist Program*. MIT Press.

Chomsky, N., and H. Lasnik. 1993. The Theory of Principles and Parameters. In *Syntax: An International Handbook of Contemporary Research*, ed. J. Jacobs et al. Walter de Gruyter. Reprinted as chapter 1 of Chomsky 1995b.

Clark, E. 1970. How Young Children Describe Events in Time. In *Advances in Psycholinguistics*, ed. G. Flores d'Arcais and W. Levelt. North-Holland.

Clark, E. 1971. On the Acquisition of the Meaning of Before and After. *Journal of Verbal Learning and Verbal Behavior* 10: 266–275.

Clark, E. 1973. What's in a Word? On the Child's Acquisition of Semantics in His First Language. In *Cognitive Development*, ed. T. Moore. Academic Press.

Coates, J. 1983. *The Semantics of the Modal Auxiliaries*. Croom Helm.

Coffa, J. A. 1991. *The Semantic Tradition from Kant to Carnap*. Cambridge University Press.

Coker, P. 1978. Syntactic and Semantic Factors in the Acquisition of Before and After. *Journal of Child Language* 5: 261–277.

Comrie, B. 1976. *Aspect*. Cambridge University Press.

Comrie, B. 1985. *Tense*. Cambridge University Press.

Cooper, R. 1979. The Interpretation of Pronouns. In *Syntax and Semantics 10.,* ed. E. Heny and H. Schnelle. Academic Press.

Craig, W. L. 1990. God and Real Time. *Religious Studies* 26: 335–347.

Craig, W. L. 1996a. Tense and the New B-Theory of Language. *Philosophy* 71: 5–26.

Craig, W. L. 1996b. The New B-Theory's *Tu Quoque* Argument. *Synthese* 107: 249–269.

Cresswell, M. 1985. *Structured Meanings*. MIT Press.

Cresswell, M. 1990. *Entities and Indices*. Kluwer.

Cromer, R. F. 1968. The Development of Temporal Reference During the Acquisition of Language. Ph.D. thesis, Harvard University.

Davidsen-Nielsen, N. 1988. Has English a Future? Remarks on the Future Tense. *Acta Linguistica Hafniensia* 21: 5–20.

Davidson, D. 1967a. Truth and Meaning. *Synthese* 17: 304–323. Reprinted in *Inquiries Into Truth and Interpretation* (Oxford University Press, 1984).

Davidson, D. 1967b. The Logical Form of Action Sentences. Reprinted in *Essays on Actions and Events* (Oxford University Press, 1980).

Davidson, D. 1986. A Nice Derangement of Epitaphs. In *Truth and Interpretation: Perspectives on the Philosophy of Donald Davidson*, ed. E. Lepore. Blackwell.

Davidson, D. 1987. Knowing One's Own Mind. *Proceedings of the American Philosophical Association* 60: 441–458.

Davies, M. 1981a. *Meaning, Quantification, Necessity*. Routledge and Kegan Paul.

Davies, M. 1981b. Meaning, Structure, and Understanding. *Synthese* 48: 135–161.

Davies, M. 1987. Tacit Knowledge and Semantic Theory: Can a Five Per Cent Difference Matter? *Mind* 96: 441–462.

Davies, M., and T. Stone, eds. 1995a. *Folk Psychology: The Theory of Mind Debate.* Blackwell.

Davies, M., and T. Stone, eds. 1995b. *Mental Simulation: Evaluations and Applications.* Blackwell.

den Dikken, M., R. Larson, and P. Ludlow. 1996. Intensional Transitive Verbs. *Rivista di Linguistica* 8. Abridged version reprinted in *Readings in the Philosophy of Language*, ed. P. Ludlow (MIT Press, 1997).

Devitt, M. 1993. *Coming to Our Senses.* Cambridge University Press.

Dieks, D. 1988. Special Relativity and the Flow of Time. *Philosophy of Science* 55: 456–460.

Donnellan, K. S. 1966. Reference and Definite Descriptions. *Philosophical Review* 77: 281–304.

Dowty, D. 1982. Tenses, Time Adverbs, and Compositional Semantic Theory. *Linguistics and Philosophy* 5: 23–55.

Dreyfus, H., ed. 1982. *Husserl, Intentionality, and Cognitive Science.* MIT Press.

Dummett, M. 1964. Bringing About the Past. *Philosophical Review* 73: 338–359. Reprinted in Dummett 1978.

Dummett, M. 1969. The Reality of the Past. *Proceedings of the Aristotelian Society* 69: 239–258. Reprinted in Dummett 1978.

Dummett, M. 1973. *Frege: Philosophy of Language.* Harvard University Press.

Dummett, M. 1975. What Is a Theory of Meaning? In *Mind and Language*, ed. S. Guttenplan. Oxford University Press.

Dummett, M. 1978. *Truth and Other Enigmas.* Harvard University Press.

Dummett, M. 1991. *The Logical Basis of Metaphysics.* Harvard University Press.

Einstein, A. 1955. A Letter of Condolence to the Family of M. Besso. Reprinted in H.-D. Zeh, *The Physical Basis for the Direction of Time* (Springer-Verlag, 1989).

Enç, M. 1986. Towards a Referential Analysis of Temporal Expressions. *Linguistics and Philosophy* 9: 405–426.

Enç, M. 1987. Anchoring Conditions for Tense. *Linguistic Inquiry* 18: 633–657.

Etchemendy, J. 1990. *The Concept of Logical Consequence.* Harvard University Press.

Evans, G. 1977. Pronouns, Quantifiers, and Relative Clauses (I). *Canadian Journal of Philosophy* 7: 467–536. Reprinted in Evans 1985.

Evans, G. 1981. Understanding Demonstratives. In *Meaning and Understanding*, ed. H. Parret and J. Bouveresse. Walter de Gruyter. Reprinted in *Collected Papers* (Oxford University Press).

Evans, G. 1982. *The Varieties of Reference.* Oxford University Press.

Evans, G. 1985a. Does Tense Logic Rest Upon a Mistake? In *Collected Papers*. Oxford University Press.

Evans, G. 1985b. Semantic Theory and Tacit Knowledge. In *Collected Papers*. Oxford University Press.

Farmer, D. 1990. *Being in Time: The Nature of Time in the Light of McTaggart's Paradox*. University Press of America.

Field, H. 1991. Metalogic and Modality. *Philosophical Studies* 62: 1–22.

Fleischman, S. 1982. *The Future in Thought and Language*. Cambridge University Press.

Fodor, J. 1975. *The Language of Thought*. Crowell.

Fodor, J., and E. Lepore. 1997. Morphemes Matter: the Continuing Case Against Lexical Decomposition. Draft manuscript, Rutgers University.

Fodor, J., and E. Lepore. 1998. The Emptiness of the Lexicon. *Linguistic Inquiry* 29, no. 2: 269-288

Forbes, G. 1996. Substitutivity and the Coherence of Quantifying In. *Philosophical Review* 105: 337–372.

Foster, J. 1976. Meaning and Truth Theory. In *Truth and Meaning*, ed. G. Evans and J. McDowell. Oxford University Press.

Frege, G. 1956. The Thought. *Mind* 65: 289–311.

French, L. A. 1986. The Language of Events. In *Event Knowledge: Structure and Function in Development*, ed. K. Nelson. Erlbaum.

French, L. A., and Brown, A. L. 1977. Comprehension of *before* and *after* in Logical and Arbitrary Sequences. *Journal of Child Language* 4: 247–256.

Gale, R., ed. 1967. *The Philosophy of Time*. Doubleday.

Geach, P. 1962. *Reference and Generality*. Cornell University Press.

Giorgi, A., and F. Pianesi. 1997. *Tense and Aspect*. Oxford University Press.

Giorgi, A., and F. Pianesi. 1998. Sequence of Tense Phenomenon in Italian: A Morphosyntactic Analysis. Manuscript.

Gödel, K. 1949. A Remark About the Relationship Between Relativity Theory and Idealistic Philosophy. In *Albert Einstein—Philosopher-Scientist*, ed. P. Schilpp. Open Court. Reprinted in Yourgrau 1990.

Goodglass, H., S. E. Blumstein, J. Berko-Gleason, M. R. Hyde, E. Green, and S. Statlender. 1979. The Effect of Syntactic Encoding on Sentence Comprehension in Aphasia. *Brain and Language* 7: 201–209.

Goodz, N. S. 1982. Is *before* Really Easier to Understand than *after*? *Child Development* 47: 822–825.

Gottlieb, D. 1980. *Ontological Economy: Substitutional Quantification and Mathematics*. Oxford University Press.

Gould, S. J. 1980. *The Panda's Thumb*. Norton.

Gould, S. J., and R. Lewontin. 1979. The Spandrels of San Marco and the Panglossian Program: A Critique of the Adaptionist Programme. *Proceedings of the Royal Society of London* 205: 281–288.

Groenendijk, J., and M. Stokhof. 1991. Dynamic Predicate Logic. In *Logics in AI, European Workshop JEELIA 1990*, ed. J. van Eijk. Springer-Verlag.

Grimshaw, J. 1990. *Argument Structure*. MIT Press.

Guenthner, F. 1979. Time Schemes, Tense Logic, and the Analysis of English Tenses. In *Formal Semantics and Pragmatics for Natural Languages*, ed. F. Guenthner and S. Schmidt. Reidel.

Haïk, I. 1983. Syncategormatic Adjectives. Manuscript, MIT.

Hale, K., and Keyser, J. 1987. A View from the Middle. Lexicon Project Working Papers 10, Center for Cognitive Science, MIT.

Hale, K., and Keyser, J. 1993. Argument Structure. In *The View from Building 20: Essays in Linguistics in Honor of Sylvain Bromberger*, ed. K. Hale and J. Keyser. MIT Press.

Hall, H. 1982. Was Husserl a Realist or an Idealist? In *Husserl, Intentionality, and Cognitive Science*, ed. H. Dreyfus. MIT Press.

Hayes, B. 1995. *Metrical Stress Theory: Principles and Case Studies*. University of Chicago Press.

Heim, I. 1982. The Semantics of Definite and Indefinite Noun Phrases. Ph.D. thesis, University of Massachusetts.

Higginbotham, J. 1983. Is Grammar Psychological? In *How Many Questions: Essays in Honor of Sydney Morgenbesser*, ed. L. Cauman et al. Hackett.

Higginbotham, J. 1985. On Semantics. *Linguistic Inquiry* 16: 547–594.

Higginbotham, J. 1986a. Linguistic Theory and Davidson's Program in Semantics. In *Truth and Interpretation: Perspectives on the Philosophy of Donald Davidson*, ed. E. Lepore. Blackwell.

Higginbotham, J. 1986b. Discussion, Peacocke on Explanation in Psychology. *Mind and Language* 1: 358–361.

Higginbotham, J. 1989. Elucidations of Meaning. *Linguistics and Philosophy* 12: 465–418.

Higginbotham, J. 1990. Contexts, Models, and Meanings: A Note on the Data of Semantics. In *Mental Representations: The Interface Between Language and Reality*, ed. R. Kempson. Cambridge University Press.

Higginbotham, J. 1991. Belief and Logical Form. *Mind and Language* 6: 344–369.

Higginbotham, J. 1995. Tensed Thoughts. *Mind and Language* 10: 226–249.

Hinrichs, E. 1981. Temporale Anaphora im Englishen. Staatsexamen thesis, University of Tübingen.

Hinrichs, E. 1986. Temporal Anaphora in Discourses of English. *Linguistics and Philosophy* 9: 63–82.

Hinrichs, E. 1988. Tense, Quantifiers, and Contexts. *Computational Linguistics* 14: 3–14.

Hintikka, J. 1962. *Knowledge and Belief.* Cornell University Press.

Hintikka, J. 1969a. Semantics for Propositional Attitudes. In *Philosophical Logic*, ed. J. Davis et al. Kluwer.

Hintikka, J. 1969b. On Kant's Notion of Intuition (Anschauung). In *Kant's First Critique*, ed. T. Penelhum and J. MacIntosh. Wadsworth.

Hintikka, J. 1972. Kantian Intuitions. *Inquiry* 17: 341–345.

Hintikka, J. 1975. *Intentions for Intentionality and Other New Models for Modality*. Reidel.

Hofmann, F. 1995. Externalism and Memory. Manuscript, Department of Philosophy, University of Tübingen.

Hornstein, N. 1984. *Logic as Grammar*. MIT Press.

Hornstein, N. 1990. *As Time Goes By*. MIT Press.

Hornstein, N. 1995. *Logical Form: from GB to Minimalism*. Blackwell.

Huddleston, R. 1976. An Introduction to English Transformational Syntax. Longman.

Husserl, E. 1972. *Ideas: General Introduction to Pure Phenomenology*. Collier.

Iatridou, S. 1996. The Grammatical Ingredients of Counterfactuality. Manuscript, MIT.

Ioup, G. 1977. Specificity and the Interpretation of Quantifiers. *Linguistics and Philosophy* 1: 233–245.

Isard, S. 1974. What Would You Have Done If . . . *Theoretical Linguistics* 1: 233–255.

Izvorski, R. 1997. The Present Perfect as an Epistemic Modal. *Proceedings of SALT 7*, Stanford University.

Jackendoff, R. 1972. *Semantic Interpretation in Generative Grammar*. MIT Press.

Jackendoff, R. 1983. *Semantics and Cognition*. MIT Press.

Jackendoff, R. 1992. *Languages of the Mind: Essays on Mental Representation*. MIT Press.

Jackendoff, R. 1993. *Patterns in the Mind: Language and Human Nature*. Harvester Wheatsheaf.

Jenkins, L. 1972. Modality in English Syntax. Ph.D. thesis, MIT.

Jesperson, O. 1940. *A Modern English Grammar on Historical Principles*. Copenhagen: Ejnar Munksgaard.

Johnson-Laird, P. 1983. *Mental Models*. Cambridge University Press.

Kamp, H. 1971. Formal Properties of 'Now'. *Theoria* 37: 227–273.

Kamp, H. 1984. A Theory of Truth and Semantic Representation. In *Truth, Interpretation, and Information*, ed. J. Groendijk et al. Foris.

Kamp, H., and U. Reyle. 1993. *From Discourse to Logic*. Kluwer.

Kant, I. 1910–1983. *Kants gesammelte Schriften*, volumes 1–29. De Gruyter & Reimer.

Kaplan, D. 1977. Demonstratives. Manuscript, UCLA. Reprinted in *Themes from Kaplan*, ed. J. Almog et al. (Cornell University Press, 1989).

Kaplan, D. 1979. On the Logic of Demonstratives. *Journal of Philosophical Logic* 8: 81–98.

Kaplan, D. 1990. Thoughts on Demonstratives. In Yourgrau 1990.

Karttunen, L. 1976. Discourse Referents. In *Syntax and Semantics 7: Notes from the Linguistic Underground*, ed. J. McCawley. Academic Press.

Katz, J. 1972. *Semantic Theory*. Harper.

Katz, J. 1981. *Language and Other Abstract Objects*. Rowman and Littlefield.

Katz, J., and Fodor, J. A. 1963. The Structure of a Semantic Theory. *Language* 39: 170–210.

Katz, J., and Postal, P. 1964. *An Integrated Theory of Linguistic Description*. MIT Press.

Kayne, R. 1984. *Connectedness and Binary Branching*. Foris.

Kayne, R. 1994. *The Antisymmetry of Syntax*. MIT Press.

Keller-Cohen, D. 1974. The Acquisition of Temporal Reference in Pre-School Children. Ph.D. thesis, SUNY Buffalo.

Keller-Cohen, D. 1987. Context and Strategy in Acquiring Temporal Connectives. *Journal of Psycholinguistic Research* 16: 165–183.

Kneale, W. 1949. Is Existence a Predicate? In *Readings in Philosophical Analysis*, ed. H. Feigel and W. Sellars. Appleton-Century-Crofts.

Kornblith, H., ed. 1994. *Naturalizing Epistemology*, second edition. MIT Press.

Kratzer, A. 1989. An Investigation of the Lumps of Thought. *Linguistics and Philosophy* 12: 607–653.

Kretzman, N. 1976. Aristotle on the Instant of Change. *Proceedings of the Aristotelean Society* 50 (supplement): 91–114.

Kripke, S. 1976. Is There a Problem About Substitutional Quantification? In *Truth and Meaning*, ed. G. Evans and J. McDowell. Oxford University Press.

Kripke, S. 1979. A Puzzle About Belief. In *Meaning and Use*, ed. A. Margalit. Reidel.

Kripke, S. 1980. *Naming and Necessity*. Harvard University Press.

Ladusaw, W. 1977. Some Problems with Tense in PTQ. *Texas Linguistics Forum* 6: 89–102.

Larson, R., and P. Ludlow. 1993. Interpreted Logical Forms. *Synthese* 95: 305–356.

Larson, R., and G. Segal. 1995. *Knowledge of Meaning*. MIT Press.

Larson, R., M. den Dikken, and P. Ludlow. 1997. Intensional Transitive Verbs and Abstract Clausal Complementation. Manuscript, SUNY Stony Brook and Frei Universiteit Amsterdam.

Lasnik, H., and J. Kupin. 1977. A Restrictive Theory of Transformational Grammar. *Theoretical Linguistics* 4: 173–196.

Lepore, E. 1983. What Model Theoretic Semantics Cannot Do. *Synthese* 54: 167–187.

Lepore, E., and B. Loewer. 1981. Translational Semantics. *Synthese* 48: 121–133.

Lepore, E., and B. Loewer. 1983. Three Trivial Truth Theories. *Canadian Journal of Philosophy* 13: 433–447.

Lepore, E. and B. Loewer. 1987. Dual Aspect Semantics. In *New Directions in Semantics*, ed. E. Lepore. Academic Press.

Lepore, E., and K. Ludwig. 1998. Truth Conditional Semantics for Tense. In *Tense, Time and Reference*, ed. Q. Smith. Oxford University Press.

Lewis, D. 1969. *Convention*. Harvard University Press.

Lewis, D. 1972. General Semantics. In *Semantics of Natural Language*, ed. D. Davidson and G. Harman. Reidel.

Lewis, D. 1975a. Language and Languages. In *Language, Mind and Knowledge*, ed. K. Gunderson. University of Minnesota Press.

Lewis, D. 1979. Score-keeping in a Language Game. *Journal of Philosophical Logic* 8: 339–359.

Lewis, H. A. 1985. Substitutional Quantification and Nonstandard Quantifiers. *Noûs* 19: 447–451.

Ludlow, P. 1985. The Syntax and Semantics of Referential Attitude Reports. Ph.D. thesis, Columbia University.

Ludlow, P. 1989. Psychology, Semantics, and Mental Events Under Descriptions. Technical Report CSLI-89-135, Center for the Study of Language and Information, Stanford University.

Ludlow, P. 1992. Formal Rigor and Linguistic Theory. *Natural Language and Linguistic Theory* 10: 335–344.

Ludlow, P. 1993. Do T-theories Display Senses? *Electronic Journal of Analytic Philosophy* 1: 4.

Ludlow, P. 1994. Conditionals, Events, and Unbound Pronouns. *Lingua e Stile* 29: 165–183.

Ludlow, P. 1995. Social Externalism, Self-Knowledge, and Memory. *Analysis* 55: 157–159.

Ludlow, P. 1996. Social Externalism and Memory: a Problem? *Acta Analytica* 14. Reprinted in Ludlow and Martin 1998.

Ludlow, P. ed. 1997a. *Readings in the Philosophy of Language*. MIT Press.

Ludlow, P. 1997b. Semantics, Tense, and Time: On Tenseless Truth Conditions for Token-Reflexive Tensed Sentences. *Protosociology* 10: 190–195.

Ludlow, P. 1998. LF and Natural Logic. Manuscript, SUNY Stony Brook.

Ludlow, P., forthcoming. Referential Semantics for I-Languages? In *Chomsky and His Critics*, ed. N. Hornstein and L. Antony. Blackwell.

Ludlow, P., and N. Martin, eds. 1998. *Externalism and Self-Knowledge*. CSLI Publications.

Ludlow, P., and S. Neale. 1991. Indefinite Descriptions: In Defense of Russell. *Linguistics and Philosophy* 14: 171–202.

Malotki, E. 1983. *Hopi Time: a Linguistic Analysis of Temporal Concepts in the Hopi Language*. Mouton.

May, R. 1977. The Grammar of Quantification. Ph.D. thesis, MIT.

May, R. 1985. *Logical Form: Its Structure and Derivation*. MIT Press.

McCawley, J. 1974. On Identifying the Remains of Deceased Clauses. *Language Research* 9: 73–85. Reprinted in *Adverbs, Vowels, and Other Objects of Wonder* (University of Chicago Press, 1979).

McDowell, J. 1978. On "The Reality of the Past." In *Action and Interpretation*, ed. C. Hookway and P. Pettit. Cambridge University Press.

McDowell, J. 1980. On the Sense and Reference of a Proper Name. In *Truth Reality and Reference*, ed. M. Platts. Routledge and Kegan Paul.

McNeill, D. 1979. *The Conceptual Basis of Language*. Erlbaum.

McTaggart, J. 1908. The Unreality of Time. *Mind* 68: 457–474.

McTaggart, J. 1927. *The Nature of Existence*, volume 2. Cambridge University Press.

Meinong, A. 1904. Über Gegenstandstheorie. Translated as The Theory of Objects in *Realism and the Background of Phenomenology*, ed. R. Chisolm (Free Press, 1960).

Mellor, D. H. 1981. *Real Time*. MIT Press.

Merleau-Ponty, M. 1962. *The Phenomenology of Perception*. Routledge and Kegan Paul.

Monk, R. 1996. *Bertrand Russell: The Spirit of Solitude*. Free Press.

Montague, R. 1960. On the Nature of Certain Philosophical Entities. *Monist* 53: 159–194. Reprinted in *Formal Philosophy*.

Montague, R. 1974. *Formal Philosophy* . Yale University Press.

Munro, J., and Wales, R. 1982. Changes in the Child's Comprehension of Simultaneity and Sequence. *Journal of Verbal Learning and Verbal Behavior* 21: 175–185.

Neale, S. 1990. *Descriptions*. MIT Press.

Neale, S., and P. Ludlow. Forthcoming. Syntax. In *The Cambridge Encyclopedia of Philosophy*. Cambridge University Press.

Nirenberg, S., and V. Raskin. 1987. The Subworld Concept Lexicon and the Lexicon Management System. *Computational Linguistics* 13: 276–289.

Nolan, R. 1970. *Foundations for an Adequate Criterion of Paraphrase*. Mouton.

Palmer, F. R. 1986. *Mood and Modality*. Cambridge University Press.

Palmer, F. R. 1990. *Modality and the English Modals*, second edition. Longman.

Papineau, D. 1993. *Philosophical Naturalism*. Blackwell.

Parmenides. 1984. *Parmenides of Elea*. University of Toronto Press.

Parsons, C. 1971a. A Plea for Substitutional Quantification. *Journal of Philosophy* 68: 231–237.

Parsons, C. 1971b. Ontology and Mathematics. *Philosophical Review* 80: 158–159.

Parsons, T. 1978. Pronouns as Paraphrases. Manuscript, University of Mass. at Amherst.

Parsons, T. 1980. *Nonexistent Objects*. Yale University Press.

Parsons, T. 1985. Underlying Events in the Logical Analysis of English. In *Actions and Events: Perspectives on the Philosophy of Donald Davidson*, ed. E. Lepore and B. McLaughlin. Blackwell.

Parsons, T. 1991. *Events in the Semantics of English*. MIT Press.

Partee, B. 1973. Some Structural Analogies Between Tenses and Pronouns in English. *Journal of Philosophy* 70: 601–609.

Partee, B. 1974. Opacity and Scope. In *Semantics and Philosophy*, ed. M. Munitz and P. Unger. NYU Press.

Partee, B. 1984. Nominal and Temporal Anaphora. *Linguistics and Philosophy* 7: 243–286.

Peacocke, C. 1986. Explanation in Computational Psychology: Language, Perception, and Level 1.5. *Mind and Language* 1: 101–123.

Perry, J. 1969. The Problem of the Essential Indexical. *Nous* 13: 3–21.

Perry, J. 1977. Frege on Demonstratives. *Philosophical Review* 86: 474–497.

Pinker, S. 1994. *The Language Instinct*. William Morrow.

Pinker, S., and P. Bloom. 1990. Natural Language and Natural Selection. *Behavioral and Brain Sciences* 13: 707–784.

Prior, A. N. 1967. *Past, Present and Future*. Oxford University Press.

Prior, A. N. 1968. *Time and Tense*. Oxford University Press.

Prior, A. N. 1971. *Objects of Thought*. Oxford University Press.

Pustejovsky, J. 1995. *The Generative Lexicon*. MIT Press.

Pustejovsky, J., and S. Bergler, eds. 1991. *Lexical Semantics and Knowledge Representation*. Springer-Verlag.

Putnam, H. 1967. Time and Physical Geometry. *Journal of Philosophy* 64: 240–247.

Putnam, H. 1975. The Meaning of 'Meaning'. In *Language, Mind and Knowledge*, ed. K. Gunderson. University of Minnesota Press.

Quine, W. V. O. 1953. On What There Is. In W. V. O. Quine, *From a Logical Point of View*. Harper & Row.

Quine, W. V. O. 1960. *Word and Object*. MIT Press.

Quine, W. V. O. 1969. *Ontological Relativity and Other Essays*. Columbia University Press.

Reiber, S. 1997. A Semiquotational Solution to Substitution Puzzles. *Philosophical Studies* 86: 267–301.

Reichenbach, H. 1947. *Elements of Symbolic Logic*. Macmillan.

Reichenbach, H. 1956. *The Direction of Time*. University of California Press.

Reichenbach, H. 1958. *The Philosophy of Space and Time*. Dover.

Reinhart, T. 1976. The Syntactic Domain of Anaphora. Ph.D. dissertation, MIT.

Richard, M. 1990. *Propositional Attitudes*. Cambridge University Press.

Rips, L. 1986. Mental Muddles. In *The Representation of Knowledge and Belief*, ed. M. Brand and R. Harnish. University of Arizona Press.

Ross, J. R. 1976. To Have and to Have Not. In *Linguistic and Literary Studies in Honor of Archibald Hill*, ed. E. Polomé et al. Peter de Ridder.

Routley, R. 1980. *Exploring Meinong's Jungle and Beyond*. Research School of Social Sciences, Australian National University, Canberra.

Russell, B. 1905. On Denoting. *Mind* 14: 479–493.

Russell, B. 1910–11. Knowledge by Acquaintance and Knowledge by Description. *Proceedings of the Aristotelean Society*. Reprinted in *Mysticism and Logic* (Allen and Unwin, 1917; Doubleday, 1957).

Russell, B. 1915. On the Experience of Time. *Monist* 25: 212–233.

Salmon, N. 1986. *Frege's Puzzle*. MIT Press.

Schein, B. 1993. *Plurals and Events*. MIT Press.

Segal, B. 1989. A Preference for Sense and Reference. *Journal of Philosophy* 86: 73–89.

Sellars, W. 1963. Abstract Entities. *Review of Metaphysics* 16: 627–671.

Semenza, C., and M. Zetin. 1989. Evidence from Aphasia for the Role of Proper Names as Pure Referring Expressions. *Nature* 342: 678–679.

Shimony, A. 1993. The Transient *Now*. In A. Shimony, *Search for the Naturalistic World-View*, volume II. Cambridge University Press.

Shimony, A., and D. Nails, eds. 1987. *Naturalizing Epistemology: a Symposium of Two Decades*. Reidel.

Sidner, C. 1983. Focusing in the Comprehension of Definite Anaphora. In *Computational Models of Discourse*, ed. M. Brady and R. Berwick. MIT Press.

Sklar, L. 1974. *Space, Time, and Spacetime*. University of California Press.

Sklar, L. 1981. Time, Reality, and Relativity. In *Reduction, Time and Reality*, ed. R. Healey. Cambridge University Press. Reprinted in *Demonstratives*, ed. P. Yourgrau (Oxford University Press, 1990).

Smart, J. J. C. 1963. *Philosophy and Scientific Realism*. Routledge & Kegan Paul.

Smart, J. J. C. 1966. The River of Time. In *Essays in Conceptual Analysis*, ed. A. Flew. Routledge and Kegan Paul.

Smith, C. 1975. The Analysis of Tense in English. *Texas Linguistic Forum* 1: 71–89.

Smith, C. 1978. The Syntax and Semantics of Temporal Expressions in English. *Linguistics and Philosophy* 2: 43–99.

Smith, D. W. 1983. Kantifying In. *Synthese* 54: 261–274.

Smith, Q. 1993. *Language and Time*. Oxford University Press.

Soames, S. 1987. Direct Reference, Propositional Attitudes, and Semantic Content. *Philosophical Topics* 15: 47–87.

Sorabji, R. 1983. *Time, Creation, and the Continuum*. Cornell University Press.

Stalnaker, R. 1984. *Inquiry*. MIT Press.

Stanley, J. 1997a. Rigidity and Content. In *Language, Truth, and Logic: Essays in Honor of Michael Dummett*, ed. R. Heck. Oxford University Press.

Stanley, J. 1977b. Names and Rigid Designation. In *A Companion to the Philosophy of Language*, ed. B. Hale and C. Wright. Blackwell

Stein, H. 1968. On Einstein-Minkowski Space-Time. *Journal of Philosophy* 65: 5–23.

Stowell, T. 1994. Syntax of Tense. Manuscript, Department of Linguistics, UCLA.

Strawson, P. F. 1950. On Referring. *Mind* 59: 320–344.

Strawson, P. 1959. *Individuals*. Methuen.

Teichmann, R. 1998. Is a Tenseless Language Possible? *Philosophical Quarterly* 48: 176–188.

Thompson, M. 1972–73. Singular Terms and Intuitions in Kant's Epistemology. *Review of Metaphysics* 26: 314–343.

Trosborg, A. 1982. Children's Comprehension of 'before' and 'after' Reinvestigated. *Journal of Child Language* 9: 381 -402.

van Benthem, J. 1982. Later than Late: On the Logical Origin of the Temporal Order. *Pacific Philosophical Quarterly* 63: 193–203.

van Fraassen, B. 1980. *The Scientific Image*. Oxford University Press.

Venuti, L. 1995. *The Translator's Invisibility: A History of Translation*. Routledge.

Vickner, S. 1985. Reichenbach Revisited: One, Two, or Three Temporal Relations. *Acta Linguistica Hafniensia* 19: 81–98.

Wallace, J. 1972. On the Frame of Reference. In *Semantics of Natural Language*, ed. D. Davidson and G. Harman. Reidel.

Weil, J., and Stenning, K. 1978. A Comparison of Young Children's Comprehension and Memory for Statements of Temporal Relations. In *Recent Advances in the Psychology of Language*, ed. R. Campbell and P. Smith. Plenum.

Weist, R. M. 1986. Tense and Aspect. In *Language Acquisition*, second edition, ed. P. Fletcher and M. Garman. Cambridge University Press.

Wekker, H. 1976. *The Expression of Future Time in Contemporary British English*. North-Holland.

Wettstein, H. 1986. Has Semantics Rested on a Mistake? *Journal of Philosophy* 83: 185–209.

Whorf, B. 1956. *Language, Thought, and Reality*. MIT Press.

Willett, T. 1988. A Cross-Linguistic Survey of the Grammaticization of Evidentiality. *Studies in Language* 12: 51–97.

Williams, D. C. 1951. The Myth of Passage. *Journal of Philosophy* 48: 457–472.

Williams, E. 1983. Semantic vs. Syntactic Categories. *Linguistics and Philosophy* 6: 423–446.

Wittgenstein, L. 1961a. *Notebooks, 1914–1916*, ed. G. von Wright and G. Anscombe. Harper & Row.

Wittgenstein, L. 1961b. *Tractatus Logico-Philosophicus*. Routledge and Kegan Paul.

Wright, C. 1983. *Frege's Conception of Numbers as Objects*. Aberdeen University Press.

Wright, C. 1986. Theories of Meaning and Speakers' Knowledge. In *Philosophy in Britain Today*, ed. S. Shanker. SUNY Press.

Wright, C. 1993. *Realism, Meaning, and Truth*, second edition. Blackwell.

Yourgrau, P. 1987. The Dead. *Journal of Philosophy* 84: 84–101.

Yourgrau, P., ed. 1990. *Demonstratives*. Oxford University Press.

Yourgrau, P. 1991. *The Disappearance of Time: Kurt Gödel and the Idealistic Tradition in Philosophy*. Cambridge University Press.

Zalta, E. 1983. *Abstract Objects: an Introduction to Axiomatic Metaphysics*. Reidel.

Zalta, E. 1988. *Intensional Logic and the Metaphysics of Intensionality*. MIT Press.

Index

Subjects

over events, 73, 74, 77, 84–86, 121
over properties, 69
over semantic values, 66, 76
over times, 77, 78, 84–86, 100
substitutional, 74–76, 127, 128
Quantifier raising (QR), 182–184

Realism, 75, 149, 150, 177
scientific, 178
Reason, categories of, 4, 179
Reference
vs. denotation, 112,113
to future and past events, 15, 77–86, 99, 104, 113, 156
implicit, 9
of modals, 160
to properties, 46
temporal, 103–106, 111, 130
and temporal adverbs, 124, 125
to times, 113, 140, 144, 156
to utterances, 89–93
Referring expressions, 47
Relativity Theory, 3
Representation, 171, 172
Rigidity, 71, 72
Russellian propositions, 49

Scope, 167
as c-command, 182, 186, 187
of descriptions and modals, 60, 71, 72
of quantified expressions, 115, 117, 182–184
of tense morphemes, 101, 104, 121
Self-referential expressions, 89
Semantic markers, 28, 29
Semantics, 13, 20, 27–64
absolute, 14, 28, 31–38, 57, 65, 82
A-theory, 15, 97–141, 144, 209–213
austerity in, 54
B-theory, 6–8, 15, 77–96, 99, 132, 137, 138, 203–207
and epistemology, 72, 99, 100
Fregean, 58, 59
and language/world connections, 27–31, 36–38, 171–173
and metaphysics, 4, 5, 14, 64–76, 95, 84, 85, 95, 96, 99, 100, 141, 163, 171
model-theoretic, 28, 30, 31
possible-world, 50
and psycholinguistics, 39–42
referential, 14, 172–179
structural, 28–31
of Tense, 4, 47, 77–135
truth-conditional, 14, 28, 31–46, 50–52, 57, 64–76
Semantic values, 32–36, 45, 46, 48–52, 66–71, 74

Senses, 42–46, 57–59, 61, 97, 98
Sequences, 185
Simulation theory, 63
Slow-switching, 153–156
S-substance, 175, 177
Stoffen, 75, 76
Synonymy, 168, 169
Syntax, 166, 167, 169, 181–185, 191, 192, 197, 203, 209

Teleological Explanation, 20–22
Temporal becoming, 1–7, 77, 106
Temporal conjunctions, 11–12, 80, 81, 101, 111, 118–135, 139–141, 156
Temporal discourse, 6, 87–91, 97, 98, 137
Temporal egocentrism, 140
Temporal perception, 96
Tense(s)
absolute, 117, 118, 120
acquisition of, 15, 138–141
as aspect, 157, 162
complex, 9, 78–80, 101, 104, 111–124, 156
as constituent of language, 166
elimination of, 15, 95, 96, 156–163
embedded (nested), 82–84, 102, 103, 126
as evidentiality, 161–163
as modality, 157–160
as predicate of proposition-like objects, 50, 100, 156
sequence of, 82–84, 131–133
Tensed nature of world, 96
Tensed Nominals, 82, 130, 131
Thought, 4, 166
in animals, 24, 54
imagistic, 25, 26
language of, 14, 21–28, 54, 95, 165–169
and mental models, 26
nonlinguistic, 25, 26, 166–169
and sense, 58, 59
tensed nature of, 95, 96
Time
A-series conception of. See A-series
B-series conception of. See B-series
consciousness of, 96
experience of, 141–144
flow of, 106–109, 142–144
future and past, 151
phenomenology of, 15, 137, 141–144
as physical property, 2–4
tensed conception of, 2
untensed (tenseless) conception of, 1, 2, 77, 78, 144, 163
Token-reflexives. See Truth-conditions
Translation, 165
Trans-world Identity, 72

DATE DUE

			Printed in USA